Gun Digest® Buyer's Guide to
TACTICAL RIFLES

Phillip Peterson

Published by

Gun Digest® Books, an imprint of F+W Media, Inc.
Krause Publications • 700 East State Street • Iola, WI 54990-0001
715-445-2214 • 888-457-2873
www.krausebooks.com

To order books or other products call toll-free 1-800-258-0929
or visit us online at www.krausebooks.com, www.gundigeststore.com
or www.Shop.Collect.com

Library of Congress Control Number: 2010928614

ISBN-13: 978-1-4402-1446-2
ISBN-10: 1-4402-1446-8

Cover & Interior Design by Tom Nelsen
Edited by Dan Shideler

Printed in United States of America

CONTENTS

DEDICATION

To my wife Kelly and my sons Eric and Evan. Thank you for helping my American dream come true!

INTRODUCTION

Gun Digests Buyers Guide to Tactical Firearms includes a variety of firearms that might be categorized as "tactical" by many who have knowledge of or interest in firearms.

What is a Tactical Firearm? Most associate tactical with military or law enforcement applications. Those services do use such guns in performance of their duties but there are countless American civilians who own this class of guns as well. For the purposes of this book it is a semi-automatic rifle or pistol that accepts detachable magazines that hold over 20 rounds of ammunition. A few, such as the Barrett M-82 .50 Cal rifle and the SVD Draganov Sniper rifle, which have 10-round magazines, are included as they certainly need to be in such a guide.

Most firearms found within are versions of existing fully automatic firearms or new designs that borrow from and blend the features of those guns. In recent years, tactical has also come to be applied to guns with M-1913 picatinny rails for mounting high-tech optical devices or other accessories.

There are some things that carry a "tactical" label that are not covered in this work. That would include shotguns, bolt action rifles and conventional handguns with rails for attaching lasers or optical sights. Such firearms are certainly "tactical" in nature, but since even some revolvers now have tactical rails built into them, we just had to draw the line somewhere.

I know some will question the use of the term *tactical*. The thing is, there is no generally accepted term or classification for this type of gun. Many still prefer the term "assault weapon" but that name has been made into a media whipping post by anti-gun politicians. Other names have been tried for this class of firearm: black guns, EBR (Evil Black Rifle), homeland defense rifles, military pattern semi-automatics, para-military firearms, sport utility firearm. I'm sure there are more. But none of these names has caught on.

Using this book

The firearm entries in *Gun Digest® Buyers Guide to Tactical Rifles* are listed in alphabetical order. Most entries are listed by manufacturer. Some foreign firearms are listed under an importer name if it is more commonly associated with the model that the actual company that manufactured it. A few are listed by model name if the gun is usually known by that. We also try to include crossreferences for some obscure items, in case the reader knows the model name but the actual manufacturer or importer is not clear.

Pricing

The firearms prices listed in this book are RETAIL PRICES, that is, the prices at which you can reasonably expect to buy firearms from a dealer or private seller. Any firearm can bring more or less, depending on many variables. If you choose to sell your gun to a dealer, you will not receive the retail price but instead a wholesale price based on the markup that particular dealer needs to realize a profit.

The prices listed here come from four main sources: prices realized at internet or live auctions, asking prices at retail shops and gun show prices. We give more weight to actual sold prices from auctions over gun shop or gun show tag prices, which sometimes can be negotiated

downward. A seller can ask $1800 for his 1993 vintage Colt Sporter AR but it is not likely to sell for that. A price guide would be pretty inaccurate if every overpriced item observed was factored into the listings. There was no specific methodology in collecting this data. The fourth source for pricing is my own opinion based on trends in the firearm business. I have been a FFL holder since 1988 so I have a feel for the market. It would be nearly impossible to find actual market price examples for each individual model or variation.

In recent years, internet sales of tactical firearms have become a major factor in this market. Auction sites such as www.GunBroker.com and specialty retailer web sites have mostly overtaken storefront or gun show purchases for many owners. In my own business, I find that the auction sites bring me more buyers with more money than I ever had from traditional venues. I usually set up at gun shows to buy merchandise and then sell it online so as to reach more buyers. The better-quality arms I find rarely ever get displayed on my gun show table; they sell online first – frequently for more than they will bring locally. The downside of this for those not participating in the internet revolution is that they are missing out on a lot of interesting firearms that will never be offered through any other venue. This internet selling has leveled out the market. Any pricing found online is going to reflect a nationwide trend. In the "old days" one could find seasonal and regional differences in the prices of firearms. A small gun or pawn shop in the middle of farm country might have had a FN FAL priced at $1200 sit on the shelf for years. None of the local shooters had a taste for that type of firearm. Now these local dealers need only offer these slow-selling guns on the internet and they suddenly have the entire country as potential customers. Throw that FAL up on an internet auction and it will go for $2000-3000.

Buyers will sometimes pay higher prices for a firearm that they need to fill out their collection, when in most circumstances they will not be willing to pay market price if they don't need the gun. Then there are persons or companies that buy up tactical firearms in speculation that future legislation will drive the prices up. Their primary goal is to make a large profit in times of panic buying. The point here is that prices paid for firearms is an ever-changing affair based on a large number of variables. The prices in this book are a *GENERAL GUIDE* as to what a willing buyer and willing seller might agree on. You may find the item for less, and then again you may have to pay more depending on the variables of a particular situation. There is a saying among collectors that goes *"I didn't pay too much for this gun, I bought it too soon."* This reflects a solid trend with firearms that the prices continue to rise with each year. This is especially true with semi-automatic tactical firearms. With the likelihood that future federal, state or local legislation will restrict or completely stop the manufacture or import of these type of firearms, the prices can rapidly fluctuate. If news of any significant change in the status of these guns reaches the public, watch out for a buying panic that will drive prices through the roof. It has happened before and will undoubtedly occur again in the future.

In the final analysis, the prices listed here are given to assist the shooter and collector in pursuing their hobby with a better understanding of what is going on in the marketplace. If this book can expand one's knowledge, then it will have fulfilled its purpose.

Condition Ratings

This guide uses five condition categories: MSRP, NIB, Excellent, Very Good, and Good.

MSRP (Manufacturer Suggested Retail Price)

If a manufacturer lists a suggested retail price in its catalogs or on a website, that price is included here. The price listed is for the base model firearm as described in company sources. Please remember that many current production firearms are offered with a variety of options that can change the actual price to be paid. While the price of a few of these add-on options might be mentioned, it is not possible to list every feature in this book.

Another thing to bear in mind when reading a MSRP is that guns rarely sell at MSRP. The retail mark up in the firearms business varies by seller. With a lot of wholesale pricing available to the public, few retailers can expect to charge full MSRP. There is great competition among retailers and any who insist on charging full MSRP may be sitting on inventory for quite a while. However, with the nature of supply and demand, some hard-to-get models may actually bring more than MSRP – especially if there is any legislation pending that could ban or limit future manufacture.

NIB (New in Box)

For currently manufactured merchandise that is not advertised with a MSRP, the NIB price reflects the trend in price at retailer outlets. We have decided not to list out of production items with a NIB price. The reason is that there are too many variables in pricing this way that cannot be reflected in this sort of guide. For instance, you can have a 30-year-old FN FAL that is unfired in the box, along with all items that were originally shipped with the rifle. That would likely add $250-1000 to the price for a collector who wants the best possible example of this model. But what about lightly used but still in the box? What is a box worth? On the FAL it would still add quite a bit to the price with some buyers. With a Norinco AK-47/s, maybe not so much. One must also consider which items originally were included in the box with the firearm. How much to subtract from a price for missing magazines, cleaning kits or instruction manuals?

Excellent

The firearm must retain at least 98 percent of the factory original finish. Synthetic stocks, forearms and pistol grips should have no appreciable wear or scratches. The firearm must also be in 100 percent original factory condition without refinishing, repair, alterations, or additions of any kind. Sights must be factory original as well. The price listed includes one standard capacity original magazine. Prices for extra magazines and add-ons such as optics are not included in pricing.

Very Good

Firearms must be in working order and retain approximately 90 percent metal and wood finish. Synthetic stocks, forearms and pistol grips can have minor cosmetic scratches and surface wear. It must be 100 percent factory original, but may have some small repairs, alterations, or non-factory additions. No refinishing is permitted in this category. The bore should remain bright and shiney with no sign of wear or corrosion.

Good

Firearms must retain at least 80 percent metal and wood finish. Synthetic stocks, forearms and pistol grips might have obvious surface wear or scratches. They should not have cracks or pieces chipped off. Small repairs, alterations, or non-factory additions are sometimes encountered in this class. Factory replacement parts are permitted. The overall working condition of the firearm must be good as well as safe. The bore may exhibit wear or some corrosion.

Tactical firearms are rarly found in a condition that rates below good. The oldest of these firearms is just over 50 years old and most were made for the civilian market and have not seen much actual use.

I separate Tactical Firearms into a few loose categories:

The Classics

Many semi-automatic firearm designs over the last 50 years are based on existing select-fire models being used in military service around the world. Some are made by the original manufacturer while some are copies made by other companies wishing to cash in on the U.S. civilian arms market. The "Original Equipment Manufacturer" or OEM guns are the ones I refer to as classics.

Doing research for this book I was surprised to find out how many of the manufacturers of the world's true assault weapons have offered semi-automatic versions on the American market. The oldest one I came across is the FN FAL. I have a July, 1961 *American Rifleman* magazine with an ad for Browning Arms Co. listing the FAL rifle for a whopping (for the time) $175.00. The CETME and HK-41 are other early 1960's models that are very rare today. Colt introduced their AR-15 in 1964, with very little notice from the shooting public.

Most of the Classic designs were made overseas. The HK-41, CETME, Valmet, Galil, Steyr AUG, FAMAS, SIG AMT and more were legally imported in the 1960's through the 1980's. When these models were first offered on the American market, they were not great sellers. Most were too expensive to appeal to the average shooter. Some of these classics were imported in limited numbers, as few as 100 pieces.

Within the classification of classics I also include many independent designs that were made by fans of the classics that incorporated desirable features in new models. Guns that fit in this category include the Ruger Mini-14, Bushmaster ARM pistol, Halloway HAC-7, Wilkinson Arms Terry and Linda, and the Australian Leader. Some of these were made in small quantities and the companies folded quietly after a few years. Some models have achieved a bit of success. The Ruger Mini-14 continues to be a popular model to this day.

In the mid 1980's demand for military lookalike guns grew faster than it had in the previous 20 years. This might be attributed to a new generation of shooters coming of age, one whose members had grown up viewing this type of firearm in the news and movies. The WWII-era generation preferred walnut and steel guns. The younger group of shooters was more accepting of lightweight alloy parts and synthetic stocks. Around this time the American firearm industry press began to use the term *assault weapon* to identify this evolving class of firearm.

Unfortunatly, the 1980's saw the growth in the criminal misuse of firearms. When a criminal used a semi-automatic UZI carbine to murder 20 people in a fast food restaurant in San Ysidro, California, in 1984 the national media focused attention on the kind of firearm used. Other mass shootings followed. Despite the fact that very few of this type of firearm were used in everyday street crime, the media and anti gun politicians jumped on the bandwagon to demonize this class of guns and the people who owned them.

Subsequently, California passed a ban on sale or import into the state of new semi-automatic "assault weapons." Those who owned them could keep them but no new ones could be brought into the state. This legislation was the first large-scale effort to regulate guns based on model name and external features.

The classic era for imported guns ended in 1989 when the Reagan administration banned the import of firearms that did not meet a "sporting use" criteria as set forth in Federal law. The sporting use rules had been in place since the Gun Control Act of 1968 but the definition was re-interpreted in 1989 to ban the import of previously acceptable models.

The import ban affected foreign firearms but domestic production continued as before. In 1989 there were not that many domestic products on the market. Prices for "pre-ban" imported guns shot through the roof. The period from 1989 to 1994 saw an increased demand for many models that had been slow sellers before the ban. Ever eager to fulfill the wants of American buyers, some U.S. companies began building new firearms using new American-made receivers with imported parts. The government moved to close this "loophole" by imposing the part count rules set forth in Federal regulation CFR 922r.

As they watched with horror the growing demand for tactical firearms among American shooters, the anti-gun forces were relieved when a like-minded president was elected in 1992. The Clinton administration joined with congress to push through the infamous Assault Weapons Ban of 1994. This law was one of the least effective pieces of firearm legislation ever passed. First, it "grandfathered" all existing firearms and allowed them to be owned and transferred as before. Next, it defined "assault weapon" by the external characteristics of the firearm, listing several features that were found on pre ban models. The list of features includes: pistol grip, folding or collapsible stock, bayonet mount, flash hider. A semi-automatic gun could have a single feature, but not two or more. (See the Legal appendix to see the text of this law, 922r and other Federal regulations relating to tactical firearms.)

Finally, in order to get this law passed, they added a 10-year sunset provision to mollify some pro-gun factions. This meant that unless congress voted to renew the law in 10 years, it would expire. Which, thankfully, it did.

Ban Era Guns

The decade from 1994-2004 saw the American firearms industry build or import guns that complied with the definitions set forth in the law. This resulted in such oddities as thumbhole "sporter" stocks on numerous models, AR-15's with the telescoping stock permanently pinned in the extended position, permanent muzzle compensators, and a whole list of models that had a single banned feature. Of course the antigun congresspersons who fought for the law complained that these were violating the spirit of the law. Several manufactures produced their ban-compliant models for a decade and the only thing that really happened was that the American people developed a taste for more and more of this type of gun. During this time the Clinton administration also imposed a ban on importation of rifled firearms from China, thus cutting off a huge source of new models and re-made classics.

The New Boom

In September 2004 the decade long Assault Weapon Ban expired. There were several groups that tried to get it renewed but the Bush administration did not wish to take on the issue of firearm laws as this had cost the Clintons dearly. In anticipation of this sunset, many U.S. manufacturers were prepared to begin supplying the American public the guns they had wanted for a decade. It was the dawn of a new age for the American firearms industry. For the last six years, while other parts of the firearm industry are static or slowly shrinking, the demand for Tactical Firearms has continued to expand.

A significant part of this growth is due to the election of Barak Obama and a Democratic majority in Congress in 2008. This set off a new arms race in America. Manufactures could not keep up with demand and prices shot above MSRP for some models. After almost

three years, as of this writing, things have returned to "normal" and most items can be found easily. The struggling American economy has not affected the firearms market as much as other sectors. There are always buyers for guns at realistic prices.

Even though the new administration has not, as yet, made any major movement to reinstate an assault weapon ban or any other firearm legislation, the common belief is that they will try at some point. One can be assured that anti-gun politicians have drafted new laws without any sunset clause that define assault weapons broadly enough to prevent continued manufacture in any configuration. When and if this happens, the pricing in this guide will be a bit "low." A panic market drives things through the roof.

Heavy Iron

One growing segment of the tactical firearm market is semi-automatic versions of classic machine guns and sub-machine guns. This had begun in the pre ban era with Thompsons, Uzis, Browning M1919, and others but this new generation of designs uses original parts with new American made receivers and barrels. Many of the models offered are Soviet bloc designs. The main reason for this is the availability of parts kits on the world arms market. Former Communist guns such as the AK-47, PPSh, and DP-28 are cheap and plentiful. The importers cut the receivers and barrels and bring in the rest of the parts. New mechanisms are engineered that require significant alterations to stock parts. These new guns must receive approval from the BATFE that their semi-automatic mechanism can't be converted back to full auto. The U.S. customs department and BATFE have attempted to curtail this market by adding barrels to the receiver as parts that must be flame cut, not sawed, in three pieces before importation. But this is a minor inconvenience compared to the re-engineering that had to take place to get the semi-automatic mechanism to function reliably. A barrel is one of the easier parts to make here in the U.S.

Home Gunsmithing

Finally, I must address another significant trend that started as far back as the 1970's. I call it "rolling your own." This is when a new receiver is purchased by the end user, who builds a functional firearm using new or surplus parts. There have been semi-auto AR-15 receivers available since the 1970's but since 2004 the number of home assembled firearms has grown significantly. Besides the AR, one can currently purchase BATFE approved semi-automatic receivers for the AK-47, PPSh, CETME, HK 91-93-MP5, FN FAL, AK series, MG-34, MG-42, MP-40, Bren, BAR and many more.

If you are examining an AR or any type of tactical firearm that bears a name not listed in this book, is is probably a home-built gun. There are several makers of AR receivers that are not included in this guide since the company did not offer complete guns.

Due to the fact that each non factory firearm is unique, this book does not include pricing for these "kit" guns. If you want a general idea what someone's kit gun is worth, look at a listing for similar models built by one of the licensed manufacturers. Value should be in the ball park, if the gun was properly assembled on a good receiver.

When examining an unfamiliar "home built" firearm, it is important to consider the skills of the builder and the quality of the parts used. This is especially true of the countless AR-15-type firearms out there. With all the major manufacturers selling their lower receivers and any combination of upper assemblies available, it is nearly impossible to be sure you are looking at a factory gun or one assembled in a hobbyist's garage. It has gotten so hard to be sure a gun is completely factory, the only way to be sure is to get it new yourself, from a dealer.

Be careful when buying – and enjoy your Tactical Firearms responsibly.

AMERICAN TACTICAL IMPORTS
Rochester, New York
Website: www.americantactical.us

Importer of rifles made by German Sports Guns.

ATI also sells the Del ton line of AR-15 type rifles. See listing under DEL-TON.

■ GSG 5

A .22LR semi-automatic carbine patterned after the Heckler and Koch MP-5 sub-machine gun. 16-1/4 inch barrel covered with an outer tube to simulate a suppressor. Total length 33.5 inches. Fixed stock, 22 round magazine. Weight: 6.7 lbs. The first shipment cleared BATF approval in January, 2008. In 2009 Heckler Koch sued GSG over trademark infringement by this design. The manufacturer made some production changes and the case was settled. At some future point there may be a divergence in pricing between "pre HK suit" and post suit versions.

MSRP	EXC.	V.G.	GOOD
550	475	425	350

GSG 5 SEMI AUTO .22LR

■ GSG 5SD

A .22LR semi-automatic carbine patterned after the Heckler and Koch MP-5SD sub-machine gun. 16-1/4 inch barrel covered with a forearm and outer tube that simulates an integral suppressor. Total length 33.5 inches. Fixed stock, 22 round magazine. Introduced in 2009. Discontinued 2010.

MSRP	EXC.	V.G.	GOOD
575	500	425	375

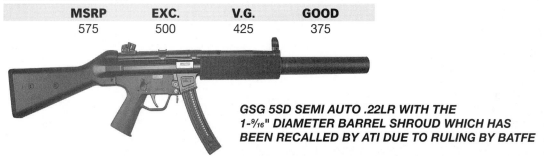

GSG 5SD SEMI AUTO .22LR WITH THE 1-⁹⁄₁₆" DIAMETER BARREL SHROUD WHICH HAS BEEN RECALLED BY ATI DUE TO RULING BY BATFE

NOTE: There was a BATFE ruling declaring the fake supressor on this model to be a violation of the NFA. ATI will replace the tube with an approved version. The notification from ATI:

To all retail customers:

On January 2010 American Tactical Imports Inc received official notification from the Bureau of Alcohol, Tobacco, Firearms and explosives that the original barrel shroud (aka: fake suppressor) supplied with your GSG 5 SD model must be replaced. **It has been determined that this shroud is regulated under the National Firearms Act.** American Tactical will provide a replacement shroud at no charge for each GSG 5 SD model sold or currently in inventory.

Consumers in possession of a GSG 5 SD model with the original shroud in place on the firearm are now in violation of the NFA. To avoid continued violation of the NFA, ATI asks that all persons in possession obtain a replacement shroud as soon as possible. We anticipate arrival of the new shrouds to begin by the middle of February 2010.

IMPORTANT: THE ORIGINAL SD MODEL SHROUD MUST BE RETURNED ACOMPANIED BY THE FIREARM SERIAL NUMBER BEFORE A REPLACEMENT SHROUD IS ISSUED. THE DIAMETER OF THE SD SHROUD IS 1-9/16". DO NOT RETURN THE SMALLER CARBINE SHROUD.

WHAT TO DO:

If possible return your old shroud to the dealer where purchased and show him this notice. The shroud will be returned to ATI along with a list of serial numbers from the guns that the shrouds were removed. ATI will send replacements to the dealer for pick up at your convenience; ATI will be sending replacements as fast as logistics allow. If your dealer is out of business or difficult to reach, or you purchased your gun used, from a consumer, return the shroud directly by US mail or UPS to American Tactical Imports Inc. 100 Airpark Drive Rochester, NY 14624.

PLEASE TRY NOT TO CALL US. We will provide comprehensive information on our web site www.americantactical.us , and www.ar15.com or by e-mail to atiexchange@americantactical.us

REMEMBER, INCLUDE THE FIREARM SERIAL NUMBER WITH EACH SHROUD OR A REPLACEMENT WILL NOT BE ISSUED.

This action IS NOT being instituted through any fault and is strictly due to NFA compliance. American Tactical will assume the responsibility to satisfy the requirements in an effort to minimize the impact on our customers and protect your investment.

We at American Tactical Imports Inc. sincerely apologize for any inconvenience caused by this unfortunate situation.

Sincerely,
Anthony DiChario
President C.E.O.

■ GSG 5P

A .22LR semi-automatic pistol patterned after the Heckler and Koch MP-5 sub-machine gun. 9-inch barrel with flash hider. Total length 18.6 inches. Fixed stock, 10 or 22 round magazine. Introduced In 2008. Discontinued 2010.

MSRP	EXC.	V.G.	GOOD
550	475	400	350

GSG 5 PISTOL

■ GSG 5PK

A .22LR semi-automatic pistol patterned after the Heckler and Koch MP-5K sub-machine gun. 4.7 Inch barrel. Total length 15.2 Inches. 10 or 22 round magazine. Introduced in 2009. Discontinued 2010.

MSRP	EXC.	V.G.	GOOD
550	475	400	350

■ GSG KALASHNIKOV

A .22LR semi-automatic carbine patterned after the legendary AK-47. 16.5-inch barrel. Total length: 34.5 inches. Wood or black synthetic furniture. 24 round magazine.

MSRP	EXC.	V.G.	GOOD
500	475	425	375

GSG KALISHNIKOV .22LR RIFLE

■ AT-94A2

A copy of the HK MP-5 in 9mm. 16-inch barrel. HK Fixed stock. Uses MP-5 magazines.   pattern sights.

MSRP	EXC.	V.G.	GOOD
1499	1250	1100	950

ATI AT-94A2 9MM RIFLE

■ AT-94K

A copy of the HK MP-5K. Caliber 9mm, with a 4.75-inch barrel.

MSRP	EXC.	V.G.	GOOD
1450	1250	1100	950

◼ AT-94P

As above with a 16.25-inch barrel. No forearm. No stock. Legally considered a handgun.

MSRP	EXC.	V.G.	GOOD
1450	1250	1100	950

◼ AT-47M

New for 2010. Assembled in the U.S. from un-issued Bulgarian and US made parts. Milled receiver. Wood stock.

MSRP	EXC.	V.G.	GOOD
875	800	750	675

◼ AT-47S

As above. With a stamped steel receiver.

MSRP	EXC.	V.G.	GOOD
750	700	650	600

ARMALITE
Costa Mesa, California

In business 1959 through the 1970's.

◼ AR-180

5.56mm/.223 semi-automatic. 18.25-inch barrel. Side folding stock. Originally designed to be a low-cost alternative to the M-16, the fully-automatic AR-18 used steel stampings for major components instead of machined parts. No major military contracts were placed for the select-fire version but the semi-automatic AR-180 found some success on the civilian market. It was manufactured by three makers under the Armalite name.

◆ Armalite 1969-72

EXC.	V.G.	GOOD
1500	1200	900

◆ Howa, Japan 1972-74

EXC.	V.G.	GOOD
1400	1100	800

◆ Sterling, England 1976-1979

EXC.	V.G.	GOOD
1100	900	750

ARMALITE MODEL AR-180 RIFLE CAL .223 W/ SIDE FOLDING STOCK

ARMALITE, INC.
Geneseo, Ill.
Website: www.armalite.com

Current manufacturer. Formed in 1995, after Eagle Arms purchased the old Armalite name.

Armalite currently offers an extensive line of rifles based on the AR-15 design. The following list is taken from their current catalog. Includes base model features listed. The Armalite product code is listed after each description. Many other features are available on a special-order basis. Armalite also sells assembled uppers and lowers as well as lower receivers.

■ 7.62X51MM/.308 RIFLES

Note: The AR-10 series uses modified M-14 7.62mm magazines. These are available from Armalite with a MSRP of $45.00.

◆ AR-10A2

The 7.62mm equivalent of the famed M16A2. 20-inch chrome-lined double-lapped barrel. A2 style upper receiver, with carry handle and A2 rear sight. Weight 9.8lbs. Available with green or black furniture.

Item: 10A2 or 10A2B (black)

MSRP	EXC.	V.G.	GOOD
1561	1250	1100	1000

ARMALITE MODEL AR-10 RIFLE, CAL. 7.62MM

◆ AR-10A2 Carbine

Similar to above with 16-inch barrel and collapsible stock, mid-length handguard, double-lapped, chrome-lined barrel. Weight 9 lbs. Available with green or black furniture.

Item: 10A2C or 10A2CB (black)

MSRP	EXC.	V.G.	GOOD
1561	1250	1100	1000

ARMALITE AR-10A2 CARBINE

◆ AR-10A4 SPR

20 inch barrel, picatinny rail receiver, and gas block of the AR-10(T) rifle, removable conventional sights with ArmaLite telescopic sight mounts, double-lapped chrome-lined barrel. Available with green or black furniture.

MSRP	EXC.	V.G.	GOOD
1557	1250	1100	1000

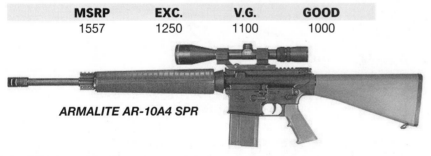

ARMALITE AR-10A4 SPR

◆ AR10A4 Rifle w/ Stainless Steel Barrel

Same as above but fitted with a 20-inch 416R stainless steel barrel. Black furniture.

MSRP	EXC.	V.G.	GOOD
1657	1350	1100	1000

◆ AR-10A4 Carbine

Removable conventional sights with ArmaLite telescopic sight mounts, 16-inch barrel, collapsible stock. Post-ban model available with pinned stock.

MSRP	EXC.	V.G.	GOOD
1506	1250	1100	950

ARMALITE MODEL AR-10A4 FLAT TOP CARBINE, WITH ADDED SCOPE

◆ AR-10A4NM Rifle (National Match)

National Match two-stage trigger, matched receivers, extended elevation NM sights installed into ArmaLite detachable sight bases, and ArmaLite 20-inch stainless steel match barrel mated to ArmaLite MIL STD 1913 free float rail handguard. Weight: 10.4lbs.

MSRP	EXC.	V.G.	GOOD
2365	1950	1750	1500

◆ AR-10B

A retro version of the original AR-10 produced in the 1960's. The AR-10B features the unique charging handle in the carry handle of the first AR-10 rifles, brown Sudanese style furniture, elevation scale window, and the famed ArmaLite Pegasus Logo. 20-inch barrel.

DISC	EXC.	V.G.	GOOD
N/A	1500	1300	1100

ARMALITE AR-10B

◆ AR-10 Super SASS Rifle

Adjustable gas system to optimize rifle function with suppressor as well as the AR designed enhancements that our engineers have made standard on every Armalite AR-10; improved reliability of feeding, extraction and ejection. 20-inch stainless steel match grade barrel. 1 min MOA claimed. Weight: 14 lbs.

MSRP	EXC.	V.G.	GOOD
3078	2500	2100	1600

ARMALITE AR-10 SUPER SASS RIFLE

◆ AR-10 (T) Rifle

20-inch triple lapped stainless steel barrel; picatinny rail on the upper receiver and the gas block allows for rapid and repeatable interchange of removable iron or scope sights. Features ArmaLite machined, tool-steel National Match two-stage trigger group. Armalite's top of the line rifle.

MSRP	EXC.	V.G.	GOOD
1892	1700	1550	1400

ARMALITE, INC.

◆ AR-10 (T) Carbine

As above with a 16-inch stainless steel barrel. Black furniture.

MSRP	EXC.	V.G.	GOOD
1892	1700	1550	1400

◆ AR-10 (T) Rifle Caliber .338 Federal

Chambered in .338 Federal. Features include one piece aluminum handguard allowing custom mounting of bipods, sights and optional MIL-STD 1913 rails. 22-inch stainless steel match barrel. Weight: 9.4 lbs.

MSRP	EXC.	V.G.	GOOD
1912	1700	1600	1500

◆ AR10 Lower Receiver

Lower receiver only. Black anodized.

MSRP	EXC.	V.G.	GOOD
227	N/A	N/A	N/A

■ 5.56MM/.223 RIFLES

◆ M15A2 Rifle Service Model

Semi-automatic civilian version of the famed M-16A2 service rifle. 20-inch double-lapped and chrome lined barrel. Includes ArmaLite's front sight base with bayonet lug and flash suppressor. Green or black furniture.

MSRP	EXC.	V.G.	GOOD
1150	900	750	600

◆ M15A2 Carbine

Carbine version of the M-15A2 rifle. Features include ArmaLite's exclusive mid-length handguards, 16-inch barrel, optimal gas pulse to power the operating system.

MSRP	EXC.	V.G.	GOOD
1150	900	750	600

ARMALITE M15A2 CARBINE

◆ M15A2 National Match

Features include a special, triple-lapped barrel, National Match 1/4 windage - 1/2 elevation sights with clear digits, floating barrel sleeve in the industry. Green or black furniture.

MSRP	EXC.	V.G.	GOOD
1388	1200	1000	800

ARMALITE M15A2 NATIONAL MATCH

◆ M15A4 SPR Rifle

Standard grade .223 caliber rifle with picatinny rail; accepts removable front sights and carry handles and other devices conforming to MIL STD 1913 (Picatinny) rail. 20-inch barrel. Weight 7.8 lbs.

MSRP	EXC.	V.G.	GOOD
1060	900	750	600

ARMALITE M15A4 SPR RIFLE

◆ M15A4 Carbine

Flat-top .223 caliber model of the AR-10A4 Carbine. 16-inch barrel. Weight: 7 lbs.

MSRP	EXC.	V.G.	GOOD
1060	900	750	600

ARMALITE M15A4 CARBINE

◆ SPR Model 1 Midlength Carbine

Forged, one-piece upper receiver/rail system with detachable side and bottom rails. Three detachable rails at three o'clock, six o'clock, and nine o'clock (three extra rails standard with a low insert for bare rail with a low profile and plain insert with a quick detach sling swivel hole). One-piece construction for continuous optic platform (COP). 16 inch-barrel. Weight: 6.5lbs. Black furniture.

MSRP	EXC.	V.G.	GOOD
1554	1200	1000	800

◆ SPR Mod1 LE Carbine

As above but with a short gas system and shorter handguard.

Item: 15SPR1LB

MSRP	EXC.	V.G.	GOOD
1529	1200	1000	800

◆ M15A4 SPR II National Match Rifle

Features include a 20-inch special, triple-lapped stainless steel barrel, forged flattop receiver, removable carry handle with National Match sights.

MSRP	EXC.	V.G.	GOOD
1413	1200	1000	800

M15A4 SPR II NATIONAL MATCH RIFLE

◆ M15A4 (T) Rifle

Similar to AR-10(T) Rifle in .308 but in .223 caliber. 20-inch triple-lapped stainless steel barrel floats within a rugged fiberglass handguard and the Military Standard sight base (Picatinny rail) on the upper receiver and gas block allow rapid and repeatable interchange of removable iron or scope sights. The M-15A4(T) features the Armalite National Match two-stage trigger. Weight: 8.6 lbs.

MSRP	EXC.	V.G.	GOOD
1296	1150	1000	850

M15A4 SPR II NATIONAL MATCH RIFLE

◆ M15 Lower Receiver

Lower receiver only. Black andodized.

MSRP	EXC.	V.G.	GOOD
159	N/A	N/A	N/A

◆ AR-180B Rifle

Features polymer lower made of a high strength polymer with trigger group and magazine well of the AR-15 so that magazines and repair parts are readily available. The AR-180B upper is formed sheet metal similar to 1st Generation AR-180 and features the AR-180 gas system to keep operating gases outside the receiver. The chrome moly barrel features an integral muzzle brake and adjustable front sight base. The new AR-180B upper and lower receiver groups are interchangeable with those of the 1st Generation AR-180, so earlier models may now be repaired by replacing the upper or lower half. Discontinued 2009.

EXC.	V.G.	GOOD
700	650	550

ARMALITE MODEL AR-180B RIFLE CAL. .223

■ 6.8MM SPC, 7.62X39MM RIFLES

◆ M14A4 6.8mm Carbine

Built on the same platform as the tactical M-15A4 Carbine but in 6.8 SPC. Mid-length handguard and gas system, green or black furniture.

MSRP	EXC.	V.G.	GOOD
1107	900	775	675

ARMALITE M14A4

◆ M15A4 Carbine 7.62x39mm

As above, chambered for 7.62x39mm. 16-inch barrel. Weight: 7 lbs.

MSRP	EXC.	V.G.	GOOD
1107	950	750	600

ARMI JAGER
Milano, Italy

Manufacturer of a series of .22LR rifles copied from famous assault rifles. They have been imported by Bingham Ltd., Mitchell Arms and others.

■ AP-74 /M-16

A copy of the U.S. M-16 rifle. Upper and lower receivers are made from cast alloy. The early models have triangular handguards. The newer versions have round handguards. 15 round magazine.

EXC.	V.G.	GOOD
325	250	200

Note: There was a 7.65mm/.32 ACP version of this rifle. A few were imported, although sales were slow because of the price of ammunition. 10 round magazine. Values are as follows:

EXC.	V.G.	GOOD
400	350	300

■ AK-22

A .22-caliber copy of the Soviet AK-47. The receiver is made from cast alloy. Sheet steel top cover. 15 and 30 round magazines.

EXC.	V.G.	GOOD
400	350	300

■ GALIL-22

A .22-caliber copy of the Israeli Galil. It uses the same action as the AK-22 with a different bolt handle and rear sight. 15 and 30 round magazines.

EXC.	V.G.	GOOD
400	350	300

■ MAS-22

A .22-caliber copy of the French FAMAS rifle. Bull pup design. Same action as the AK-22. 15 and 30 round magazines.

EXC.	V.G.	GOOD
500	425	350

**MITCHELL/ ARMI JAGER MAS-22
SEMI AUTOMATIC CARBINE**

ARMITAGE INTERNATIONAL
Seneca, South Carolina

■ SCARAB SKORPION PISTOL

A 9mm semi-automatic based on the Czech Model 61 Skorpion machine pistol. It has a 4-5/8 inch barrel with threaded muzzle. Black finish. Magazines hold 12 or 30 rounds. Approximately 600 were manufactured 1989-90. This model was recently put back in production by Leinad.

EXC.	V.G.	GOOD
550	475	400

**ARMITAGE INTERNATIONAL
SCARAB SKORPION PISTOL**

ARMSCOR
Marikina City, Philippines

Manufacturer based in the Philippines. Maker of a line of low-cost .22LR rifles that resemble the M-16 and AK. Has been imported under several names over the years, including Armscor Precision, KBI and Squires Bingham.

■ MODEL 1600

A copy of the U.S. M-16 rifle with an 18-inch barrel. Plastic stock. 10 or 15 round magazine.

EXC.	V.G.	GOOD
200	150	125

ARMSCORP M1600 RIFLE

■ MODEL 1600R

As above with collapsible wire stock.

EXC.	V.G.	GOOD
225	170	140

■ MODEL 1600W

As above with mahogany stock.

EXC.	V.G.	GOOD
200	150	125

■ MODEL AK22

A .22LR copy of the Soviet AK-47. 18-inch barrel. 10 or 15 round magazines. Mahogany stock.

EXC.	V.G.	GOOD
225	190	150

■ MODEL AK22F

As above with folding wire stock.

EXC.	V.G.	GOOD
250	200	175

ARMSCORP AK22 RIFLE WITH FOLDING STOCK

ARMSCORP OF AMERICA
Baltimore, Maryland

Manufacturer and importer 1982-94. They have offered custom built M-14 rifles assembled to customer specifications. Since each one is a unique item it is not practical to list all variations in this guide.

■ M-14 R RIFLE

7.62mm/.308 Excellent condition USGI M-14 parts set assembled on a new U.S. made semi-automatic receiver. Introduced 1986.

EXC.	V.G.	GOOD
1400	1000	800

M-14 BEGINNING NATIONAL MATCH
Built with excellent condition USGI parts and an air gauged premium barrel. Made 1993-96.

EXC.	V.G.	GOOD
1500	1100	950

M-14 NM (NATIONAL MATCH)
Offered with three barrel weights, National Match sights, operating rod and other parts. Introduced 1987.

EXC.	V.G.	GOOD
1600	1250	1000

M-21 MATCH RIFLE
National Match rear-lugged receiver. Custom barrel, stock and sights.

EXC.	V.G.	GOOD
2000	1750	1500

T-48 FAL ISRAELI PATTERN RIFLE
7.62mm/.308 manufactured with U.S.-made receiver and Israeli parts in original metric dimensions. Parts are interchangeable with FN Belgium made parts. Offered 1990-92.

EXC.	V.G.	GOOD
1250	1000	800

T-48 FAL L1A1 PATTERN
Copy of English L1A1. Add $200 for wood furniture.

EXC.	V.G.	GOOD
1200	900	750

T-48 BUSH MODEL
Similar to Israeli pattern but with 18-inch barrel.

EXC.	V.G.	GOOD
1250	1000	800

FRHB
Assembled with Israeli parts. Heavy barrel with bipod. Offered 1990 only.

EXC.	V.G.	GOOD
1800	1500	1100

FAL
New Armscorp manufactured receiver with Argentine made parts. 21-inch barrel. Offered 1987-90

EXC.	V.G.	GOOD
1250	1000	800

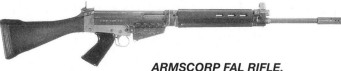

ARMSCORP FAL RIFLE.
IMAGE COURTESY ROCK ISLAND AUCTION.

FAL BUSH MODEL
As above with 18-inch barrel with flash hider. Offered 1989 only.

EXC.	V.G.	GOOD
1400	1100	900

FAL PARATROOPER MODEL
A Bush Model with side folding metal stock. Offered 1989 only.

EXC.	V.G.	GOOD
1900	1600	1250

M36 SNIPER MODEL
A 7.62mm/.308 bullpup type rifle that used a M-14 receiver. 22-inch free floating barrel with integral flash hider. Folding bipod. Copied from an Israeli design. According to some sources, only 10 pieces were made in 1989.

EXC.	V.G.	GOOD
5000	4500	4000

ARSENAL

Bulgaria

This commercial branch of the Bulgarian state arms industry made semi-automatic rifles for the U.S. market. Imported by DIG of Virginia Beach, Virginia, in the 1990's.

■ SLR-93 RIFLE

A milled receiver AK-47 imported to the U.S. 1994-1998. Caliber 7.62x39. Made with a wood thumbhole "sporter" type stock.

EXC.	V.G.	GOOD
1000	850	650

■ SLR-95 RIFLE

As above but made with a synthetic thumbhole stock. Offered with a muzzle brake or without.

EXC.	V.G.	GOOD
1000	850	650

ARSENAL, BULGARIA SLR-95 RIFLE WITH MUZZLE BREAK

ARSENAL, INC.

Las Vegas, Nevada

Website: www.arsenalinc.com

This is the current importer for AK type rifles made in Bulgaria. They bring in approved "sporting" rifles and refit them with enough U.S. made parts to qualify as American made, thus legal in most configurations. Government action suspended most parts importation and several variations have been discontinued since 2008. Not every variation is listed here. Pricing is in the same range as those listed.

■ 7.62X39MM RIFLES

◆ SLR-107F

Stamped receiver. 7.62x39 with a 16-1/4-inch barrel. Black or desert tan synthetic stocks. Left-side folding butt stock. Total length is 36-7/8 inches with stock open or 27-3/8 with stock folded. Flash hider, bayonet lug, accessory lug, stainless steel heat shield, 2 stage trigger, and Russian type scope rail on the Left side. Also available as a "ban" model without muzzle threads and bayonet mount.

MSRP	EXC.	V.G.	GOOD
859	750	700	600

ARSENAL SLR-107F

◆ SLR 107CF

Stamped receiver, 7.62x39 with a 16-1/4 inch barrel. Front sight block/gas block combination, 500m rear sight, cleaning rod. Stainless steel heat shield. Black or desert tan polymer stocks. Left-side folding butt stock, Total length is 34-1/2 inches with stock open or 25 inches with stock folded. Two-stage trigger and scope rail.

MSRP	EXC.	V.G.	GOOD
979	850	775	700

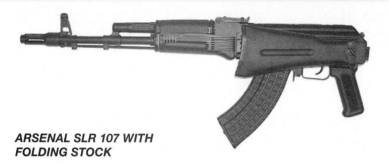

ARSENAL SLR 107 WITH FOLDING STOCK

◆ SLR-107UR

Stamped receiver, 7.62x39 caliber, short gas system, front sight block/gas block combination, cleaning rod, black polymer furniture, stainless steel heat shield, left-side folding polymer stock, two-stage trigger and scope rail. Discontinued.

	EXC.	V.G.	GOOD
	850	775	700

ARSENAL SLR 107UR

◆ SLR-108

Stamped receiver. Standard AK type rifle in 7.62x39mm. 16-1/4-inch barrel. Slant muzzle compensator. Fixed black polymer stock.

MSRP	EXC.	V.G.	GOOD
650	600	550	500

◆ SA M-7

A milled receiver AK rifle in 7.62x39. Black polymer fixed stock. Available with or without threaded muzzle and bayonet lug.

MSRP	EXC.	V.G.	GOOD
1550	950	825	750

◆ SA M-7 Classic

As above fitted with blond wood furniture. Discontinued.

	EXC.	V.G.	GOOD
	1000	850	750

◆ SAS M-7

Milled receiver, front sight block with bayonet lug. 16-1/4-inch barrel with flash hider. Black polymer furniture, with collapsible underfolding buttstock. Discontinued.

	EXC	V.G.	GOOD
	1000	900	800

◆ SAS M-7 Classic

As above made with blond wood forearm and pistol grip. Discontinued.

	EXC	V.G.	GOOD
	1000	900	800

◆ SLR-101/SLR-96

A assault weapon ban era AK rifle with polymer thumb hole stock. Caliber 7.62x39mm. Milled receiver. Pinned muzzle break. Similar to the older SLR-95. Discontinued.

	EXC.	V.G.	GOOD
	950	750	600

ARSENAL, INC.

◆ SA RPK-7

US made milled receiver. Caliber 7.62x39mm. 21-inch RPK heavy barrel, 14mm muzzle threads, muzzle nut, folding bipod, cleaning rod inside bipod, no bayonet lug, blond wood furniture, paddle style butt stock. Limited production. Discontinued.

■ 5.56MM/.223 RIFLES

◆ SLR-106F

Stamped receiver, 5.56 NATO caliber, Left side folding polymer stock. 16-1/4-inch barrel with muzzle brake, bayonet lug, accessory lug, stainless steel heat shield and 2-stage trigger. Discontinued.

EXC.	V.G.	GOOD
700	625	550

ARSENAL SLR 106F

◆ SLR-106F With Metal Stock

Stamped receiver, 5.56 NATO caliber, original metal left-side folding stock, 16-1/4-inch barrel with muzzle brake, bayonet lug, accessory lug, stainless steel heat shield and 2 stage trigger. Discontinued.

EXC	V.G.	GOOD
675	600	525

◆ SLR-106UR

Stamped receiver. Cal. 5.56mm NATO. 16-1/4-inch barrel. Short gas system. Black polymer furniture. Left side folding stock. Replica dummy suppressor.

MSRP	EXC.	V.G.	GOOD
1179	1000	N/A	N/A

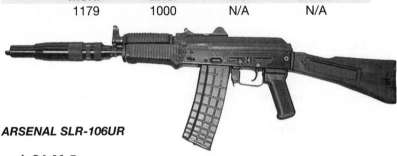

ARSENAL SLR-106UR

◆ SA M-5

US made milled receiver. Caliber 5.56mm Nato. 16-1/4 inch barrel. Muzzle brake, cleaning rod, bayonet lug, black polymer furniture. NATO pact buttstock. Discontinued

EXC.	V.G.	GOOD
800	700	600

◆ SA RPK-5

US made milled receiver. 21-inch RPK heavy barrel, cal 5.56mm. Folding bipod, cleaning rod inside bipod, no bayonet lug, blond wood furniture, paddle style buttstock. Discontinued.

EXC.	V.G.	GOOD
750	700	650

AUTO ORDNANCE
West Hurley, New York

Website: auto-ordnance.com

A manufacturer of the Thompson submachine guns through 1986, they also made several semi-automatic versions of the classic sub gun. Became a division of Kahr Arms in 1999. Add 20% for pre-Kahr Arms/AOC West Hurley, NY, production.

Note: Kahr Arms offers variants of its Thompson M1 and 1927 models in ÒSBÓ (short barrel) variations modeled after the original 10.5 inch, full-auto Thompson submachine guns. These short-barreled rifles are subject to the same ownership restrictions as submachineguns. See www.tommygun.com for more information.

■ THOMPSON 1927A-1 STANDARD CAL. 45 ACP

16-inch plain barrel. Horizontal forearm. Shipped with a 30-rd stick magazine. Discontinued.

	EXC.	V.G.	GOOD
	950	850	700

■ THOMPSON 1927A-1 DELUXE

Similar to abover but with 16-1/2 inch finned barrel and compensator. Available with a blued steel receiver.

MSRP	EXC.	V.G.	GOOD
1221	1100	950	850

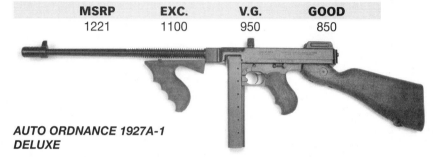

AUTO ORDNANCE 1927A-1 DELUXE

■ THOMPSON 1927 A-1 DELUXE WITH DETACHABLE BUTTSTOCK

As above but has a detachable buttstock similar to that on the 1928 SMG. Introduced in 2007.

MSRP	EXC.	V.G.	GOOD
1675	1400	1200	1000

AUTO ORDNANCE 1927A-1 DELUXE COMPARED TO A GENUINE THOMPSON 1928 SMG

■ THOMPSON 1927 A-1C LIGHTWEIGHT DELUXE

Same as the Deluxe model but with an aluminum alloy receiver.

MSRP	EXC.	V.G.	GOOD
986	850	750	600

■ THOMPSON 1927 A-1 COMMANDO

Replaced the standard model in the AO/Kahr lineup. Horizontal forearm. 16-1/2-inch finned barrel with compensator. Has a parkerized finish on the steel and a black finish on the stocks. Introduced in 1998.

MSRP	EXC.	V.G.	GOOD
1200	950	800	700

KAHR/AUTO-ORDNANCE
THOMPSON 1927A-1 COMMANDO

■ THOMPSON 1927 A-4

Pistol version made with an alloy receiver, 13 inch barrel, pistol grip forearm. No provision for mounting a stock. Discontinued in 1994. Reintroduced with 10.5 inch barrel and horizonal fore-arm as Model T5 by Kahr Arms in 2008.

EXC.	V.G.	GOOD
1500	1250	900

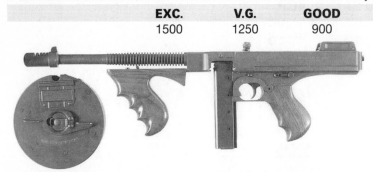

AOC 1927-A4 THOMPSON PISTOL. COURTESY ROCK ISLAND AUCTION.

NOTE: *Add $300 for 50 round drum magazine or $100 for 39-round drum XL magazine that accompanied many Thompson 1927 models. For 100 round drum add $300.*

■ THOMPSON M-1

A semi-automatic version of the WWII era M1A1 sub-machine gun. 16-inch barrel, horizontal forearm. Cocking knob is on the right side of the receiver instead of on top as the 1927 models. Does not accept drum magazines.

MSRP	EXC.	V.G.	GOOD
1148	950	800	700

■ THOMPSON 1927-A3 .22 CAL.

Has a 16-inch finned barrel with compensator. Alloy frame and receiver. Walnut stock. Pistol grip forearm. 30 round curved magazine. Discontinued 1994.

EXC.	V.G.	GOOD
1250	1100	950

AOC THOMPSON MODEL 1927A-3 .22LR. COURTESY ROCK ISLAND AUCTION.

■ AUTO-ORDNANCE M-1 CARBINE

A close copy of the classic U.S. Carbine Cal. .30 M-1. New manufacture. Has walnut or synthetic stock.

MSRP	EXC.	V.G.	GOOD
777	600	450	350

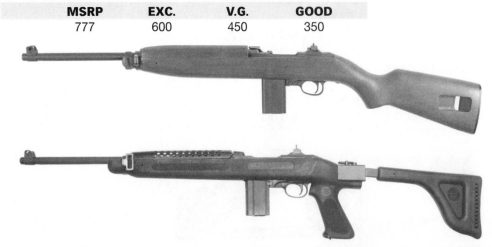

AUTO-ORDNANCE M-1 CARBINE WALNUT STOCK (TOP); FOLDING SYNTHETIC STOCK (BOTTOM)

BARRETT F.A. MFG CO.
Murfeesboro, Tennessee

Website: www.barrett.net

■ MODEL 82 RIFLE

A .50 Browning semi-automatic rifle. 37-inch barrel with a muzzle compensator. 11 round detachable magazine. Parkerized finish. Approx weight 35 lbs. Manufactured 1985-87.

EXC.	V.G.	GOOD
7000	6000	5000

■ MODEL 82A1 /M107

Updated version of the Model 82. Offered with 29- or 20-inch barrel. Weight approx 30 lbs. Currently issued to the U.S. military as the M107. Price for gun without optics.

MSRP	EXC.	V.G.	GOOD
9350	8000	7500	6500

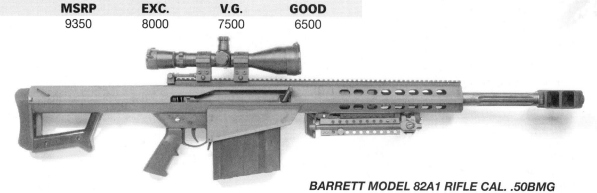

BARRETT MODEL 82A1 RIFLE CAL. .50BMG

■ REC7

AR-15 type rifle with a gas piston operating system. Cal. 5.56mm or 6.8mm SPC. 16-inch barrel. Flat top receiver. A.R.M.S. SIR rail system. Four-position telescoping stock. Weight: 7.6 lbs.

MSRP	EXC.	V.G.	GOOD
2520	2000	1500	1200

BARRETT MODEL REC7 RIFLE 5.56MM CAL.

BENELLI USA
Accokeek, Md.

Website: www.benelliusa.com

This manufacturer of shotguns has added a semi automatic rifle to its line.

■ MR1

A 5.56mm semi-automatic rifle utilizing the ARGO (Auto Regulating Gas Operated) action. It has a 16-inch barrel, adjustable sights, picitinny rail on top of receiver. Uses standard AR-15 magazines. Weight: 7.9 lbs. New for 2010.

MSRP	EXC.	V.G.	GOOD
1299	1150	N/A	N/A

BENELLI USA

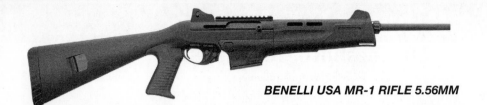

BENELLI USA MR-1 RIFLE 5.56MM

BERETTA, PIETRO
Gardonne, Italy

■ AR-70

A 5.56mm/.223 semi-automatic rifle. 17.7-inch barrel. Black epoxy finish with a black plastic stock. Sold with 8 and 30 round magazines. Weight 8-1/2 lbs. Made in Italy by Beretta. Imported by the Berben Corp. of NY, NY. Importation discontinued in 1989.

EXC.	V.G.	GOOD
2000	1750	1500

AR-70

■ BM-59

A 7.62mm/.308 version of the M-1 Garand that takes detachable 20 round magazines. A few were imported by Springfield Armory in the 1980s. Springfield Armory also manufactured their own version of this model. (Bottom illustration shows receiver markings.)

EXC.	V.G.	GOOD
2300	2000	1700

BERETTA BM-59 RIFLE 7.62MM

*RECEIVER MARKINGS
ON A BERETTA BM-59*

BERETTA U.S.A.
Accokeek, Maryland
website: www.berettausa.com

■ CX4 STORM

A semi-automatic carbine with a 16-5/8 inch barrel. Offered in 9mm, .40S&W or .45ACP. Uses the same magazines from Beretta handguns in these calibers. Synthetic stock. Introduced in 2003.

MSRP	EXC.	V.G.	GOOD
915	750	625	500

BERETTA MODEL CX4 STORM RIFLE 9MM

BUSHMASTER FIREARMS
Portland/Bangor, Maine

■ BUSHMASTER ARMS PISTOL

A 5.56mm semi-automatic pistol built in a bull pup configuration. 11-1/2-inch barrel. Alloy or steel frame. Operating handle is on top, later changed to the side. Pistol grip housing can be adjusted sideways to allow for left or right hand operation. Parkerized finish. Uses AR-15/M-16 magazines. Discontinued in 1988.

EXC.	V.G.	GOOD
900	800	700

BUSHMASTER ARM PISTOL CAL. .223

■ BUSHMASTER RIFLE

A rifle built with the same operating mechanism as above, but not a bull pup. 18-1/2-inch barrel. Side-folding stock. Fixed wood stock was available as an option. Discontinued.

EXC.	V.G.	GOOD
800	700	600

BUSHMASTER FIREARMS
Windham, Maine
Website: www.bushmaster.com

This company was formed in 1986 when Ouality Parts Co. bought the old Bushmaster trademark. They currently manufacture a variety of AR-15 type rifles. Bushmaster recently purchased Professional Ordnance and has added the Carbon 15 series of firearms to their offerings. Owned by Cerberus Capital, who also owns Remington and Marlin as part of its Freedom Group.

■ BUSHMASTER ACR - ADAPTIVE COMBAT RIFLE

Features include a 16-1/2-inch cold hammer-forged barrel (1x7 and 1x9 twist available); adjustable, two-position gas-piston-driven system; tool-less quick-change barrel system available in 16.5-inch and 18-inch lengths and in multiple calibers; multi-caliber bolt carrier assembly quickly changes from 223/5.56mm NATO to 6.8mm Rem SPC; free-floating MIL-STD 1913 monolithic top rail for optic mounting; fully ambidextrous controls including magazine release, bolt catch and release, fire selector and non-reciprocating charging handle; high-impact composite handguard with heat shield that accepts rail inserts; Magpul MBUS front/rear flip sights. Availible in black or tan. New in 2010.

MSRP	EXC.	V.G.	GOOD
2685	2500	2200	2000

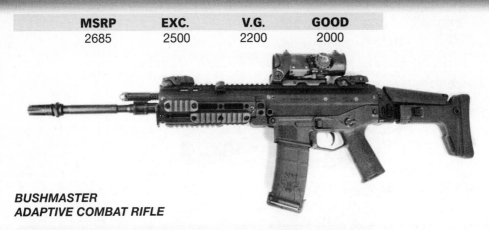

BUSHMASTER
ADAPTIVE COMBAT RIFLE

■ BUSHMASTER ACR ENHANCED CONFIGURATION

As above but with a folding six-position high-impact polymer stock with rubber butt pad and sling mounts.

MSRP	EXC.	V.G.	GOOD
3061	2850	2500	2200

■ BUSHMASTER GAS PISTON RIFLE

Operates on piston rather than direct impingement. Features a M4 flat top receiver with removable carry handle. 1913 gas block. 16-inch barrel. Telescoping stock. Weight: 6.5 lbs. without magazine.

MSRP	EXC.	V.G.	GOOD
1850	1250	1100	1000

BUSHMASTER GAS PISTON RIFLE

■ BUSHMASTER M4A3 CARBINE

Features include M4 barrel profile (M203 compatible); six position telestock; 1913 flat top upper receiver; removable A2 type carry handle.

MSRP	EXC.	V.G.	GOOD
1300	1000	850	700

■ BUSHMASTER M4A2 CARBINE

As above but with a standard A2 type upper receiver.

MSRP	EXC.	V.G.	GOOD
1300	1000	850	700

■ BUSHMASTER O.R.C. (OPTICS READY CARBINE)

Shipped without iron sights. Various add-on rear iron sights can be easily attached to the flat-top upper receiver; Bushmaster's BMAS front flip-up sight for V Match rifles can be mounted over the milled gas block. The premium 16-inch M4 profile barrel is chrome lined in both bore and chamber.

MSRP	EXC.	V.G.	GOOD
1180	950	825	700

■ BUSHMASTER .308 O.R.C. (OPTICS READY CARBINE)

.308 Win./7.62 NATO; 16-inch heavy profile barrel with mid-length gas system and A2 birdcage flash hider, receiver length picatinny optics rail with two 1/2-inch optics risers, milled gas block, heavy oval handguards, six position telescoping stock, shipped in a lockable hard case with operator's safety manual, 20 round magazine, yellow safety block and black web sling. Weight 7.75 lbs. without magazine.

MSRP	EXC.	V.G.	GOOD
1395	1200	1050	900

BUSHMASTER 308 OPTICS READY CARBIN

■ BUSHMASTER A.R.M.S. M4 TYPE CARBINE

5.56mm / .223 Rem. Features include front and rear flip sights, allowing for optics and iron sights in the same carbine; 16-inch chrome-lined barrel; Magpul MOE adjustable buttstock with a strong A-frame design; Hogue non-slip pistol grip.

MSRP	EXC.	V.G.	GOOD
1395	1200	1050	850

■ BUSHMASTER M.O.E. (MAGPUL ORIGINAL EQUIPMENT) M4 TYPE CARBINE

5.56mm / .223 Rem. Features include 16-inch M4 profile barrel with A2 birdcage flash hider, receiver length picatinny optics rail with Magpul MBUS rear flip sight, Magpul MOE polymer handguard that accepts MOE rail inserts (not included), Magpul MOE adjustable buttstock or MOE collapsible stock, pistol grip, polymer handguard, MBUS rear flip sight and PMAG. Available with black, flat dark earth or foliage green furniture.

MSRP	EXC.	V.G.	GOOD
1295	1150	1000	850

■ BUSHMASTER MODULAR CARBINE

5.56mm NATO/.223 Rem. Features include chrome-lined, free-floated 16-inch chrome-moly vanadium steel barrel; Bushmaster modular accessories including B.M.A.S. four rail tubular forend which free-floats the barrel from the barrel nut forward; molded rubber Sure-Grip rail covers; rear sight detachable dual aperture B.M.A.S. rear flipup unit with windage calibrated to 1/2 MOA; front sight B.M.A.S. clamp-on designed to fit directly over the milled front gas block; birdcage flash suppressor. The modular carbine is available with either a lightweight skeleton stock or a six-position telescoping stock.

MSRP	EXC.	V.G.	GOOD
1780	1400	1250	1100

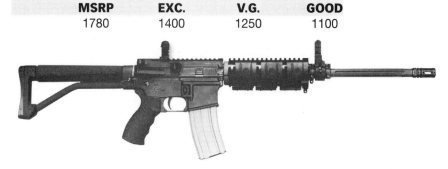

BUSHMASTER MODULAR CARBINE CAL. .223

■ BUSHMASTER CARBON 15 9MM CARBINE

9mm Parabellum. Features include 16-inch barrel; carbon fiber receivers; AR15 type operating controls; six-position telestock; and receiver-length picatinny optics rail.

MSRP	EXC.	V.G.	GOOD
1080	950	850	750

BUSHMASTER CARBON 9 CARBINE, CAL. 9MM

■ BUSHMASTER CARBON 15 TOP LOADING CARBINE

5.56mm NATO/.223 Rem. Developed specifically for the California market (and other locales with similar restrictions) prohibiting detachable magazines. Features include carbon fiber composite molded receivers; 16-inch M4 profile barrel; 10 round internal magazine; otherwise identical in function to basic AR.

MSRP	EXC	V.G.	GOOD
1070	950	850	750

■ BUSHMASTER CARBON 15 M4 FLAT TOP CARBINE

5.56mm NATO/.223 Rem. Features include carbon 15 composite molded receivers for light weight and rugged durability; 16-inch M4 profile barrel; lightweight carbon 15 composite receivers; matte black finish throughout; anodized aluminum picatinny rail for unlimited sight, scope or optics mounting. 16-inch M4 profile chrome-lined barrel with standard threaded muzzle; Izzy flash suppressor; AR type base with post front sight adjustable for elevation; B.M.A.S. dual aperture flip-up rear sight, adjustable for windage; six-position telestock; carbine-length handguards with internal aluminum shields.

MSRP	EXC.	V.G.	GOOD
1190	1000	900	800

BUSHMASTER CARBON 15 M-4 CARBINE, CAL. .223

■ BUSHMASTER "AK" CARBINES

5.56mm NATO/.223 Rem. Features include 16-inch chrome-lined chrome-moly vanadium steel heavy barrel; forged aluminum receiver; six position telestock; carbine length handguard; birdcage flash suppressor; AK47 type muzzle brake; 5.5-inch suppressors permanently pinned and welded onto barrels to achieve legal length; A2 or A3 upper receiver; dual aperture rear sights on A2 models have 1 MOA elevation adjustments and 1/2 MOA windage adjustments with a 300-800 meter range. A3 type carbines (removable carry handle included) have 1/2 MOA adjustments for both elevation and windage with a 300-600 meter range. A3 upper has a picatinny rail for the attachment of sights, scopes, or night vision optics. A2 front post type sights are adjustable for elevation.

MSRP	EXC.	V.G.	GOOD
1215	1000	875	750

BUSHMASTER "AK" CARBINE .223, WITH AK MUZZLE BRAKE

■ BUSHMASTER CARBON 15 R4 RIFLE

5.56mm / .223 Rem. Features include carbon 15 composite molded receiver; color-coded safety lever markings on both sides of receiver for quick visual check of firing condition; 14.5-inch M4 profile barrel – chrome lined chrome-moly steel – that includes an Izzy flash suppressor pinned and welded in place to achieve 16-inch overall barrel length; receiver-length raised picatinny optics rail with integral dual aperture rear sight (windage adjustable). Front sight is standard A2 post type gas block adjustable for elevation. Six-position telestock reduces overall length by 4 inches when retracted.

MSRP	EXC.	V.G.	GOOD
1190	1000	875	750

BUSHMASTER CARBON 15 R4 RIFLE

■ BUSHMASTER SUPERLIGHT CARBINES

5.56mm/.223 Rem. Features include a 16-inch barrel design based on original G.I. "pencil barrel" profile; six-position telestock or a "stubby stock." Bushmaster's lightest aluminum carbine.

MSRP	EXC.	V.G.	GOOD
1250	1100	950	800

■ BUSHMASTER DISSIPATOR CARBINE

5.56mm/.223 Rem. Features include 16-inch carbine length barrel, full-length handguards and the sight radius of the original AR rifle design. Available with A2 fixed or 6-position telestock.

MSRP	EXC.	V.G.	GOOD
1240	1050	875	700

BUSHMASTER DISSIPATER CARBINE, WITH FULL-LENGTH HANDGUARD

■ BUSHMASTER M4 TYPE "POST BAN" CARBINE

5.56mm/.223 Rem. This model offers features that make it legal for sale in states where restrictions similar to the Assault Weapons Ban of 1994 are still in place. Features include 14.5-inch chrome lined M4 type barrel with a permanently attached Izzy brake for 16-inch overall length (BATFE legal) barrel; fixed length "tele-style" unit, not collapsible in order to conform with regulations. Magazine capacity is limited to 10 rounds; bayonet lug is milled off.

MSRP	EXC.	V.G.	GOOD
1265	1100	950	800

■ BUSHMASTER TARGET MODEL RIFLE A2 20-INCH

5.56mm/.223 Rem. Standard A2 type rifle with 20-inch heavy barrel.

MSRP	EXC.	V.G.	GOOD
1095	900	750	600

■ BUSHMASTER TARGET MODEL RIFLE A2 STAINLESS 20-INCH

As above with a stainless steel barrel.

MSRP	EXC.	V.G.	GOOD
1125	950	800	650

■ BUSHMASTER TARGET MODEL RIFLE A3 20-INCH

5.56mm/.223 Rem. Standard rifle featuring an A3 upper with detachable carry handle.

MSRP	EXC.	V.G.	GOOD
1195	1000	900	800

■ BUSHMASTER TARGET MODEL RIFLE A3 STAINLESS 20-INCH

5.56mm/.223 Rem. As above with a stainless steel barrel.

MSRP	EXC.	V.G.	GOOD
1235	1050	950	850

■ BUSHMASTER TARGET MODEL A3 24-INCH

5.56mm/.223 Rem. The A3 target rifle fitted with a 24-inch barrel.

MSRP	EXC.	V.G.	GOOD
1205	1000	900	800

■ BUSHMASTER DCM XR SERIES COMPETITION RIFLE A2 MODEL

5.56mm/.223 Rem. Features include 20-inch 1:8 extra heavy chrome-moly vanadium steel competition barrel with full 1" diameter under the free float tube, precision button rifled with 1:8 right hand twist; M16A2 dual aperture rear sight; competition front sight; buttstock weight; two-stage competition trigger.

MSRP	EXC.	V.G.	GOOD
1150	1050	900	750

■ BUSHMASTER VARMINTER

5.56mm/.223 Rem. Features include 24-inch fluted DCM extra heavy (1-inch dia.) competition barrel with 11° competition crowned muzzle. 5 round magazine, front bipod swivel. Weight: 8.8 lbs.

MSRP	EXC.	V.G.	GOOD
1350	1100	950	800

■ BUSHMASTER PREDATOR

Built as a result of numerous requests by the hunters who wanted a slightly shorter barrel and lighter weight in a carry rifle for predator hunting/calling, this is a 20-inch barreled version of the Varminter.

MSRP	EXC.	V.G.	GOOD
1350	1100	950	800

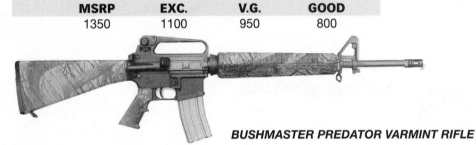

BUSHMASTER PREDATOR VARMINT RIFLE

■ BUSHMASTER STAINLESS VARMINT SPECIAL

As above with a stainless steel match grade barrel.

MSRP	EXC.	V.G.	GOOD
1365	1100	950	800

BUSHMASTER STAINLESS VARMINT SPECIAL

■ CARBON 15 .22 LR RIMFIRE

.22 LR rimfire. AR-style blowback rifle similar in appearance and construction to Carbon 15 centerfire rifle.

MSRP	EXC.	V.G.	GOOD
790	700	625	550

BUSHMASTER CARBON 15 .22 LR RIMFIRE

■ BUSHMASTER .450 RIFLE AND CARBINE

.450 Bushmaster. Features include chrome-moly 1:24 chrome lined steel barrel (rifle 20-inch, carbine 16-inch); free floating aluminum forend; forged aluminum receiver; A2 pistol grip and solid A2 buttstock with trapdoor storage compartment. All operating controls are the same as any AR type rifle. Shipped with one 5 round magazine, a black web sling, operators safety manual, and orange safety block in a lockable hard plastic carrying case.

MSRP	EXC.	V.G.	GOOD
1350	1200	1050	900

BUSHMASTER .450 RIFLE AND CARBINE

■ BUSHMASTER 6.8 SPC RIFLE

6.8mm SPC. Features include 16-inch M4 profile barrel with IzzyÓbrake; six-position telescoping stock;; other stocks are available as optional installations; 26 round magazine; A2 or A3 upper receivers.

MSRP	EXC.	V.G.	GOOD
1330	1100	1000	850

■ BUSHMASTER M17S

A bullpup style rifle in 5.56mm/.223. It has a 20-inch barrel. The receiver is made from machined aluminum. Uses AR-15 magazines. Discontinued.

EXC.	V.G.	GOOD
750	675	600

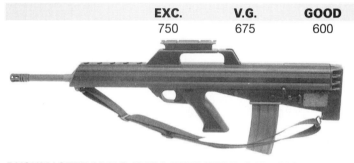

BUSHMASTER M17 S "BULL PUP" RIFLE, CAL. .223

■ BUSHMASTER PISTOLS

◆ Carbon 15 Type 21S Pistol

Pistol version of AR. 5.56mm/.223 Rem. Features include full length picatinny rails with integral iron sights; receivers, forend and other parts are molded of Carbon 15 composite; 7-1/4 inch stainless steel match grade barrel with A2 flash suppressor. The total length of the pistol is 20 inches. The bolt carrier is black oxide finished, and other critical steel parts are manganese phosphate finished for corrosion and rust protection. Upper receiver includes a full length picatinny optics rail with integral dual aperture rear sight (windage adjustable), and an A2 type square post front sight adjustable for elevation. Uses AR-15 magazines.

MSRP	EXC.	V.G.	GOOD
1080	850	750	650

BUSHMASTER CARBON 15 TYPE 21S .223 PISTOL

◆ Bushmaster Carbon 15 Type 97 Pistol

Pistol version of AR. 5.56mm/.223 Rem. Features include receivers and other parts molded of durable carbon fiber composite; match grade 7-1/4-inch stainless steel barrel stainless steel fluted match grade barrel; ghost ring type rear sight; blade front sight; quick-detach compensator; Hogue overmolded pistol grip. Uses AR-15 magazines.

MSRP	EXC.	V.G.	GOOD
1020	850	750	650

◆ Bushmaster Carbon 15 Type 97S Pistol

Similar to Type 97 but with additional picatinny accessory mounting rail for lasers or flashlights and other refinements Uses AR-15 magazines.

MSRP	EXC.	V.G.	GOOD
1130	900	800	700

BUSHMASTER TYPE 97S PISTOL CAL. .223

◆ Bushmaster Carbon 15 9mm Pistol

Similar to Type 97S pistol but chambered in 9mm Parabellum.

MSRP	EXC.	V.G.	GOOD
1055	850	750	650

BUSHMASTER CARBON 15 PISTOL IN 9MM

CALICO LIGHT WEAPONS SYSTEMS
Hillsboro, Oregon
Website: www.calicolightweaponsystems.com

■ CALICO M-100

A .22LR semi-automatic carbine. It has a 16-1/8-inch barrel that ends in a flash hider. Synthetic handguards. Folding steel stock. The Calico firearms utilize a unique high capacity helical magazine that holds 100 rounds. Manufactured 1989-98. Re-introduced in 2004, after expiration of the assault weapon ban. Weight: 5.7 lbs. with loaded 100 round magazine.

MSRP	EXC.	V.G.	GOOD
651	500	400	300

CALICO M100 RIFLE .22LR
WITH 100 ROUND MAGAZINE

■ M100 TACTICAL
A Model 100 fitted with a quad rail forearm.

MSRP	EXC.	V.G.	GOOD
726	600	500	400

■ MODEL 100P/M-110
A pistol version of the M-100. It has a 6-inch barrel that ends with a muzzle brake. No shoulder stock.

MSRP	EXC.	V.G.	GOOD
688	500	425	375

CALICO MODEL 100 PISTOL
WITH A 100 ROUND MAGAZINE

■ MODEL 100S SPORTER/M-105
A Model 100 carbine with solid walnut stock and forearm. Discontinued.

EXC.	V.G.	GOOD
600	525	450

■ MODEL 100 FS
A model 100 fitted with a synthetic fixed stock. For markets with folding stock restrictions.

MSRP	EXC.	V.G.	GOOD
651	500	400	300

■ MODEL 100 MAGAZINE
Calico 22LR 100 round magazine.

MSRP	EXC.	V.G.	GOOD
141	100	75	50

■ MODEL 900 / LIBERTY 1
A 9mm semi-automatic carbine. It uses a unique retarded blowback method of operation. 16-inch barrel. Fixed rear sight. Adjustable front sight. Collapsible shoulder stock. Manufactured 1989-90 and 1992-93. Re-introduced after 2004 as the Liberty series. Sold with 50 or 100 round helical magazine. The 100 round version runs approximatly $50 more.

MSRP	EXC.	V.G.	GOOD
807	700	600	500

■ LIBERTY 100 TACTICAL
As above with a quad rail forearm. Shipped with a 100 round magazine. Deduct $50 if supplied with a 50 round magazine. Introduced 2010.

MSRP	EXC.	V.G.	GOOD
890	700	600	500

■ MODEL 900-S / LIBERTY II
As above with a fixed synthetic shoulder stock.

MSRP	EXC.	V.G.	GOOD
963	700	575	500

■ LIBERTY II TACTICAL RIFLE

As above with a quad rail forearm.

MSRP	EXC.	V.G.	GOOD
1038	800	700	600

■ MODEL 950 PISTOL / LIBERTY III PISTOL

A handgun version of the model 900. It has a 6-inch barrel. Shipped with a 50 round magazine.

MSRP	EXC.	V.G.	GOOD
890	700	600	500

CALICO MODEL 950 PISTOL

■ MODEL 951T TACTICAL RIFLE

A Model 950 with the addition of a muzzle brake and a hand grip on the forearm. Manufactured 1990-94.

EXC.	V.G.	GOOD
750	675	600

■ CALICO 9MM 50 ROUND HELICAL MAGAZINE

MSRP	EXC.	V.G.	GOOD
131	100	75	50

■ CALICO 9MM 100 ROUND HELICAL MAGAZINE

MSRP	EXC.	V.G.	GOOD
157	125	100	75

CENTURY INTERNATIONAL ARMS
St. Albans, Vermont/
Georgia, Vermont
Website: www.centuryarms.biz

Century Arms has been known for years as the largest importer of military surplus firearms for the U.S. market. As the overseas supplies of surplus firearms legal for importation has dwindled, Century Arms has expanded their offerings to include a wide variety of semi-automatic versions of classic assault rifles. Not every variation is listed here.

■ CENTURY AKM

Century currently has several variations of the Automat Kalishnikov series available. These are manufactured by Century Arms using U.S. made receivers and barrels and other parts necessary to comply with U.S. code 922(r), along with original AK parts imported from over seas. These are offered with both Draganov style thumbhole stocks as well as standard military pattern stock sets. Some models only accept a 10 round single column magazine and lack the recoil compensator and bayonet mount in order to comply with laws in several states and cities. Others accept the original high capacity magazines but lack the features banned by some laws.

NOTE: *AKM Type rifles that accept a 10 round low capacity magazine will not accept standard AK magazines.*

■ CENTURY CUT AWAY GP WASR-10

As above but a cut away rifle for training gunsmiths and others. Allows viewing of internal parts and their functional relationship. Still requires paperwork, just like any modern firearm. Includes a cutaway 10 round magazine.

NIB	EXC.	V.G.	GOOD
425	350	325	300

CENTURY INTERNATIONAL AKM WITH VERTICAL FOREND (TOP) AND STANDARD CONFIGURATION (BOTTOM)

■ CENTURY WASR-2

Semi-auto rifle low capacity rifle with military style stock, cal. 5.45x39mm.

NIB	EXC	V.G.	GOOD
350	325	300	275

CENTURY INTERNATIONAL WASR-2

■ CENTURY WASR-3

Semi-auto rifle, low capacity w/ military style stock, cal. .223. Shipped with two 10 round magazines.

NIB	EXC	V.G.	GOOD
350	325	300	275

AKM TYPE RIFLES THAT ACCEPT STANDARD CAPACITY MAGAZINES AND DRUM MAGAZINES

■ CENTURY GP WASR-10 HI-CAP

Semi-auto rifle with Dragunov style stock, Cal. 7.62x39mm. 16-1/4-inch barrel. Weight is 7-1/2 lbs. Shipped with two 30 round magazines.

NIB	EXC.	V.G.	GOOD
375	325	300	275

■ CENTURY WASR-2 HI-CAP

Semi-auto rifle with military stock, Cal. 5.45x39mm. No recoil compensator or bayonet lug. Shipped with two 30 round magazines.

NIB	EXC	V.G.	GOOD
400	375	350	325

■ CENTURY WASR-3 HI-CAP

Semi-auto rifle with military style stock, Cal. .223. No recoil compensator or bayonet lug. Shipped with two 30 round magazines.

NIB	EXC	V.G.	GOOD
400	375	350	325

■ CENTURY GP WASR-10 HI-CAP SIDE FOLD

Semi-auto rifle with side folding composite stock and original Romanian pattern wood forward pistol grip, Cal. 7.62x39mm. Has recoil compensator and bayonet lug. Shipped with two 30 round magazines and a bayonet.

NIB	EXC	V.G.	GOOD
475	450	525	400

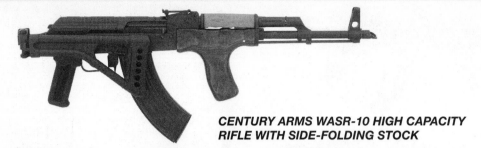

CENTURY ARMS WASR-10 HIGH CAPACITY RIFLE WITH SIDE-FOLDING STOCK

■ CENTURY GP WASR-10 HI-CAP SLIDE STOCK

Semi-auto rifle with CAR-15 style collapsible stock, cal. 7.62x39mm. Wood forearm. Has recoil compensator and bayonet lug. Shipped with two 30 round magazines and a bayonet.

NIB	EXC	V.G.	GOOD
450	425	400	375

■ CENTURY GP WASR-10 HI-CAP

Galil handguard and CAR-15 type collapsible stock, cal 7.62x39mm. Has recoil compensator and bayonet lug. Shipped with two 30 round magazines and a bayonet.

NIB	EXC	V.G.	GOOD
450	425	400	375

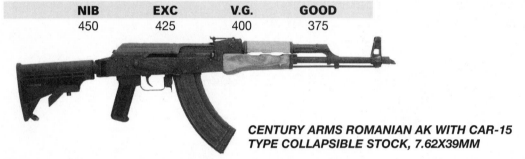

CENTURY ARMS ROMANIAN AK WITH CAR-15 TYPE COLLAPSIBLE STOCK, 7.62X39MM

■ CENTURY M72 HEAVY BBL SEMI-AUTO SPORTER

Cal. 7.62x39mm. 21-1/4-inch barrel. Based on the Yugoslavian M72 light machine gun. Folding bipod. Has recoil compensator. Shipped with two 40 round magazines.

NIB	EXC	V.G.	GOOD
650	600	575	550

■ CENTURY M70B1 SEMI-AUTO SPORTER

Cal. 7.62x39mm. Same as the Yugoslavian Model 70 rifle. Original wood stock has the issue rubber recoil pad. 16-1/4-inch barrel features a recoil compensator. No bayonet mount. Weight 8-1/2 lbs. Shipped with two 30 round magazines.

NIB	EXC	V.G.	GOOD
525	500	475	450

■ CENTURY M70AB2

Sporter with under-folding stock, cal. 7.62x39mm. Based on the Yugoslavian Model 70AB paratrooper rifle with under folding stock. Original parts are refinished to like new condition. Has recoil compensator and bayonet lug. Shipped with two 30 round magazines and a bayonet.

NIB	EXC	V.G.	GOOD
550	500	475	450

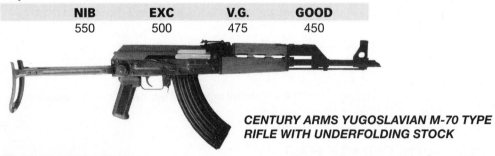

CENTURY ARMS YUGOSLAVIAN M-70 TYPE RIFLE WITH UNDERFOLDING STOCK

■ CENTURY AMD65

Hungarian AMD65 pattern semi-auto sporter with sidefolding stock and pistol grip forearm. Cal. 7.62x39mm.

NIB	EXC	V.G.	GOOD
600	550	500	425

***CENTURY ARMS HUNGARIAN AMD-65 TYPE
RIFLE WITH SIDEFOLDING STOCK. 7.62X39MM***

■ CENTURY GP 1975 RIFLE

Cal. 7.62x39mm. It has a T6 adjustable collapsible stock for perfect length adjustment. Top and bottom handguard from Fobus. Accepts 30 round mags. 16-1/4-inch barrel (without compensator). Overall length 34 inches (37.5 inches with fully extended stock). Weight: 6.9 lbs.

NIB	EXC	V.G.	GOOD
575	550	525	500

■ CENTURY GP WASR-10 ROMANIAN UNDER FOLDER RIFLE

Cal. 7.62x39mm. Has recoil compensator and bayonet lug. Shipped with two 30 round magazines and a bayonet. Product ID: RI1405

NIB	EXC	V.G.	GOOD
475	450	425	400

■ CENTURY AES-10B HI-CAP SEMI-AUTO RIFLE

Cal. 7.62x39mm. Basically an AES-10 with a heavy barrel and bipod to make it look almost exactly like the famous RPK. Comes with two 40 round mags. Barrel: 21-1/4 inches; overall length 40 inches. Weight 10.75 lbs.

NIB	EXC	V.G.	GOOD
500	475	450	425

■ CENTURY 1975 AK BULLPUP RIFLE

Cal. 7.26x39mm. An AK type rifle reconfigured in bullpup design. Comes with two 30 round magazines. Barrel: 16-1/4 inches, overall length 27 inches. Weight: 7 lbs.

NIB	EXC	V.G.	GOOD
525	500	475	450

***CENTURY ARMS AKM TYPE RIFLE WITH
NEW BULL PUP STOCK, CAL. 7.62X39MM***

■ CENTURY TANTAL SPORTER

Cal. 5.45x39mm. Copy of the Polish Issue AK-74 design. 18-inch barrel with muzzle break, folding steel stock. Comes with two 30 round magazines.

NIB	EXC	V.G.	GOOD
600	500	450	400

CENTURY ARMS TANTAL RIFLE 5.45X39MM

■ CENTURY CENTURION 39 RIFLE

New all U.S. made AK type rifle in 7.62x39mm. 16.5-inch barrel with muzzle break. Features a milled steel receiver. Handguard has 4 picitinny rails. Synthetic stock. Weight: 8.2 lbs.

NIB	EXC	V.G.	GOOD
875	800	700	600

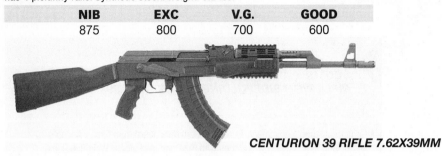

CENTURION 39 RIFLE 7.62X39MM

■ CENTURY ROMANIAN DRAGUNOV SEMI-AUTO RIFLE

Cal. 7.62x54R. A copy of the classic Russian sniper rifle from the Cold War. 26-1/2-inch barrel. Overall length 45-1/2 inches. Weight 9 lbs. Comes with LPS 4x60 TIP2 scope and mount, compensator and two 10 round magazines.

NIB	EXC	V.G.	GOOD
900	850	750	650

CENTURY ARMS ROMANIAN DRAGUNOV SNIPER RIFLE, CAL. 7.62X54RMM

■ CENTURY M-76 SNIPER RIFLE

Cal. 8x57mm. A semi-auto-only version of the famous Yugoslavian M76; has a brand new US-made receiver and barrel. 21-1/2 inch barrel (without flash hider), Overall: 44.5 inches. Weight 11.3 lbs. Comes with original scope, mount, and 10 round magazine.

NIB	EXC	V.G.	GOOD
1500	1350	1200	1000

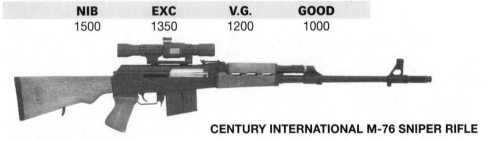

CENTURY INTERNATIONAL M-76 SNIPER RIFLE

NON-AK RIFLES

■ CENTURY CETME

Semi-Auto Sporter, cal. .308 Win. Built with original CETME parts kit on a Century Arms receiver. Originally offered with wood stock and forearm. Current model has a synthetic black or camouflage stock and forearm.

Note: Some owners have reported function issues with early Century Arms CETME sporters. It took them a while to fine tune production and assembly procedures. It is also reported that Century has willingly fixed or replaced affected guns.

NIB	EXC	V.G.	GOOD
600	550	500	450

CENTURY INTERNATIONAL CETME

■ CENTURY VZ58 2008 SPORTER SEMI-AUTO RIFLE

Cal. 7.62x39mm. Based on the Czechoslovakian Model Vz-58. The action is not Kalishnikov based. 16-inch barrel. Folding wire stock, synthetic forearm. Weight 6.9 lbs. Standard AKM magazines will not work. Shipped with two 30 round magazines, bayonet, sling and cleaning kit.

NIB	EXC	V.G.	GOOD
775	700	550	400

VZ2008 SPORTER FROM CENTURY ARMS

■ CENTURY M53 BELT FED SEMI-AUTO RIFLE

Cal. 8mm. Based on the German WWII issue MG-42 machine gun. Comes with 100 round belt and can. Barrel: 21 inches, overall length 48 inches. Weight: 25.5 lbs. Limited production. Product ID: RI1399

NIB	EXC	V.G.	GOOD
2600	2250	2000	1750

CENTURY ARMS M-53 BELT FED SEMI AUTO, GERMAN MG-42 TYPE. CAL. 8X57MM

■ CENTURY GOLANI SEMI-AUTO SPORTER RIFLE

Cal. .223. A copy of the Galil rifle. New receiver and barrel with original Galil parts. Comes with a spare 35 round magazine. 21 inch barrel. Overall: 29 inches (folded), Weight: 8.13 lbs. Product ID: RI 1410

NIB	EXC	V.G.	GOOD
850	750	650	550

CENTURY ARMS GOLANI RIFLE. ASSEMBLED WITH ISRAELI GALIL PARTS. CAL. .223

■ CENTURY L1A1 SPORTER

A semi-automatic version of the FN FAL rifle in 7.62mm/.308. Plastic stock and forearm. Some were made with a thumbhole stock during the 1994 AWB. Discontinued.

	EXC.	V.G.	GOOD
	700	600	500

■ CENTURY G-3 RIFLE

A copy of the Heckler and Koch G-3. cal. 7.62mm/.308. Synthetic stock and forearm. Discontinued.

	EXC.	V.G.	GOOD
	650	550	475

■ CENTURY C-93 RIFLE

A copy of the HK-93 rifle. Caliber 5.56mm, U.S.-made 16.25-inch barrel and receiver. Original HK parts. Synthetic stock and forearm. Uses original HK magazines. Shipped with two 40 round mags. Weight: 8.2 lbs.

NIB	EXC	V.G.	GOOD
525	500	475	450

CIA C-93 5.56MM RIFLE

■ CENTURY GORYUNOV SA-43 RIFLE

A new semi-automatic rifle built with original Russian SG-43 machine gun parts on a new U.S. made receiver. Belt feed 7.62x54Rmm. Includes the wheeled mount with shield and a 250 round belt with can. Weight: 96 lbs. complete.

NIB	EXC	V.G.	GOOD
4750	3500	N/A	N/A

CIA GORYUNOV SG-43
SEMI-AUTOMATIC RIFLE 7.62X54R

■ CENTURY DP-28 RIFLE

A semi-automatic recreation of the Russian DP-28 machine gun. 7.62x54Rmm with a 24-inch barrel. Feeds from a pan magazine on top of receiver. Weight: 23 lbs. There is also a version of this called a DPM that features a pistol grip stock.

NIB	EXC	V.G.	GOOD
2600	2400	2000	1650

CIA DPM SELF-LOADING RIFLE 7.62X54R

■ CENTURY STERLING TYPE 1 & 2

A semi-automatic carbine patterned after the English Sterling SMG. Cal 9mm with a 16.2-inch barrel. Folding stock. Shipped with two 34 round magazines. Weight: 8.2 lbs. The Type 2 Sterling has an extended heat shield that covers the whole barrel.

NIB	EXC	V.G.	GOOD
675	550	500	450

CIA STERLING SEMI-AUTO CARBINE, CAL. 9MM

■ CENTURY STERLING TYPE 3

As the Type 1 but chambered in 7.62x25mm. Shipped with two 20 round magazines.

NIB	EXC	V.G.	GOOD
675	550	500	450

■ CENTURY COLEFIRE MAGNUM PISTOL

A pistol in 7.62x25mm or 9mm. Based on the Sterling design with a 4.5-inch barrel. Total length is 13.25 inches. Weight: 4.7 lbs.

NIB	EXC	V.G.	GOOD
540	500	450	400

CIA COLEFIRE PISTOL IN 7.62X25MM OR 9MM

CETME
(CENTRO DE ESTUDIOS TŽCNICOS DE MATERIALES ESPECIALES)
Santa Barbara, Spain

Importer: Mars Equipment, Chicago, Illinois

■ CETME

CETME was actually the name of a Spanish government design organization from the 1950's. They designed the CETME rifle using the roller locking system first tried by Germany during WWII in the experimental Mauser StG45. After the war, Mauser engineer Ludwig Vorgrimmler came to Spain and helped design a new rifle. The rifle ended up bearing the name of the design group. Spain adopted the Cetme select fire rifle in 1957. It was chambered in 7.62x51mm. The design was licensed by Heckler and Koch and was adopted by West Germany as the G-3 rifle in 1958. In the early 1960s the semi-automatic CETME Sport rifle was imported to the U.S. by the Mars Equipment Co. of Chicago, Ill. These are the only true Spanish made CETMEs ever imported. See CETME listings under Century Arms.

EXC.	V.G.	GOOD
3000	2600	2200

CETME

CETME RIFLE IMPORTED BY MARS EQUIPMENT CO., CAL .30

MARS CETME RIFLE RECEIVER MARKINGS

CLARIDGE HI-TEC
North Hollywood, California

■ MODEL S9 PISTOL

A 9mm semi-automatic pistol. It has a 5-inch barrel. 16, 20 and 30 round magazines. Manufactured 1990-93. This design was based on the Goncz pistol and the owner of that design reportedly successfully sued Claridge for patent infringement. The company was forced to cease operations.

EXC.	V.G.	GOOD
450	400	350

CLARIDGE MODEL S9

■ MODEL L9 PISTOL

As above with a 7-1/2- or 9-1/2-inch barrel with a ventilated shroud. Some variations exist. None significantly affects price.

EXC.	V.G.	GOOD
450	400	350

■ C9 RIFLE

A rifle version using the Claridge action. 16-1/8-inch barrel. Wood stock and forearm.

EXC.	V.G.	GOOD
550	500	450

CMMG
Fayette, Mo.
Website: cmmginc.com

Manufacturer of AR-15 pattern firearms. Base models are listed. Numerous options are available on a custom build basis.

■ 11.5-INCH CARBINE W/ 5-INCH FLASH HIDER

Cal. 5.56mm. Features a 11-1/2-inch barrel with permanently attached 5-inch flash hider. A3 flat top receiver with removable A2 carry handle. CAR telescoping stock.

MSRP	EXC.	V.G.	GOOD
1125	900	800	700

■ 14.5-INCH M-4 CARBINE

Cal. 5.56mm. Features a 14-1/2 inch M-4 contour barrel with permanently attached 2-inch Phantom muzzle break or A2 style flash hider. A3 flat top receiver with removable A2 carry handle. CAR telescoping stock.

MSRP	EXC.	V.G.	GOOD
1125	900	800	700

■ 16-INCH M-4 CARBINE

Cal. 5.56mm. Features a 16-inch M-4 contour barrel with A2 flash hider. A3 flat top receiver with removable A2 carry handle. CAR telescoping stock.

MSRP	EXC.	V.G.	GOOD
1075	900	800	700

■ 14.5-INCH MID LENGTH CARBINE

Cal. 5.56mm. Features a 14-1/2-inch barrel with permanently attached 2 inch Phantom muzzle break or A2 style flash hider. A3 flat top receiver with removable A2 carry handle. Mid length gas system and handguard. CAR telescoping stock.

MSRP	EXC.	V.G.	GOOD
1125	900	800	700

■ 20-INCH GOVERNMENT A2 RIFLE

Cal. 5.56mm. Features a 20-inch barrel with A2 flash hider. A3 flat top receiver with A2 carry handle. Standard A2 stock.

MSRP	EXC.	V.G.	GOOD
1075	900	800	700

■ 14.5-INCH M-4 CARBINE

Cal. 5.56mm. Features a 14-1/2-inch M-4 contour barrel with permanently attached 2 inch Phantom muzzle break or A2 style flash hider. A3 flat top receiver with removable A2 carry handle. CAR telescoping stock.

MSRP	EXC.	V.G.	GOOD
1125	900	800	700

COBB MANUFACTURING, INC.
Dallas, Ga.

This company made an AR-15 type rifle. In business 2005-2007. They were purchased by Bushmaster, later purchased by Cerberus.

■ MCR RIFLE

MCR stands for Multi-Caliber-Rifle and it was built on the AR type design. MCR Semi-Automatic rifles came in four different models which interchange with each other from one series to the next. To change calibers for example from a .223 (MCR100) to .308 (MCR200) you simply change the upper receiver and magazine module.

EXC.	V.G.	GOOD
1850	1500	1200

COBB MANUFACTURING MULTI CALIBER RIFLE

COBRAY INDUSTRIES/S.W.D. INC.
Atlanta, Ga.

This company was one manufacturer of the MAC-10 pattern semi-auto pistols.

■ M-11 PISTOL

A 9mm semi-automatic pistol. Made from steel stampings. Fires from a closed bolt. Parkerized finish. 12 and 32 round magazines. Guns made until 1994 have a threaded muzzle.

EXC.	V.G.	GOOD
325	275	250

■ M-12 PISTOL

As above but chambered in .380 ACP.

EXC.	V.G.	GOOD
325	275	250

COBRAY M-12 PISTOL, CAL. .380

■ TM-11 CARBINE

A 9mm semi-automatic rifle. Constructed from steel stampings. 16-1/4-inch barrel. Back half is covered with a shroud. Metal shoulder stock that can be removed. 12 and 32 round magazines. Factory made steel magazines bring a premium over the more common zytel (plastic) magazines. Based on the M-11 semi-auto pistol. Discontinued.

EXC.	V.G.	GOOD
350	300	250

■ TM-12 CARBINE

As above, but chambered in .380 ACP.

EXC.	V.G.	GOOD
400	350	300

COLT'S PATENT FIREARMS MANUFACTURING COMPANY
Hartford, Connecticut

Website: www.coltsmfg.com

■ AR-15

When Eugene Stoner submitted the early M-16 rifles for government testing in 1958, no one had any idea that it was the beginning of a significant chapter in U.S. gun making history. The first M-16 select fire rifles were made by Armalite on contract for the U.S. Air Force in 1961. When a flood of contracts overwhelmed the Armalite Company the manufacturing rights were transferred to Colt. Colt began filling military orders in 1964. For those interested in learning more about the history and development of this firearm I recommend the book *The Gun Digest Book of The AR-15* by Patrick Sweeney, available from Gun Digest publications.

Colt began offering a semi-automatic version of the new rifle on the civilian market in 1964. This was dubbed an AR-15, which was the name that Armalite had used for the design until the government adopted it as the M-16. It should be noted that while the name "AR-15" has become synonymous with semi-automatic versions of the M-16, Colt holds the trademark on that name.

Pricing for pre-ban Colt AR-15 rifles peaked in the 1990s due to demand for rifles with the then-banned features such as the collapsible stock, bayonet lug and flash hider. Since the 2004 expiration of the AWB, the demand for pre-ban rifles has dropped as many buyers can now get new rifles made by several other manufacturers with whatever features they want. Those who insist on owning a Colt-made gun are still willing to pay extra for the name.

Colt lists eight models of AR-15 in their 2010 commercial sales catalog. They also manufacture a line of law enforcement models featuring a telescoping buttstock. Colt policy restricts these models to law enforcement sales only; however, these models frequently end up in the retail market.

■ AR-15 SPORTER (MODEL #6000) RECEIVERS MARKED SP-1 UNTIL 1985

Introduced into the Colt product line in 1964. Similar in appearance and function to the military version, the M-16, but with no capability for automatic fire. Chambered for the .223 cartridge. It is fitted with a standard 20-inch barrel with no forward assist, no case deflector, but with a bayonet lug. Weighs about 7.5 lbs. The first production rifles had the three prong flash hider. This was soon changed to the birdcage flash hider. Dropped from production in 1985. Bottom photo shows receiver markings.

EXC.	V.G.	GOOD
1400	1150	900

COLT AR-15 SP-1 RIFLE CAL .223

COLT AR-15 SP-1 RECEIVER MARKINGS

■ AR-15 SPORTER W/COLLAPSIBLE STOCK (MODEL #6001)

Same as above but fitted with a 16-inch barrel and sliding stock. Weighs approximately 5.8 lbs. Introduced in 1978 and discontinued in 1985.

EXC.	V.G.	GOOD
1750	1500	1250

■ AR-15 CARBINE (MODEL #6420)

Introduced in 1985 this model has a 16-inch standard weight barrel. All other features are the same as the previous discontinued AR-15 models. This version was dropped from the Colt product line in 1987.

EXC.	V.G.	GOOD
1500	1250	1000

AR-15 9MM CARBINE (MODEL #6450)

Chambered for the 9mm cartridge. Has the collapsible stock. Weighs 6.3 lbs. Discontinued in 1987.

EXC.	V.G	GOOD
1750	1500	1250

COLT AR-15 9MM CARBINE

AR-15A2 (MODEL #6500)

Introduced in 1984, this was an updated version with a heavier barrel and forward assist. The AR sight was still utilized. Weighs approximately 7.8 lbs.

EXC.	V.G.	GOOD
1100	900	800

AR-15A2 GOVT. MODEL CARBINE (MODEL #LE6520)

Added to the Colt line in 1988, this 16-inch standard barrel carbine featured for the first time a case deflector, forward assist, and the improved A2 rear sight. This model is fitted with a four-position telescoping buttstock. Weighs about 5.8 lbs. Colt restricts this model from civilian sales.

NIB	EXC.	V.G.	GOOD
1750	1500	1250	1000

AR-15A2 GOVERNMENT MODEL (MODEL #6550)

This model was introduced in 1988; it is the rifle equivalent to the Carbine. It features a 20-inch A2 barrel, forward assist, case deflector, but still retains the bayonet lug. Weighs about 7.5 lbs. Discontinued in 1990.

EXC.	V.G.	GOOD
1250	1000	800

COLT AR-15A2 GOVERNMENT CARBINE

AR-15A2 H-BAR (MODEL #6600)

Introduced in 1986, this version features a special 20-inch heavy barrel. All other features are the same as the A2 series of AR15s. Discontinued in 1991. Weighs about 8 lbs.

EXC.	V.G.	GOOD
1250	1000	800

AR-15A2 DELTA H-BAR (MODEL #6600DH)

Same as above but fitted with a 3x9 Tasco scope and detachable cheekpiece. Dropped from the Colt line in 1990. Weighs about 10 lbs. Equipped with a metal carrying case.

EXC.	V.G.	GOOD
1800	1500	1250

SPORTER LIGHTWEIGHT RIFLE

This lightweight model has a 16-inch barrel and is finished in a matte black. It is available in either a .223 Rem. caliber (Model #6530) that weighs 6.7 lbs., a Model #6430 w/A1 sights, 9mm caliber weighing 7.1 lbs., or a Model #6830 7.65x39mm that weighs 7.3 lbs. The .223 is furnished with two five round box magazines as is the 9mm and 7.65x39mm. A cleaning kit and sling are also supplied with each new rifle. The buttstock and pistol grip are made of durable nylon and the handguard is reinforced fiberglass and aluminum lined. The rear sight is adjustable for windage and elevation. These newer models are referred to simply as Sporters and are not fitted with a bayonet lug and the receiver block has different size pins.

EXC.	V.G.	GOOD
850	750	600

■ SPORTER TARGET MODEL RIFLE (MODEL #6551)

This 1991 model is a full size version of the Lightweight Rifle. The Target Rifle weighs 7.5 lbs. and has a 20-inch barrel. Offered in .223 Rem. caliber only with target sights adjustable to 800 meters. New rifles are furnished with two 5 round box magazines, sling, and cleaning kit. Same as the Model 6550 except for a rib around the magazine release. Bottom photo shows receiver markings.

EXC.	V.G.	GOOD
1200	850	700

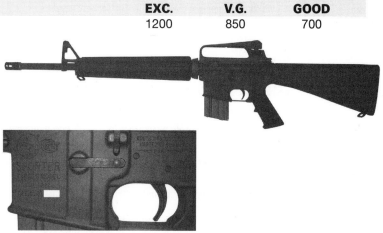

COLT SPORTER TARGET MODEL RIFLE (TOP); RECEIVER MARKINGS (BOTTOM)

■ SPORTER MATCH H-BAR (MODEL #6601)

This 1991 variation of the AR-15 is similar to the Target Model but has a 20-inch heavy barrel chambered for the .223 caliber. This model weighs 8 lbs. and has A2 sights adjustable out to 800 meters. Supplied with two five round box magazines, sling, and cleaning kit.

NIB	EXC.	V.G.	GOOD
1218	1100	900	700

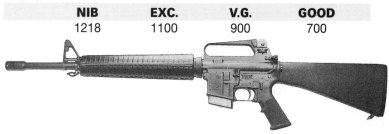

COLT SPORTER MATCH H-BAR

■ SPORTER MATCH DELTA H-BAR (MODEL #6601 DH)

Same as above but supplied with a 3x9 Tasco scope. Has a black detachable cheekpiece and metal carrying case. Weighs about 10 lbs. Discontinued in 1992. Deduct $150 if there is no scope or hard case.

EXC.	V.G.	GOOD
1350	1200	1000

COLT SPORTER MATCH DELTA H-BAR

■ MATCH TARGET H-BAR COMPENSATED (MODEL MT6601C)

Same as the regular Sporter H-BAR with the addition of a compensator.

NIB	EXC.	V.G.	GOOD
1219	1100	900	700

■ SPORTER COMPETITION H-BAR (MODEL #6700)

Introduced in 1992, the Competition H-Bar is available in .223 caliber with a 20-inch heavy barrel counterbored for accuracy. The carry handle is detachable with A2 sights. With the carry handle removed the upper receiver is dovetailed and grooved for Weaver-style scope rings. This model weighs approximately 8.5 lbs. New rifles are furnished with two 5 round box magazines, sling, and cleaning kit.

NIB	EXC.	V.G.	GOOD
1230	1100	950	850

■ SPORTER COMPETITION H-BAR SELECT W/SCOPE (MODEL #6700CH)

This variation, also new in 1992, is identical to the Sporter Competition with the addition of a factory mounted scope. The rifle has also been selected for accuracy and comes complete with a 3-9X Tasco rubber armored variable scope, scope mount, carry handle with iron sights, and nylon carrying case. Discontinued.

EXC.	V.G.	GOOD
1200	850	700

■ MATCH TARGET COMPETITION H-BAR COMPENSATED (MODEL MT6700C)

Same as the Match Target with a compensator.

NIB	EXC	V.G.	GOOD
1287	1200	850	700

■ AR-15A3 CARBINE FLAT-TOP HEAVYWEIGHT/MATCH TARGET COMPETITION (MODEL #6731)

This variation in the Sporter series features a heavyweight 16-inch barrel with flat-top receiver chambered for the .223 cartridge. It is equipped with a fixed buttstock. Weight is about 7.1 lbs.

NIB	EXC.	V.G.	GOOD
1207	1000	850	700

■ AR-15A3 TACTICAL CARBINE (MODEL #LE6721)

This version is similar to the above model with the exception of the buttstock which is telescoping and adjusts to four positions. Chambered for the .223 cartridge with a weight of about 7 lbs.

NIB	EXC.	V.G.	GOOD
1850	1600	1300	1100

■ AR-15A3 CARBINE (MODEL #LE6920)

AR-15 carbine with a flat top receiver and removable carry handle. Telescoping buttstock adjusts to four positions. M4 contour barrel. Chambered for the .223 cartridge with a weight of about 7 lbs. About 130 rifles were shipped before the 1994 ban. One of these will bring a slight premium. A majority of these guns were for law enforcement only.

NIB	EXC.	V.G.	GOOD
1750	1600	1300	1100

■ AR-15A3 ADVANCED LE CARBINE (MODEL #LE6940)

The Colt LE6940 Monolithic Advanced Law Enforcement Carbine is an evolution of the 6920. This rifle feature's Colt's new monolithic upper receiver. In addition to an uninterrupted full-length front rail, this upper receiver allows for a free-floated barrel. This rifle also features a gas-block mounted front flip-up sight with bayonet lug and a MaTech backup rear sight. The barrel is Colt's standard 16.1-inch chrome lined M4 barrel with an A2 flash hider up front.

NIB	EXC.	V.G.	GOOD
1850	1700	1400	1200

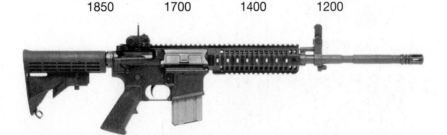

COLT AR-15A3 ADVANCED LE CARBINE

■ COLT ACCURIZED RIFLE CAR-A3 (MODEL CR6724)

This variation was introduced in 1996 and features a free floating 24-inch stainless steel match barrel with an 11-degree target crown and special Teflon coated trigger group. The handguard is all-aluminum with twin swivel studs. Weight is approximately 9.26 lbs.

NIB	EXC.	V.G.	GOOD
1374	1200	1000	850

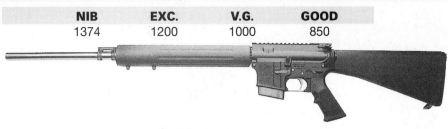

COLT COLT ACCURIZED RIFLE CAR-A3

■ **COLT TACTICAL RIMFIRE SERIES: SEE ENTRIES UNDER UMAREX**

COMMANDO ARMS
Knoxville, Tennessee

Formerly known as Volunteer Enterprises. The name was changed in 1978.

■ MARK III CARBINE

A semi-automatic rifle that resembles a Thompson sub-machine gun. 16-1/2-inch barrel with a simulated recoil compensator. .45 ACP caliber. The early versions have an pistol grip/ trigger housing made from metal alloy. Wood stock. Vertical pistol grip in front of magazine. Blued finish. Uses M3 grease gun 30 round stick magazines. Manufactured 1969-78.

EXC.	V.G.	GOOD
550	475	400

■ MARK 45

An improved version of the Mark III. The pistol grip/trigger housing is made from plastic. Wood or synthetic stock. Offered with vertical pistol grip or horizontal forearm. Blued or nickel finish. Uses modified 20 and 30 round Thompson SMG magazines. Will not take a drum magazine. Manufactured from 1978 through the early 1990s.

EXC.	V.G.	GOOD
600	525	450

COMMANDO ARMS MARK 45 RIFLE

■ MARK 9

As above but chambered in 9mm. Uses modified Sten SMG magazines.

EXC.	V.G.	GOOD
550	475	400

CZ USA
Kansas City, Kansas

website: www.cz-usa.com

The U.S. importer for Ceska Zbrojovka products.

■ VZ-58 MILITARY SPORTER

A semi-automatic version of the Czechoslovakian Vz-58 service rifle. Caliber 7.62x39mm. It has a 16-1/8-inch barrel. Total length is 36 inches. Weight is 7-1/2 lbs. 30 round magazine, not interchangeable with AK magazines.

MSRP	EXC	V.G.	GOOD
970	875	800	725

CZ USA VZ-58 MILITARY SPORTER

■ VZ-58 TACTICAL SPORTER

As above but fitted with a synthetic "sporter" stock.

MSRP	EXC.	V.G.	GOOD
990	900	825	750

CZ USA VZ-58 TACTICAL SPORTER

DAEWOO
Pusan, Korea

Imported by several companies including Stoeger and Kimber.

■ MAX I AR-100 (K2) 5.56MM RIFLE

The action is a combination of AR-15 type lock up with the gas system of a AK series. Has an 18-inch barrel. Side folding synthetic stock. Imported 1985-86. Uses AR-15 magazines.

EXC.	V.G.	GOOD
1250	1100	900

■ MAX II (K1A1)

This Daewoo has a different gas system from the MAX I. Made with a retractable wire stock.

EXC.	V.G.	GOOD
1250	1100	900

DAEWOO MAX II RIFLE

■ DR200

Introduced in 1996 this is a version of the MAX I with a thumbhole stock. Made to comply with the AWB 1994. Discontinued in 1997.

EXC.	V.G.	GOOD
750	600	500

DANIEL DEFENSE

Black Creek, Ga.

Website: www.danieldefense.com

Manufacturer of AR pattern rifles. Base models are listed. Numerous options are availible.

■ M4 CARBINE

Cal 5.56mm, 16-inch M4 contour barrel, flat top receiver, DD A1.5 rear sight, DD Omega x12.0 rail system, Magpul MOE buttstock. DD vertical foregrip.

MSRP	EXC.	V.G.	GOOD
1537	1200	1050	900

DANIEL DEFENSE M4 RIFLE WITH OMEGA X7 RAIL SYSTEM

■ M4V2

As above with Qmega x7.0 rail system.

MSRP	EXC.	V.G.	GOOD
1537	1200	1050	900

DANIEL DEFENSE M4 RIFLE WITH OMEGA X7 RAIL SYSTEM

■ M4V3

Cal 5.56mm, 16-inch M4 contour barrel, flat top receiver, DD A1.5 rear sight, mid-length gas system, DD Omega x9.0.0 rail system, Magpul MOE buttstock. DD vertical foregrip.

MSRP	EXC.	V.G.	GOOD
1537	1200	1050	900

■ DDXV

Cal. 5.56, 16-inch M4 contour barrel, flat top receiver, DD A1.5 rear sight. A2 gas block, CAR length handguard. 5 position telescoping stock.

MSRP	EXC.	V.G.	GOOD
1300	1000	850	700

■ DDXV EZ CARBINE

Cal. 5.56, 16-inch M4 contour barrel, flat top receiver, DD A1.5 rear sight. A2 gas block, EZ CAR length rail system. 5 position telescoping stock.

MSRP	EXC.	V.G.	GOOD
1368	1050	900	750

■ DDXVM

Cal 5.56mm, 16-inch M4 contour barrel, flat top receiver, DD A1.5 rear sight, mid-length gas system, round handguard, 5 position telescoping stock.

MSRP	EXC.	V.G.	GOOD
1429	1050	900	750

■ DDV6.8

Cal 6.8mm, 16-inch M4 contour barrel, flat top receiver, DD A1.5 rear sight, mid-length gas system, DD Omega x9.0.0 rail system, Magpul MOE buttstock. DD vertical foregrip. New 2010.

MSRP	EXC.	V.G.	GOOD
1537	1200	1050	900

■ AMBUSH 6.8

Cal 6.8mm, 16-inch M4 contour barrel, flat top receiver, no sights, mid-length gas system, DD modular free float tube handguard, Magpul MOE buttstock. New 2020

MSRP	EXC.	V.G.	GOOD
1537	1200 1050	900	

DANIEL DEFENSE AMBUSH RIFLE 6.8MM

DEL-TON

North Carolina
Marketed by ATI
website: www.del-ton.com

Current maker of AR-15 type rifles. NY compliant versions are available of most models.

■ A2 CARBINE H/BAR FIXED STOCK

Chambered for the .223 cartridge and fitted with a 16-inch barrel.

MSRP	EXC.	V.G.	GOOD
750	600	550	500

■ A2 CARBINE FIXED STOCK

This model features a 16-inch barrel, flat top receiver and an A2 type fixed stock.

MSRP	EXC.	V.G.	GOOD
750	600	550	500

■ A2 DT 4 RIFLE

This rifle has a M4 profile barrel, 1x9 twist, six-position M4 stock, CAR handguards with single heat shields, and A2 flash hider.

MSRP	EXC.	V.G.	GOOD
750	600	550	500

■ 16-INCH DTI-4 RIFLE

This rifle has a flat top receiver, 16-inch barrel with M4 profile, 1x9 twist, six-position M4 stock, CAR handguards with single heat shields, and A2 Flash Hider.

MSRP	EXC.	V.G.	GOOD
750	600	550	500

■ MID-LENGTH CARBINE

This rifle has a Flat top receiver. 16-inch mid-length barrel with 1x9 twist, six-position M4 stock, CAR handguards with single heat shields, and A2 flash hider.

MSRP	EXC.	V.G.	GOOD
750	600	550	500

■ MID-LENGTH RIFLE

This rifle has a A2 upper receiver with A2 rear sight, heavy profile barrel with mid-length gas system and 1x9 twist, A2 buttstock, standard length with heat shields, and A2 flash hider.

MSRP	EXC.	V.G.	GOOD
750	600	550	500

■ A2 STANDARD RIFLE

This rifle has a 20-inch heavy profile barrel with standard gas system and 1x9 twist, A2 upper reciever with iron sights, A2 buttstock, standard length handguard with heat shields, and A2 flash hider.

MSRP	EXC.	V.G.	GOOD
750	600	550	500

■ DTI STANDARD RIFLE

This rifle has a flat top receiver, 20-inch heavy profile barrel with standard gas system and 1x9 twist, A2 buttstock, standard length handguard with heat shields, and A2 flash hider.

MSRP	EXC.	V.G.	GOOD
750	600	550	500

DOUBLESTAR CORP
Winchester, Kentucky
Website: www.star15.com

Current maker of AR-15 type rifles that began business after the expiration of the AWB in 2004. Price listed is for base models. Many options available.

■ STAR EM-4

Chambered for the .223 cartridge and fitted with a 16-inch barrel. Rifle is supplied with A2 or flat top upper and Colt M4 handguard.

MSRP	EXC.	V.G.	GOOD
915	775	725	650

■ STAR-15

This model has a 20-inch barrel, A2 buttstock, and A2 handguard. Supplied with A2 or flat top upper.

MSRP	EXC.	V.G.	GOOD
880	700	650	600

■ STAR LIGHTWEIGHT TACTICAL RIFLE

Fitted with a 15-inch fluted barrel with permanently attached muzzle brake. Fitted with a short tactical buttstock. Supplied with an A2 or flat top upper. Discontinued.

EXC.	V.G.	GOOD
775	725	675

■ STAR CARBINE

This model has a 16-inch match grade barrel. Supplied with either an A2 buttstock or non-collapsing CAR buttstock. Upper receiver is A2 style or flat top.

MSRP	EXC.	V.G.	GOOD
775	700	650	600

DOUBLESTAR STAR CARBINE

■ STAR DS-4 CARBINE

This model features a 16-inch M-4 barrel with six-position buttstock, oval handguard, and A2 flash hider. Weight is about 6.75 lbs. Choice of A2 or flattop upper receiver.

MSRP	EXC.	V.G.	GOOD
910	800	750	675

DSC COMMANDO CARBINE

A2 or flat top upper, 11.5-inch barrel with permanently attached 5.5-inch flash hider, six-position buttstock.

MSRP	EXC.	V.G.	GOOD
930	750	700	650

STAR SUPER MATCH RIFLE

Choice of match grade barrel lengths of 16, 20, 22, or 24 inches. Rifle supplied with flat top upper or tactical Hi-Rise upper, free float handguard.

MSRP	EXC.	V.G.	GOOD
1030	800	750	675

STAR CRITTERSLAYER

This model is fitted with a 24-inch fluted super match barrel with a flat top upper and free floating handguard. Match 2 stage trigger. Fitted with a Harris LMS swivel bipod and Ergo grip with palm swell. Discontinued.

EXC.	V.G.	GOOD
1100	1000	900

DSC EXPEDITION RIFLE

A2 or flat top upper, 16-inch barrel with light contour in front and heavy under the HG, CAR handguard, A2 or six-position stock.

MSRP	EXC.	V.G.	GOOD
919	725	675	625

DSC PATROL RIFLE

Flat top upper, 16-inch barrel with A2 phantom flash hider, DSC 4 rail handguard, six-position M-4 buttstock. Weight: 6.5 lbs.

MSRP	EXC.	V.G.	GOOD
1215	950	850	750

DSC MARKSMAN RIFLE

Flat Top upper, 20-inch Wilson Premium stainless steel heavy barrel, full length quad rail handguard, Magpul PRS buttstock, GG&D HD swivel bipod.

MSRP	EXC.	V.G.	GOOD
1885	1400	1200	1000

DSC STAR-15 CMP SERVICE RIFLE

Fitted with a 20-inch chrome lined heavy match barrel. National Match front and rear sights. CMP free float handguard. National Match trigger. A2 upper receiver. Discontinued.

EXC.	V.G.	GOOD
900	825	750

DSC STAR CMP IMPROVED SERVICE RIFLE

Similar to the above model but with 20-inch Wilson Arms premium grade heavy match barrel. McCormick single- or two-stage Match trigger and Tippie Competition rear sight. Discontinued.

EXC.	V.G.	GOOD
1100	1000	900

DSC STAR 15 LIGHTWEIGHT TACTICAL

This model is fitted with a 16-inch fluted heavy barrel with tactical "shorty" A2 buttstock. Discontinued.

EXC.	V.G.	GOOD
800	725	650

DSC STAR DISSIPATOR

This model features a 16-inch barrel with full length handguard. Available with A2 or flattop upper receiver.

MSRP	EXC.	V.G.	GOOD
875	800	725	675

DSC STAR 15 9MM RIFLE

Chambered for the 9mm cartridge and fitted with a 16-inch heavy barrel. A2 or flattop upper receiver. Available with A2 or CAR buttstock. Discontinued.

EXC.	V.G.	GOOD
950	850	750

DPMS Inc.
(Defense Procurement Manufacturing Service)
Panther Arms
Becker, Minnesota
Website: www.dpmsinc.com

Current manufacturer of AR-15 type rifles that was established in 1996. DPMS lists rifles under the Panther trade name. They offer complete 5.56mm rifles in several configurations. DPMS also lists several rifles chambered in .223 Remington, as well as .204 Ruger, 6.8 Remington SPC, 7.62x39mm, .243 and .308 Winchester, .260 Remington, .300 Remington SAUM and more. Their website states that most rifles are built on a custom-order basis. We list many Items but not all possible variations. DPMS also sells complete kits to build most models as well as stripped lower receivers and upper/lower receiver sets.

■ ORACLE

A3 Picatinny rail flat top. Rail gas block. Cal. 5.56x45mm. 16-inch barrel. Six-position telescoping stock. Weight: 6.3lbs. New in 2010.

MSRP	EXC.	V.G.	GOOD
759	700	650	575

■ 3GI

A3 Picatinny rail flat top. Cal. 5.56mm. 18-inch black stainless barrel. Magpul adjustable stock. Weight: 7.75 lbs. New in 2010.

MSRP	EXC.	V.G.	GOOD
1499	1250	1000	850

■ THE AGENCY

A3 Picatinny rail flat top. Cal. 5.56mm. 16-inch heavy barrel. EOtech HDS M512 sight as well as a flip rear sight. SureFire M73 quad rail handguard with flashlight. Pardus six-position telescoping stock. Weight 7 lbs.

MSRP	EXC.	V.G.	GOOD
2069	1750	1500	1250

■ RAPTR

A3 Picatinny rail flat top. Cal. 5.56mm. 16-inch AP4 contour barrel, AP4 - six position, telescoping fiber reinforced polymer stock, ERGO Ambi-Sure grip , ERGO Z-Rail two-piece 4 rail carbine length handguard, MVF-515 Crimson Trace vertical grip/flashlight/laser. New for 2010.

MSRP	EXC.	V.G.	GOOD
1649	1500	1300	1100

■ CSAT PERIMETER

A3 Picatinny rail flat top. Cal. 5.56mm. 16-inch AP4 heavy barrel, 4 rail free float tube with Magpul covers. Magpul CTR adjustable stock. NEW for 2010.

MSRP	EXC.	V.G.	GOOD
1799	1600	1400	1200

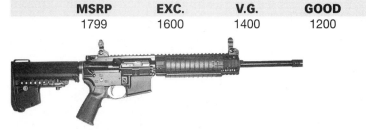

DPMS CSAT PERIMETER RIFLE

■ PRAIRIE PANTHER

A3 rail flat top receiver. Cal. .223 Rem. 20-inch Stainless steel heavy fluted barrel. Skeletonized A2 fixed stock. Availible with Desert Shadow or Mossy Oak finish. New for 2010.

MSRP	EXC.	V.G.	GOOD
1249	1050	900	750

■ SWEET SIXTEEN

This AR-15 type rifle is chambered for the .223 cartridge and fitted with a 16-inch stainless steel bull barrel. A2-style buttstock. No sights.

DPMS INC.

Barrel has 1:9 twist. Flat top receiver. Handguard is aluminum free float tube. Upper and lower receivers are hard coated black. Weight is about 9.5 lbs. Each rifle comes standard with two 7 round magazines, sling, and cleaning kit.

MSRP	EXC.	V.G.	GOOD
909	750	700	650

■ BULL 20

This AR-15 type rifle is chambered for the .223 cartridge and fitted with a 20-inch stainless steel bull barrel. A2-style buttstock. No sights. Barrel has 1:9 twist. Flat top receiver. Handguard is aluminum free float tube. Upper and lower receivers are hard coated black. Weight is about 9.5 lbs. Each rifle comes standard with two 7 round magazines, sling, and cleaning kit.

MSRP	EXC.	V.G.	GOOD
939	750	700	650

■ BULL 24

Similar to the model above but fitted with a 24-inch bull barrel. Flat top receiver. Weight is about 10 lbs.

MSRP	EXC.	V.G.	GOOD
969	800	750	700

■ BULL 24 SPECIAL

This model is fitted with a 24-inch stainless steel fluted bull barrel. Adjustable A2 style buttstock. Flat top receiver. Adjustable sniper pistol grip. Weight is about 10 lbs.

MSRP	EXC.	V.G.	GOOD
1189	900	850	750

■ PANTHER EXTREME SUPER BULL 24

This model is fitted with a 24-inch stainless steel extra heavy bull barrel (1.150 inch dia.). Skeletonized stock. Flat top receiver. Weight is about 11.75 lbs. Discontinued.

EXC.	V.G.	GOOD
925	875	800

■ BULLDOG

Fitted with a 20-inch stainless steel fluted bull barrel with black synthetic A2-style buttstock. Flat top receiver. Adjustable trigger. Weight is about 10 lbs.

MSRP	EXC.	V.G.	GOOD
1200	925	875	800

■ ARCTIC

This model is similar to the model above but with 20-inch fluted bull barrel and flat top receiver. Black A2-style buttstock with white coat finish on receiver and handguard. Black Teflon finish on barrel. Weight is about 8.25 lbs.

MSRP	EXC.	V.G.	GOOD
1099	900	825	750

■ CLASSIC

M-16A2 style. 5.56mm. Fitted with a 20-inch 4150 steel heavy barrel with square front post sight and A2 rear sight. A2 round handguard. Weight is about 9.5 lbs.

MSRP	EXC.	V.G.	GOOD
849	700	625	550

■ TACTICAL A2

As above but with a 16-inch barrel. Retains the full length handguard.

MSRP	EXC.	V.G.	GOOD
829	700	625	550

■ CLASSIC 16

As above with a 16-inch barrel. Carbine handguard.

MSRP	EXC.	V.G.	GOOD
829	700	600	500

■ CARBINE

As above with a 11.5-inch barrel with permanent 5.5-inch flash hider. Pardus six-position telescoping stock.

MSRP	EXC.	V.G.	GOOD
829	750	625	550

■ AP4 CARBINE

A3 Picatinny rail flat top Includes detachable carry handle and A2 rear sight. Cal. 5.56mm. 16-inch M4 contour barrel. Six-position telescoping stock. Also available in post-ban configuration with stock pinned in extended position.

MSRP	EXC.	V.G.	GOOD
989	800	700	600

■ DCM

This model is similar to the model above but with a .223 Remington 20-inch stainless steel heavy barrel and NM rear sight. DCM free-float handguard. Adjustable trigger. Weight is about 9.5 lbs.

MSRP	EXC.	V.G.	GOOD
1099	800	725	675

■ CLASSIC 16 POST BAN

This model is fitted with a 5.56mm 16-inch 4150 steel heavy barrel. A2-style sights. Round handguard. Weight is about 7.25 lbs. Discontinued.

MSRP	EXC.	V.G.	GOOD
775	625	575	500

■ LITE 16

A1 type upper receiver and sights. six-position Pardus collapsible stock. 5.56mm. 16-inch light contour barrel. Weight 6.1 lbs.

MSRP	EXC.	V.G.	GOOD
759	700	600	500

■ LITE 16 A3

As above with an A3 picatinny rail flattop.

MSRP	EXC.	V.G.	GOOD
759	700	600	500

■ LO-PRO CLASSIC

Flattop low-profile extruded receiver. 5.56mm 16-inch bull barrel. A2 buttstock. Weight: 7.75 lbs..

MSRP	EXC.	V.G.	GOOD
759	700	575	475

■ MINI SASS

AKA Semi Automatic Sniper System. A3 flat top 5.56mm rifle with a fluted 18-inch stainless steel bull barrel that is black Teflon coated. Four-rail free float handguard, Magpul precision stock. Weight: 10.3 lbs.

MSRP	EXC.	V.G.	GOOD
1599	1450	1300	1150

DPMS MINI SASS RIFLE

■ MK 12

A3 flat top 5.56mm rifle with an 18-inch stainless steel barrel finish in black Teflon. Four-rail free float handguard, LMT SOPMOD carbine six-position stock. Weight: 9.5 lbs.

MSRP	EXC.	V.G.	GOOD
1599	1450	1300	1150

■ SPORTICAL

A3 flat top tubular receiver, without forward assist. 16-inch light contour barrel. CAR oval handguards, Pardus six-position telescoping stock. Weight: 6.3 lbs.

MSRP	EXC.	V.G.	GOOD
715	650	600	550

DPMS SPORTICAL RIFLE

■ RACE GUN

Similar to Panther Bull but with 24-inch fluted bull barrel. Sights: JP Micro adjustable rear, JP front sight adjustable for height. Includes Lyman globe and Shaver inserts. Discontinued.

EXC.	V.G.	GOOD
1450	1300	1050

■ TUBER

Similar to Panther Bull 24 but with 16-inch barrel with cylindrical aluminum shroud. Discontinued.

EXC.	V.G.	GOOD
650	600	550

■ SINGLE SHOT RIFLE

AR-15-style single-shot rifle with manually-operated bolt, no magazine.

MSRP	EXC.	V.G .	GOOD
775	675	600	525

■ PARDUS

Similar to Panther Post-ban but with 16-inch bull barrel, telescoping buttstock and tan Teflon finish. Discontinued.

EXC.	V.G.	GOOD
1000	875	800

■ 20TH ANNIVERSARY RIFLE

Similar to Panther Post-ban but with 20-inch bull barrel and engraved, chrome-plated lower receiver. Discontinued.

EXC.	V.G.	GOOD
2000	1700	1500

■ SDM-R

Similar to Panther but with stainless steel barrel and Harris bipod.

MSRP	EXC	V.G.	GOOD
1200	1000	900	825

■ LR-204

A3 flat top receiver. Fluted 24-inch stainless steel bull barrel chambered in .204 Ruger. Standard length ribbed aluminum free float handguard. A2 fixed stock.

MSRP	EXC.	V.G.	GOOD
1029	975	900	825

■ 6.8 SPC RIFLE

A Panther DCM rifle built with a 20-inch chrome-moly barrel chambered for 6.8x43 Remington SPC. Weight: 9 lbs.

MSRP	EXC.	V.G.	GOOD
1029	950	850	750

■ 6.8 SPC CARBINE

As above with a 16-inch barrel and six-position telescoping buttstock. Weight: 7 lbs.

MSRP	EXC.	V.G.	GOOD
1019	950	850	750

■ 7.62X39 RIFLE

A Panther DCM rifle built with a 20-inch barrel chambered for 7.62x39mm.

MSRP	EXC.	V.G.	GOOD
860	800	750	700

■ 7.62X39 CARBINE

As above with a 16-inch barrel and six-position telescoping buttstock. Weight: 7 lbs.

MSRP	EXC.	V.G.	GOOD
850	800	750	700

■ REPR

A3 flat top 7.62mm rifle with a 18-inch fluted stainless steel barrel. Four-rail free float handguard, Magpul stock in coyote brown. Weight: 9.5 lbs.

MSRP	EXC.	V.G.	GOOD
2519	2100	1800	1500

308 MK 12

A3 flat top 7.62mm rifle with an 18-inch heavy stainless steel barrel. Four-rail free float handguard, Magpul CTR adjustable stock. Weight: 9.6 lbs

MSRP	EXC.	V.G.	GOOD
1709	1500	1300	1100

ORACLE 7.62 NATO

A3 flat top 7.62mm rifle with a 16-inch heavy barrel. CAR oval handguard, Pardus six-position stock. Weight: 8.3 lbs

MSRP	EXC.	V.G.	GOOD
1074	975	900	800

SPORTICAL 7.62 NATO

As above, built with a tubular receiver without forward assist.

MSRP	EXC.	V.G.	GOOD
999	950	900	800

LR-308

A3 flat top. .308 Win rifle with a 24-inch stainless steel bull barrel. Ribbed aluminum free float handguard. Standard A2 stock. Weight: 11.2 lbs

MSRP	EXC.	V.G.	GOOD
1169	1075	950	825

![DPMS LR 308 RIFLE]

DPMS LR 308 RIFLE

LR-308B

A3 flat top .308 Win. rifle with a 18-inch bull barrel. CAR length free float handguard. Standard A2 stock. Also offered in 7.62 NATO as the LR-308T. Weight: 9.7 lbs

MSRP	EXC.	V.G.	GOOD
1159	1075	950	825

LR-308L

A3 flat top 7.62mm rifle with a light contour 18-inch stainless steel barrel with black Teflon coating. Carbon fiber free float handguard, skeletonized A2 stock. Weight: 8.0 lbs

MSRP	EXC.	V.G.	GOOD
1499	1400	1250	1100

LRT-SASS

Flat top receiver. Chambered in 7.62 NATO. 18-inch stainless steel fluted barrel with black teflon finish, flip front and rear sights, four-rail standard length free float handguard, Magpul Precision Rifle stock. Harris bipod. Weight: 11.5 lbs.

MSRP	EXC.	V.G.	GOOD
2119	1800	1600	1400

DPMS LRT SASS RIFLE

LR-308C

A3 Flat top receiver with detachable A2 carry handle. Chambered in 7.62 NATO. 20-inch heavy barrel, A2 round handguard, A2 buttstock. Weight: 11.2 lbs.

MSRP	EXC.	V.G.	GOOD
1099	1000	925	850

■ LR-260/ LR-6.5

24 inch stainless steel bull barrel and chambered in .260 Remington or 6.5mm Creedmore. Also available with 20-inch barrel. Standard length ribbed aluminum free float handguard. A2 fixed stock.

MSRP	EXC.	V.G.	GOOD
1199	975	900	825

■ LR-243

Similar to LR-260 but with 20-inch stainless steel heavy barrel and chambered in .243 Win.

MSRP	EXC.	V.G.	GOOD
1199	975	900	825

DSA Inc.
Barrington, Illinois
Website: www.dsarms.com

DSA, Inc. began selling its rifles to the public in 1996. Based on actual blueprints of the famous FN/FAL rifle, DSA rifles are made in the US. All SA58 rifles are fitted with fully adjustable gas system, Type I, II, or III forged receiver, hand-lapped barrel, muzzlebrake, elevation adjustable post front sight, windage adjustable rear peep sight with 5 settings from 200 to 600 meters, detachable metric magazine, adjustable sling and hard case.

■ SA58 24-INCH BULL

Fitted with a 24-inch stainless steel barrel with .308 match chamber. Overall length is 44.5 inches. Weight is approximately 11.5 lbs. 20 round magazine. Discontinued.

EXC.	V.G.	GOOD
1500	1250	1000

■ SA58 FAL BULL BARREL RIFLE

.308 cal. chrome moly, 21-inch premium match grade bull barrel, alloy free float tube with texture finish, standard synthetic or X-series buttstock, standard synthetic pistol grip, type I receiver. 20 round magazine.

MSRP	EXC.	V.G.	GOOD
1850	1500	1250	1000

DS ARMS STG 58 RIFLE WITH BULL BARREL, CAL. .308

■ SA58 FAL MEDIUM CONTOUR RIFLE

.308 cal. 21-inch medium contour barrel with threaded Belgian short flash hider, standard synthetic handguard and pistol grip, standard synthetic or X-series buttstock, type I or type II receiver. 20 round magazine.

MSRP	EXC.	V.G.	GOOD
1700	1250	1000	850

DSA SA58 FAL MEDIUM CONTOUR RIFLE

■ SA58 CARBINE

.308 cal. 16.25-inch premium bipod-cut barrel with threaded Belgian short flash hider, standard synthetic handguard and pistol grip, standard synthetic or X-series buttstock, type I or type II receiver. 20 round magazine.

MSRP	EXC.	V.G.	GOOD
1700	1300	1150	1000

DS ARMS SA 58 CARBINE

DS ARMS SA 58 CARBINE WITH STAINLESS STEEL RECEIVER

■ SA58 FAL STANDARD RIFLE

.308 cal. 21-inch premium bipod-cut barrel with threaded Belgian short flash hider, standard synthetic handguard and pistol grip, standard synthetic or X-series buttstock, type I or type II receiver. 20 round magazine.

MSRP	EXC.	V.G.	GOOD
1700	1300	1150	1000

DSA SA58 FAL STANDARD RIFLE

■ SA58 FAL STANDARD PARA RIFLE

.308 cal. 21-inch premium bipod-cut barrel with threaded Belgian short flash hider, standard synthetic handguard and pistol grip, folding para stock, type I or type II receiver. 20 round magazine.

MSRP	EXC.	V.G.	GOOD
1975	1700	1600	1500

DSA SA58 FAL STANDARD PARA RIFLE

■ SA58 FAL CARBINE PARA RIFLE

.308 cal. 16.25-inch premium bipod-cut barrel with threaded Belgian short flash hider, standard synthetic handguard and pistol grip, folding para stock, type I or type II receiver. 20 round magazine.

MSRP	EXC.	V.G.	GOOD
1975	1700	1600	1500

■ SA58 FAL TACTICAL CARBINE

.308 cal. 16.25-inch fluted medium contour barrel with threaded A2 flash hider, shortened gas system, short military grade handguard, standard synthetic or X-series buttstock, standard synthetic pistol grip, type I or type II receiver. 20 round magazine. Discontinued.

EXC.	V.G.	GOOD
1350	1250	1150

DS ARMS SA 58 FAL TACTICAL CARBINE

■ SA58 FAL PARA TACTICAL CARBINE

.308 cal. 16.25-inch fluted medium contour barrel with threaded A2 flash hider, shortened gas system, short military grade handguard, folding para stock, standard synthetic pistol grip, type I or type II receiver. 20 round magazine.

MSRP	EXC.	V.G.	GOOD
1970	1600	1450	1300

■ SA58 FAL PARA ELITE COMPACT RIFLE

.308 cal. 13-inch barrel with permanently attached long Browning flash hider making this a 16-inch barrel semi-auto rifle. Shortened gas system, short military grade handguard, folding para stock, standard synthetic pistol grip, type I or type II receiver. 20 round magazine. Discontinued.

EXC.	V.G.	GOOD
1600	1450	1300

■ SA58 SPR (SPECIAL PURPOSE RIFLE)

This model was submitted to the U.S. Army for SASS rifle trials. It features a 19-inch fully fluted premium barrel. Rail interface handguard. Extended duty scope mount. SPR side folding adjustable stock. Dura coat finish. 20 round magazine.

MSRP	EXC.	V.G.	GOOD
4795	4000	3500	3000

■ SA58 FAL G1 FAL COLLECTORS EDITION

.308/7.62mm rifle. 21-inch premium US-made barrel with quick detach long flash hider, bipod cut steel handguard with flush folding G2 bipod, hardwood humpback with proper large sling swivel and steel buttplate, standard synthetic pistol grip, original G1 steel lower receiver. Duracoat black finish on all steel surfaces.

MSRP	EXC.	V.G.	GOOD
2000	1600	1450	1300

DS ARMS FAL G1 COLLECTORS EDITION

■ SA58 FAL CONGO RIFLE

.308 cal. 18-inch premium bipod-cut barrel with Belgian short flash hider, standard synthetic buttstock and pistol grip, type I or type II receiver with carry handle, Duracoat black finish.

MSRP	EXC.	V.G.	GOOD
1970	1600	1450	1300

DSA SA58 FAL CONGO RIFLE

■ SA58 FAL PARA CONGO RIFLE

.308 cal. 18-inch premium bipod-cut barrel with Belgian short flash hider, folding para stock, standard synthetic pistol grip, type I or type II receiver with carry handle. Duracoat black finish.

MSRP	EXC.	V.G.	GOOD
2250	1800	1600	1400

■ SA58 FAL T48 COLLECTOR SERIES RIFLE

Based on the T-48 that was tested by the U.S. military in the 1950s. .308 cal. 21-inch premium barrel with long flash hider, European walnut handguard, buttstock and pistol grip, type I receiver with carry handle. Duracoat black finish.

MSRP	EXC.	V.G.	GOOD
1995	1800	1600	1400

DSA ARMS T48 RIFLE, CAL. .308

■ SA58 FAL PREDATOR RIFLE

Offered in .308, .260 Rem., or .243. 16-inch premium medium carbine or 19 inch medium contour barrel with target crown, standard synthetic or X-series buttstock, standard synthetic pistol grape, OD green handguard, grip and stock. Type I receiver no carry handle cut. Scope mount included. Discontinued.

MSRP	EXC.	V.G.	GOOD
1695	1500	1350	1200

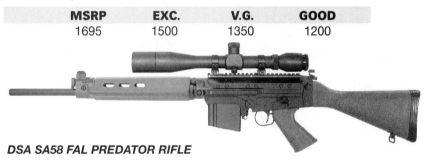

DSA SA58 FAL PREDATOR RIFLE

■ SA58 FAL GRAYWOLF RIFLE

.308 Win cal. 21-inch premium match grade bull barrel with target crown, alloy free float tube with texture finish, standard synthetic or x-series buttstock, FN saw pistol grip, type I receiver no carry handle cut. Versa-pod model 1 bipod included. Duracoat graywolf and black finish included. Discontinued.

EXC.	V.G.	GOOD
1900	1750	1600

DSA SA58 FAL GRAYWOLF RIFLE

■ STG 58 AUSTRIAN FAL STANDARD RIFLE

Austrian Pattern rifle featuring a 21-inch barrel with long flash hider, steel handguard with folding bipod,synthetic FAL buttstock.

MSRP	EXC.	V.G.	GOOD
1150	1050	950	850

■ STG 58 AUSTRIAN FAL CARBINE

As above with a 16.25- or 18-inch barrel with short flash hider.

MSRP	EXC.	V.G.	GOOD
1200	1050	950	850

DSA INC.

ZM-4 AR TYPE RIFLES

■ ZM-4 STANDARD

cal. 5.56mm, 20-inch barrel. Flat top receiver, A2 buttstock.

MSRP	EXC.	V.G.	GOOD
1050	850	750	650

■ ZM-4 MID LENGTH

Cal. 5.56mm, 16-inch fluted barrel, flat top receiver, mid length round handguard, CAR buttstock.

MSRP	EXC.	V.G.	GOOD
1050	850	750	650

■ ZM-4 STANDARD CARBINE

Cal. 5.56mm, 16-inch M4 contour barrel, flat top receiver, CAR handguard and buttstock.

MSRP	EXC.	V.G.	GOOD
1200	1050	950	850

■ ZM-4 STANDARD MRP

Cal. 5.56mm, 16- or 18-inch barrel, Multiple Rail Platform quad rail handguard, CAR buttstock.

MSRP	EXC.	V.G.	GOOD
1200	1050	950	850

■ ZM-4 A2 STANDARD CARBINE

Cal. 5.56mm, 16-inch M4 contour barrel. A2 upper receiver with A2 sight, CAR handguard and buttstock.

MSRP	EXC.	V.G.	GOOD
1095	900	800	700

■ ZM-4 A2 V1 CARBINE

Cal. 5.56mm, A2 upper receiver and rear sight, quad rail handguard, SOPMOD buttstock.

MSRP	EXC.	V.G.	GOOD
1225	1050	950	850

■ TP-9 PISTOL

A 9x19mm semi-automatic pistol based on the Steyr TMP machine pistol. Made in Switzerland by Brugger and Thomet for DSA. 6-1/2-inch barrel. Picatinney rail on top and underneath.

MSRP	EXC.	V.G.	GOOD
1250	1100	950	800

TP-9 9MM PISTOL IMPORTED FROM SWITZERLAND BY DS ARMS

EAA
(EUROPEAN AMERICAN ARMORY)
Rockledge, Florida

Website: www.eaacorp.com

■ P.A.P. 7.62 RIFLE

An AK type rifle made by Zastava. 7.62x39mm. 16-3/4-inch barrel. Standard fixed sights. Picitinny rail on top of receiver. Monte Carlo sporter-type stock. Uses a single stack 10 round magazine.

MSRP	EXC.	V.G.	GOOD
464	400	375	350

EUROPEAN AMERICAN ARMORY PAP RIFLE

Note: EAA was formerly an importer of the Izhmash Saiga series of rifles.

See: Russian American Armory Co.

EAGLE ARMS
Coal Valley, Illinois

From 1990 to 1995 Eagle Arms manufactured a line of AR type rifles. In 1995 they bought the old Armalite name and continue operations as Armalite. For post-1995 models see the Armalite listing.

■ EA-15 E-1 RIFLE

A-2 type upper receiver with fixed carry handle. Cal. 5.56mm/.223. 20-inch barrel. Manufactured 1990-93.

EXC.	V.G.	GOOD
700	650	600

■ M15 A2 H-BAR RIFLE

As above with a heavier barrel. Manufactured 1990-95.

EXC.	V.G.	GOOD
775	725	675

■ M15 A2 CARBINE

16-inch barrel. Features a CAR type collapsible stock. Changes to fixed stock in 1994. Manufactured 1990-95.

EXC.	V.G.	GOOD
750	700	650

NOTE: Deduct $100 for fixed stock version.

■ M15 A4 EAGLE SPIRIT

Designed for IPSC competition shooting. Flat top receiver. National Match 16-inch premium air gauged barrel. Fixed stock. Tubular full length aluminum handguard. Manufactured 1993-95.

EXC.	V.G.	GOOD
900	800	700

■ M15 A2 GOLDEN EAGLE

Similar to the M15 A2 with an extra heavy stainless 20-inch barrel. National Match sights. Manufactured 1991-95.

EXC.	V.G.	GOOD
900	800	700

■ M15 A4 EAGLE EYE

Designed for silhouette shooting. Flat top receiver. One inch diameter 24-inch free floating barrel. Tubular aluminum handguards. Weighted buttstock. Manufactured 1993-95.

EXC.	V.G.	GOOD
1000	900	800

■ M15 ACTION MASTER

A match rifle. National Match sights and trigger. 20-inch free floating barrel. Solid aluminum handguard tube. Fixed stock. Manufactured 1992-95.

EXC.	V.G.	GOOD
900	825	750

■ M15 A4 SPECIAL PURPOSE RIFLE

Rifle with flat top receiver with removable carry handle. 20-inch barrel. Manufactured 1994-95.

EXC.	V.G.	GOOD
750	700	650

■ M15 A4 PREDATOR

Flat top receiver with removable carry handle. National match trigger. 18-inch barrel. Fixed stock. Manufactured 1995 only.

EXC.	V.G.	GOOD
900	825	750

EMF Corp.
Santa Ana, California

Website: emf-company.com

This company is a well-known Importer of old western style revolvers and lever action rifles. In 2010 they added a semi automatic carbine to their line.

■ JUST RIGHT CARBINE

A semi-automatic pistol caliber rifle utilizing a blow back action. Available in 9mm, .40 and .45. It uses Glock magazines of the appropriate caliber. Receiver has a single rail top. Quad rail handguard. CAR type telescoping stock. Most AR accessories are compatible.

MSRP	EXC.	V.G.	GOOD
750	700	625	550

ENFIELD AMERICA, INC.
Atlanta, Georgia

■ MP-45

A blowback operated semi-automatic pistol that resembles a submachine gun. Barrels were offered in 4-1/2, 6, 8, 10, or 18 inches. All observed specimens have the shorter barrels. Steel shroud protects the barrel. Parkerized finish. 10, 30, 40 or 50 round magazines. Manufactured 1985 only. Some catalogs also mention a 9mm version. Prices are the same.

EXC.	V.G.	GOOD
450	400	350

MP-45 PISTOL BY ENFIELD AMERICA

ENTREPRISE ARMS
Irwindale, California

Website: www.entreprise.com

This company currently offers a line of FN/FAL type rifles in 7.62mm/.308. They also sell stripped receivers and parts, so not all Entreprise Arms rifles seen are factory assembled.

■ STANDARD RIFLE

Entreprise Arm Type 03 steel receiver. 21-inch barrel. Zero Climb muzzle brake. Bolt hold open on last shot, adjustable gas system and carry handle. US legal components. Built with Entreprise Arms US made parts and Brazilian Imbel parts. Parkerized finish. Weight: 9.5 lbs.

MSRP	EXC.	V.G.	GOOD
959	850	800	750

■ GOVERNMENT RIFLE

Austrian STG-58 pattern rifle features a 21-inch barrel with muzzle brake. Stamped steel handguards with folding bipod. Black synthetic stock. Carry handle.

MSRP	EXC.	V.G.	GOOD
1149	1000	900	800

■ TARGET RIFLE

Entreprise Arm Type 01 receiver. Machined aluminum free-floating handguards. 21 inch barrel with Zero Climb muzzle brake, legal configured pistol grip, bolt hold open on last shot, adjustable gas system and no carry handle.

MSRP	EXC.	V.G.	GOOD
1199	1050	950	850

■ CARBINE

Rifle is configured with 18-inch barrel. Entreprise Arm Type 03 steel receiver, Zero Climb muzzle brake, legal configured pistol grip, bolt hold open on last shot, adjustable gas system and carry handle. Synthetic stock and forearm. US legal components. Built with Entreprise Arms US parts and Imbel parts.

MSRP	EXC.	V.G.	GOOD
1199	1050	950	850

■ PARA CARBINE

Rifle is configured with 18-inch barrel. Paratrooper Folding Stock Entreprise Arm Type 03 steel receiver, Zero Climb muzzle brake, legal configured pistol grip, bolt hold open on last shot, adjustable gas system and carry handle. US legal components. Built with Entreprise Arms US parts and Imbel parts.

MSRP	EXC.	V.G.	GOOD
1249	1150	1050	950

■ MATCH TARGET STG58C

Entreprise Arm Type 01 receiver. Crosshair front sight. 24-inch barrel. No muzzle break. Bolt hold open on last shot, adjustable gas system. Aluminum free float handguards. No carry handle. Discontinued.

EXC.	V.G.	GOOD
1700	1500	1250

■ STG58C CARBINE

Entreprise Arm Type 01 receiver. Machined aluminum free-floating handguards. 16-inch barrel with Zero Climb muzzle brake. Bolt hold open on last shot. Adjustable gas system. No carry handle. Discontinued.

EXC.	V.G.	GOOD
1200	1100	1000

■ STG58SC SCOUT CARBINE

18-inch barrel with Zero Climb muzzle brake. Stamped steel handguards with folding bipod. Black synthetic stock. Bolt hold open. Carry handle. Discontinued.

EXC.	V.G.	GOOD
1050	975	900

■ STG58 C-LW LIGHTWEIGHT CARBINE

Entreprise Arm Type 01 receiver. 16-1/2-inch barrel with Zero Climb muzzle brake. Integral bipod. Bolt hold open on last shot. Adjustable gas system and carry handle. Discontinued.

EXC.	V.G.	GOOD
1050	975	900

FABRIQUE NATIONAL (FN)
Herstal, Belgium

One of the world's largest manufacturers of firearms. U.S. importers include Browning Arms Co., Steyr, Howco and others. The first FAL rifles were imported by Browning in 1961, making this the oldest classic model offered in the U.S.

BROWNING ARMS AD FOR THE FAL RIFLE, AMERICAN RIFLEMAN, JULY 1961

FABRIQUE NATIONAL FAL G SERIES RIFLE WITH WOOD STOCKS

■ FN FAL "G" SERIES (TYPE 1 RECEIVER)

The first FAL to be imported to the U.S. The receivers are capable of accepting select fire parts. These rifles are subject to interpretation by the BATFE as to their legal status. A list of BATFE legal serial numbers is shown. This information should be utilized prior to a sale in order to avoid the possibility of the sale of an illegal rifle. There was a total of 1,848 legal "G" Series FN FAL rifles imported into this country. All were grandfathered and remain legal to possess. "G" series FAL rifles have a wood buttstock and forearm.

◆ Standard

EXC.	V.G.	GOOD
6500	5000	4000

◆ Lightweight

EXC.	V.G.	GOOD
6500	5000	3000

◆ EXEMPTED FAL RIFLES

Following is the final revised listing of FAL rifles, caliber 7.62mm, that are exempt from the provisions of the National Firearms Act.

SERIES

Serial Numbers	Units Manufactured
G492 through G494	3
G537 through G540	4
G649 through G657	9
G662 through G673	12
G677 through G693	17
G709 through G748	40
G752 through G816	65
G848 through G1017	170
G1021	1
G1033	1
G1035	1
G1041 through G1042	2
G1174 through G1293	120

Serial Numbers	Units Manufactured
G1415 through G1524	110
G1570 through G1784	215
G1800 through G1979	180
G1981 through G1995	15
G3035 through G3134	100
G2247 through G2996	750
Total:	**1,815**

GL SERIES

Serial Numbers	Units Manufactured
GL749	1
GL835	1
GL1095 through GL1098	4
GL1163 through GL1165	3
GL2004 through GL2009	6
GL3135 through GL3140	6
Total:	**21**

STANDARD FAL

Serial Numbers	Units Manufactured
889768	1
889772 through 889777	6
Total Manufactured:	**7**

PARATROOP MODEL

Serial Numbers	Units Manufactured
889800 through 889801	2
889803	1
889805	1
889809	1
Total Manufactured:	**5**
TOTAL EXEMPTED FAL RIFLES:	**1,848**

■ FN-FAL

A gas-operated, semiautomatic version of the famous FN battle rifle. This weapon has been adopted by more free world countries than any other rifle. It is chambered for the 7.62 NATO or .308 and has a 21-inch barrel with an integral flash suppressor. The sights are adjustable with an aperture rear, and the detachable box magazine holds 20 rounds. The stock and forearm are made of wood or a black synthetic. This model has been discontinued by the company and is no longer manufactured.

The models listed below are for the metric pattern Type 2 and Type 3 receivers, those marked "FN MATCH." The models below are for semi-automatic rifles only. FN-FAL rifles in the "inch pattern" are found in the British Commonwealth countries of Australia, India, Canada, and of course, Great Britain.

FN-FAL HEAVY BARREL

◆ **50.00 21-inch Rifle Model**

EXC.	V.G.	GOOD
3000	2500	2000

◆ **50.63 18-inch Paratrooper Model**

EXC.	V.G.	GOOD
3500	3000	2750

◆ 50.64 21-inch Paratrooper Model

EXC.	V.G.	GOOD
3500	3000	2750

◆ 50.41 Synthetic Butt with Heavy Barrel

EXC.	V.G.	GOOD
2800	2500	2000

◆ 50.42 Wood Butt with heavy barrel

EXC.	V.G.	GOOD
3500	3000	2750

■ FNC

A lighter-weight rifle chambered for the 5.56mm cartridge. It is a gas-operated semiautomatic with an 18- or 21-inch barrel. It has a 30 round box magazine and is black, with either a fixed or folding stock. This model was also discontinued by FN.

◆ Standard

Fixed stock, 16-inch or 18-inch barrel.

EXC.	V.G.	GOOD
3500	2750	2200

◆ Paratrooper Model

Folding stock, 16-inch or 18-inch barrel.

EXC.	V.G.	GOOD
3700	3000	2500

FNC PARATROOPER RIFLE, 5.56MM

FAMAS (GIAT)
St. Etienne, France

■ F1

This bullpup design was adopted by France as a battle rifle. Fewer than 100 of a semi-automatic version were imported to the U.S. by Century Arms in the late 1980s. Caliber 5.56mm/.223. 25 round magazine.

EXC.	V.G.	GOOD
8000	7000	6000

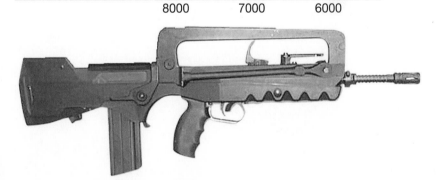

FRENCH FAMAS BULLPUP RIFLE 5.56MM

FEATHER INDUSTRIES, INC.
Trinidad, Colorado

■ AT-22

A blowback operated rifle in .22LR. Removable 1- inch barrel. 20 round magazine. Collapsible metal stock. Manufactured 1986-95. Rifles made the final year of production had the collapsible stock altered so it could not slide into the retracted position. Late production guns were sold through Mitchell Arms.

EXC.	V.G.	GOOD
375	300	250

■ F-2

Similar to the AT-22 but has a fixed synthetic stock. Made to comply with some states' "assault weapon" laws. Manufactured 1992-95.

EXC.	V.G.	GOOD
300	250	200

■ AT-9

A blowback operated 9mm rifle. Has a 16-inch barrel and collapsible metal stock. Magazines offered in 10, 25 and 30 rounds. Manufactured 1988-95.

EXC.	V.G.	GOOD
600	450	350

FEATHER USA
Eaton, Colorado

A new corporation. They bought rights to the old Feather Industries designs. Currently offering a series of firearms based on the AT-22 and AT-9 design available with many optional upgrades and accessories.

■ RAV-22LR

Basically the same rifle as the AT-22 listed above. The wire stock does not slide to a shorter position. It can be removed easily. There are several options in finish, stocks and accessories. Price listed is for the base model.

MSRP	EXC.	V.G.	GOOD
399	350	300	250

■ RAV-22HA

As above but features a tapered bull barrel.

MSRP	EXC.	V.G.	GOOD
549	475	425	375

■ RAV-22HF

A bull barrel model featuring a CAR-15 style sliding buttstock.

MSRP	EXC.	V.G.	GOOD
695	600	550	500

■ RAV-9MM

A new version of the AT-9 listed above. Several options available. Price is for the base model.

MSRP	EXC.	V.G.	GOOD
599	500	450	400

■ RAV-9HA

As above with a tapered bull barrel.

MSRP	EXC.	V.G.	GOOD
759	650	600	550

■ RAV-40S&W

Similar to the base model but in .40 S&W.

MSRP	EXC.	V.G.	GOOD
699	N/A	N/A	N/A

■ RAV-45ACP

Similar to base model but in .45 ACP.

MSRP	EXC.	V.G.	GOOD
759	650	600 5	50

■ RAV-45ACPHA

Similar to above but with tapered bull barrel.

MSRP	EXC.	V.G.	GOOD
899	750	700	650

FEDERAL ENGINEERING
Chicago, Illinois

■ XC-220

A .22LR semi-automatic rifle. Tubular construction. 16-1/2-inch barrel. 28 round magazine. Manufactured 1984-89.

EXC.	V.G.	GOOD
550	450	400

■ XC-450

As above but in .45 caliber. 30 round magazine. Manufactured 1984-89.

EXC.	V.G.	GOOD
750	600	500

■ XC-900

As above but in 9mm. 32 round magazine. Manufactured 1984-89.

EXC.	V.G.	GOOD
700	550	450

FEDERAL ORDNANCE
South El Monte, California

■ M-14

A semi-automatic version of the U.S. service rifle. New manufactured receiver assembled with USGI surplus parts. Wood or fiberglass stock. Chambered in .308/7.62 NATO. Manufactured 1986-91.

EXC.	V.G.	GOOD
800	700	600

FEG
(FEGYVER ES GAZKESZULEKGYAR)
Budapest, Hungary

Imported by Kassnar Imports of Harrisburg, Pennsylvania.

■ SA 85M

This is an AK-47 variation produced in Hungary. Caliber 7.62x39mm. Black laquer finish. Light colored wood stocks. Both fixed and folding stock versions were made. Imported 1987-89.

EXC.	V.G.	GOOD
1500	1250	1000

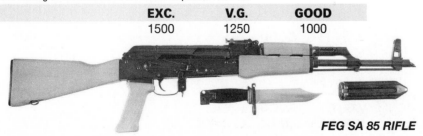

FEG SA 85 RIFLE

■ SA-2000-M

Introduced in 1999, this FEG-made AK was imported with a thumbhole stock.

EXC.	V.G.	GOOD
750	625	500

FNH USA Inc.
McLean, Virginia

The U.S. importer for FN Herstal in Belgium. They are the current incarnation of the classic manufacturer Fabrique Nationael.

■ PS-90

A semi-automatic version of the P-90 submachine gun. Chambered for the 5.7x28mm cartridge. 30 and 50 round magazines. Black or green synthetic stock.

MSRP	EXC.	V.G.	GOOD
1300	1200	1100	950

FNH MODEL PS-90 RIFLE 5.7X28MM

■ FS2000 STANDARD

A bullpup style rifle in 5.56mm/.223. 17-3/8-inch barrel. Features a 1.6x optical sighting package. Uses AR-15/M-16 magazines. Weight: 7.6 lbs.

MSRP	EXC.	V.G.	GOOD
2100	1850	1700	1600

FNH FS 2000 RIFLE 5.56MM

■ FS2000 TACTICAL

A bullpup style rifle in 5.56mm/.223. 17-3/8-inch barrel. Fixed sights. Features a picatinny rail on top. Uses AR-15/M-16 magazines. Weight: 7.6 lbs.

MSRP	EXC.	V.G.	GOOD
2100	1850	1700	1600

FNH FS 2000 TACTICAL RIFLE

SCAR 16S

A semi-automatic version of the U.S. SOCOM's newest tactical rifle. Caliber .223 with a 16-inch barrel. Folding sights. Three M-1913 rails. Utilizes a short stroke gas piston system. Side folding stock Is adjustable for comb and length of pull. Black or Desert Tan. Uses AR pattern magazines. Limited production. Weight: 7.4 lbs.

MSRP	EXC.	V.G.	GOOD
2995	2750	2500	2250

FNH SCAR-16 S RIFLE

SCAR 17S

A .308 version of the SCAR. Features are the same as the 16S. 20 round magazine. Weight: 8 lbs.

MSRP	EXC.	V.G.	GOOD
3195	2750	2500	2250

FNAR

A .308 caliber rifle. Black synthetic stock with pistol grip. No sights. M-1913 rail top. 10 or 20 round magazines. Weight: 9 lbs.

MSRP	EXC.	V.G.	GOOD
1849	1600	1250	1000

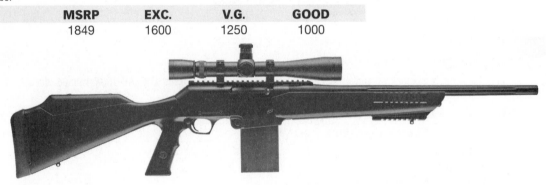

FNAR RIFLE CAL. .308

FIVE-SEVEN

A handgun chambered for the 5.7x28mm cartridge. Polymer frame. M-1913 rail underneath. Uses 10 or 20 round magazines.

MSRP	EXC.	V.G.	GOOD
1299	1000	800	600

FNH FIVE-SEVEN PISTOL 5.7X28MM

FULTON ARMORY
Savage, Maryland
Website: www.fulton-armory.com

This company manufactures a line of precision M-14 and AR-15 type rifles. They manufacture their own receivers. Most products are custom built to order and pricing changes with each feature. The base model prices are listed here.

■ M-14 SERVICE RIFLE

A new Fulton armory receiver assembled with the customer's choice of a 22- or 18-1/2-inch barrel. Chambered for 7.62mm/.308. The rest of the steel parts are original USGI. Parkerized finish. New military contour walnut stock. Optional feature available for an additional price include: national match trigger, various pattern scope mounts and even a non-functional selector switch for those who want to mirror the full appearance of the military M-14. Uses 10 and 20 round M-14 magazines. Rifle shipped with one 10 round magazine. Several upgrades availible with additional cost.

MSRP	EXC.	V.G.	GOOD
2700	2500	2200	1900

■ M-14 SOCOM MARK 14 MODEL 0 RIFLE

Tested by the U.S. military. 18- or 22-inch military contour barrel. Chambered for 7.62mm/.308. Includes Sage collapsible stock/accuracy rail system with all Sage stock accessories, tritium front night sight, vortex direct connect flash suppressor, tactical extended bolt release. Uses 10 and 20 round M-14 magazines. Rifle shipped with one 10 round magazine.

MSRP	EXC.	V.G.	GOOD
3500	3250	3000	2750

FULTON ARMORY SOCOM M-14 RIFLE

■ M-14 PEERLESS MATCH/TARGET RIFLE

A new Fulton Armory match grade receiver assembled with a Fulton 22-inch National Match stainless steel barrel. Chambered for 7.62mm/.308. Includes National Match trigger modification, national match front and rear sights, and national match operating rod spring guide. The new National Match walnut stock features Includes glass bedding, front end mod, and handguard mod. Uses 10 and 20 round M-14 magazines. Rifle shipped with one 10 round magazine.

MSRP	EXC.	V.G.	GOOD
3300	3100	2800	2500

■ TITAN FAR 308 RIFLE

An AR-10 based system. Dual-finished (hard coat anodized and black Teflon coated) 6066T6 slick-side, no-snag Titan flat top upper receiver. 20-inch or 22-inch stainless steel four groove one-in-ten Heavy barrel, genuine Smith Enterprises USGI Vortex¨ direct connect flash suppressor. Titan float tube with steel locking ring. The lower assembly begins with a dual-finished (hard coat anodized and black Teflon coated) forged 6061T6 Titan lower receiver. A2 buttstock or an optional Magpul Titan PRS buttstock. Titan SPR hand-filling pistol grip. Fulton Armory-tuned two-stage match trigger. Shipped with a 10 round magazine.

MSRP	EXC.	V.G.	GOOD
1900	1750	1500	1250

■ TITAN FAR 308 CARBINE

Dual-finished 6066T6 slick-side no-snag Titan upper receiver. 16-inch or 20-inch stainless steel four groove one-in-ten medium weight barrel. Genuine Smith Enterprises USGI Vortex¨ direct connect flash suppressor. Titan float tube with steel locking ring. Optional 3-inch to 12-inch rails for all four sides; top rail co-registers with receiver rail. Optional folding/detachable front and rear sights; requires at least one 2-inch top rail. Hard chrome bolt carrier. The lower assemble starts with a Dual-finished (hard coat anodized and black Teflon coated) Forged 6061T6 Titan lower receiver. Command Arms "Fifth Generation" collapsible stock with ambi QD swivel sockets standard. Optional Magpul Titan PRS buttstock. Titan SPR pistol grip. Fulton Armory-tuned two-stage match trigger. Shipped with a 10 round magazine.

MSRP	EXC.	V.G.	GOOD
1900	1750	1500	1250

FULTON ARMORY FAR 308 CARBINE

■ FAR-15 LEGACY

Near-exact replica of the Viet Nam era M16. The Legacy Service Rifle features new, genuine USGI M16A1 chrome lightweight 20-inch barrel in 5.56mm/.223 with 1:12 twist. Original pattern 3-prong M16-type flash suppressor. Military-contractor M16-type "Slick Side" forged upper receiver with no forward assist or case deflector. Forged steel M16 front sight base. M16 front and rear Sights. M16-type triangular handguards. M16-type buttstock with early-type solid buttplate (no door)—CAR stock optional at no extra cost. Chrome plated slick side bolt carrier has no forward assist serrations. Fulton Armory forged lower receiver. Hand-Polished and hand-fitted military trigger. A1 pistol grip. Discontinued.

EXC	V.G.	GOOD
900	800	700

■ FAR-15 M4

Based on the military issue M-4 carbine. Features a choice of flat top or A-2 type upper receiver. Fulton Armory 1:9 heavy contour or M4 contour (chrome lined bore and chamber standard) or 16-inch barrel with Fulton Armory 5.56MM match chamber. (Chrome lined bore and chamber optional) A2 flash suppressor. Forged military numbered flattop or A2 upper receiver. Forged steel front sight base with exclusive windage adjustment. Military-contract forged upper receiver. D-Fender extractor enhancer. Fulton Armory forged lower receiver. Hand-polished and hand-fitted military trigger. A2 pistol grip. Six-position collapsible stock. Choice of Black (standard) or optional Olive Drab (OD) or Tan furniture.

MSRP	EXC.	V.G.	GOOD
1100	950	850	750

■ FAR-15 A2 OR A4

Based on the military issue M-16A2, rifle features a choice of forged flat top or A-2 type upper receiver. Fulton Armory 1:9 heavy contour 20-inch barrel with Fulton Armory 5.56mm match chamber, or Fulton Armory 1:8 heavy contour barrel. A2 flash suppressor. Forged steel front sight base with exclusive windage adjustment. D-Fender extractor enhancer. Fulton Armory forged lower receiver. Hand-polished and hand-fitted military trigger. A2 pistol grip and buttstock. Choice of Black (standard) or optional Olive Drab (OD) or Tan (with A1 buttstock) furniture.

MSRP	EXC.	V.G.	GOOD
1050	900	750	600

■ FAR-15 UPR

The Universal Precision Rifle base model features: Fulton Armory Slick Side Upper Receiver, Fulton Armory 20-inch National Match 1x9 HBAR profile, Fulton Armory gas block with flip-up front sight, Fulton Armory UPR handguard float system with swivel, A2 grip, stock and flash suppressor. Weight 8.9 lbs. Numerous optional features available for additional cost.

MSRP	EXC.	V.G.	GOOD
1200	1000	900	800

■ FAR-15PVR

The Precision Varmint Rifle base model features: "Slick Side" upper receiver, 20-inch 1:12 stainless steel HBAR barrel, Fulton Armory PVR knurled handguard system with bipod stud, A2 pistol grip, A2 stock. Numerous optional features available for additional cost.

MSRP	EXC.	V.G.	GOOD
1150	1000	900	800

GALIL

See IMI.

GALIL

GRENDEL
Rockledge, Florida

◼ P-30 PISTOL

A .22 Magnum semi-automatic pistol. Frame constructed mostly of nylon. Matte black finish. It has a 5-inch barrel. 30 round magazine. Manufactured 1990-95. In 2009 Kel-Tec announced the PMR-30, a new version of the Grendel. See entry in Kel-Tec.

EXC.	V.G.	GOOD
500	400 3	00

NOTE: add $50-80 for each functional 30 round magazine.

GRENDEL P-30 PISTOL .22 MAGNUM W/30 SHOT MAGAZINE

◼ R-31 CARBINE

A semi-automatic rifle in .22 Magnum rimfire. It has a 16-inch barrel with muzzle brake, synthetic frame and forearm. Telescoping buttstock. Magazine holds 30 rounds. Discontinued in 1994.

EXC.	V.G.	GOOD
1500	1100	800

GONCZ ARMAMENT
North Hollywood, California

◼ MODEL GA

A 9mm semi-automatic pistol. This was a new design, not based on any other existing firearm. This small manufacturer built these on a prototype and special order basis from 1984-90. There were several minor variations listed in factory listings but it is unclear how many of any type were ever made. The company was taken over by Claridge Hi Tec who went on to produce another model based on this design. The designer, Lajos J. Goncz, reportedly sued Claridge over patent infringements and forced Claridge to discontinue production.

EXC.	V.G.	GOOD
2500	2000	1500

GONCZ ARMAMENT 9MM PISTOL

HECKLER AND KOCH
Oberndorf/Neckar, Germany

◼ HK41

The Heckler and Koch model HK41 is a semi-automatic rifle that was first produced in 1966. It is the civilian version of the renowned military and law enforcement G3 automatic rifle that was manufactured by Heckler and Koch, GmbH during the mid to late 1950s, and is the precursor to the HK91 semiautomatic rifle. The HK41 employs the same G3 "roller delayed blowback system" that is known for its strength, reliability and low recoil. At the time the HK41 was produced, the first digit "4" in Heckler and Koch's model numbering system signified that it is a paramilitary-type semiautomatic rifle, while the second digit "1" identified the type of ammunition the rifle is chambered for as 7.62mmx51 NATO or .308 caliber Winchester. All HK41s were manufactured at the Heckler and Koch, GmbH plant located in Oberndorf am Neckar, Germany. Only a limited number were produced for and imported into the United States. Factory records indicate fewer than 400 model 41s were ever made.

◼ HK41 (1966)

Imported in 1966 only by the Sante Fe Division of the Golden State Arms Co in Pasadena, California. These are desirable by collectors as the closest copy of a true G-3 and many were converted to full automatic operation before 1986. This has reduced the already limited numbers available on the civilian market.

EXC.	V.G.	GOOD
6000	5000	3800

◼ HK41 (1974)

Imported 1974 by SACO (Security Arms Co.) of Arlington, Virginia. The 1974 version of the 1966 HK41 had some internal changes to the receiver and trigger group due to requirements imposed by the BATF, because the 1966 version used some full automatic components.

EXC.	V.G.	GOOD
5000	3750	3000

HECKLER AND KOCH INC.
Arlington, Virginia

Website: www.hk-usa.com

Exclusive U.S. importer for H&K products. Formed in 1976.

◼ MODEL 91

This rifle is recoil-operated, with a delayed-roller lock bolt. It is chambered for the .308 Winchester/7.62 NATO cartridge and has a 17.7-inch barrel with military-style aperture sights. It is furnished with a 20 round detachable magazine and is finished in matte black with a black plastic stock. This model is a semi-automatic version of the select fire G3 rifle. Some areas of the country have made its ownership illegal. Approximately 48,000 were imported 1975-89.

EXC.	V.G.	GOOD
2800	2400	2000

HECKLER & KOCH MODEL 91 RIFLE, AKA G-3

■ MODEL 91 A3

This model is simply the Model 91 with a retractable metal stock.

EXC.	V.G.	GOOD
2800	2400	2000

■ MODEL 93

This model is similar to the Model 91 except that it is chambered for the .223 cartridge and has a 16.4-inch barrel. The magazine holds 25 rounds, and the specifications are the same as for the Model 91. This is a semi-automatic version of the select fire HK33 rifle. Approximately 18,000 were imported 1975-89.

EXC.	V.G.	GOOD
2750	2500	2100

HK MODEL 93 RIFLE 5.56MM

■ MODEL 93 A3

This is the Model 93 with a retractable metal stock.

EXC.	V.G.	GOOD
2800	2550	2200

■ MODEL 94

This is a carbine version of the Model 93 chambered for the 9mm Parabellum cartridge, with a 16.5-inch barrel. It is a smaller-scaled weapon that has a 15-shot magazine. Many have been converted to full automatic.

EXC.	V.G.	GOOD
3800	3200	2700

■ MODEL 94 A3

This model is a variation of the Model 94 with the addition of a retractable metal stock.

EXC.	V.G.	GOOD
3900	3400	2800

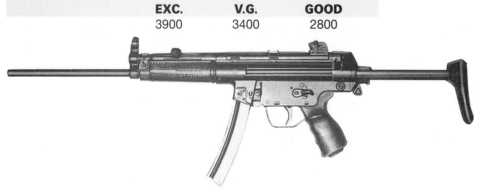

HK MODEL 94 9MM RIFLE

SP-89

A large frame semi-automatic pistol in 9mm. Based on the H&K MP-5 submachine gun. 4-1/2-inch barrel. Imported 1991-1994.

EXC.	V.G.	GOOD
3500	3000	2500

HK SP-89 PISTOL

PSG-1

A precision sniping rifle based on the HK91 with a 25-5/8-inch heavy barrel. Fine tune trigger group. Adjustable buttstock. Sold with a Hensoldt 6x42 scope. Shipped in a fitted case. Discontinued in 1989.

EXC.	V.G.	GOOD
15,000	12,500	9500

HK PSG-1 SNIPER RIFLE, CAL. .308

MODEL SR9

A sporter version of the HK91 made to comply with U.S. law. 19-3/4-inch barrel without flash suppressor. Synthetic stock with thumbhole pistol grip. Imported 1990-94.

EXC.	V.G.	GOOD
1900	1750	1400

MODEL SR9 T (TARGET)

SR9 with adjustable MSG90 buttstock, PSG-1 trigger group and hand grip. Imported 1992-94.

EXC.	V.G.	GOOD
3000	2500	2000

SR9 TC (TARGET COMPETITION)

SR9 with PSG-1 stock, trigger group and pistol grip. Imported 1993.

EXC.	V.G.	GOOD
7000	5500	4000

■ SL-8-1

A new generation .223/5.56mm rifle based on the Model G36. Gas operated action. Most parts are made from poly carbon fiber. Gray color. Thumbhole stock with cheek rest. 20-3/4-inch barrel. 10 round magazine. Introduced in 2000-2003. Reintroduced In 2007

MSRP	EXC.	V.G.	GOOD
2449	2000	1750	1500

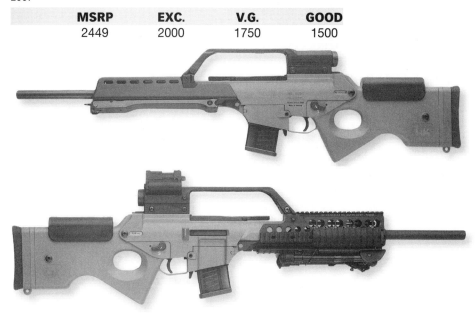

HK SL-8 RIFLE 5.56MM

■ SL-8-6

As above with a higher picatinny rail sighting system. Black finish.

MSRP	EXC.	V.G.	GOOD
2449	2000	1750	1500

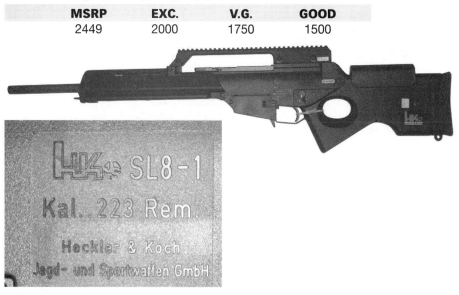

H&K SL-8-6 RIFLE (TOP) AND RECEIVER MARKINGS (BOTTOM)

■ MODEL USC

A semi-automatic blowback operated carbine in .45 ACP. It is based on H&K's UMP submachine gun. 16-inch barrel. Skeletonized synthetic stock. Gray or black color. 10 round magazine. Imported 2000-2003. Reintroduced in 2007.

MSRP	EXC.	V.G.	GOOD
1833	1600	1400	1200

HK USC RIFLE, CAL .45

■ MODEL MR556

HK's version of the AR-15. Cal. 5.56mm. 16-inch barrel. Flat top receiver. diopter rear sight, Quad rail handguard, telescoping buttstock. 10 or 30 rd magazines.

MSRP	EXC.	V.G.	GOOD
2295	2000	1750	1500

■ MODEL MR762

HK's version of the AR-10. Cal. 7.62mm Nato. 16-inch barrel. Flat top receiver. diopter rear sight, Quad rail handguard, telescoping buttstock. 10 or 30 rd magazines.

MSRP	EXC.	V.G.	GOOD
2695	1600	1400	1200

HESSE ARMS
Inver Grove Heights, Minnesota

This company is no longer in business under this name. The resale market in Hesse firearms is extremely soft.

■ FAL-H RIFLES

All FAL-H rifles include these features: military spec internal parts, new or as new barrel, military finish, post ban legal muzzlebrake, one magazine, new metric pattern Type 3 receiver, adjustable gas system, refinished or new pistol grip, hard case, carry handle, sling, and manual. All rifles chambered for .308 Winchester cartridge. Additional calibers in .22-250 and .243 are also available. Weights are from 8.5 to 14 lbs. depending on model.

◆ FALO Tactical Rifle

This model features a free floating handguard assembly.

EXC.	V.G.	GOOD
900	800	700

◆ FALO Heavy Barrel

This model features a heavy barrel and is based on the Israeli FALO rifle.

EXC.	V.G.	GOOD
750	650	550

◆ FAL-H High Grade

This model is available in any configuration and features a new walnut stock, pistol grip, and hand guard. Trigger is gold plated.

EXC.	V.G.	GOOD
1050	950	800

This is standard model that is similar in appearance to the original FAL.

EXC.	V.G.	GOOD
750	600	500

◆ FAL-H Congo Rifle
This model features a 16-inch barrel.

EXC.	V.G.	GOOD
800	700	600

◆ FALO Congo Rifle
Similar to the model above but fitted with a 16-inch heavy barrel.

EXC.	V.G.	GOOD
800	700	600

■ HAR-15 RIFLES
All of the HAR-15 rifles have these features: military spec internal parts, heavy match grade barrels, post ban legal muzzle-brake, A2 upper receiver, A2 round handguards with heat shields, A2 stock, A2 lower receiver. Each rifle comes with hard case, manual, and sling. Rifles are chambered for .223 Remington but can be chambered in other calibers as well. These include .17 Rem. (add $145), 9mm NATO (add $85), 6mm PPC (add $145), 6mmx45 (add $95), .300 Fireball (add $195), and 7.62x39 (add $45).

◆ Omega Match
Fitted with a 1-inch diameter stainless steel barrel, adjustable match trigger, E2 stock, flat top receiver, free floating handguard.

EXC.	V.G.	GOOD
800	700	600

◆ HAR-15A2 Standard Rifle
This model has all of the standard features offered for HAR-15 rifles.

EXC.	V.G.	GOOD
575	500	450

◆ HAR-15A2 National Match
This model is fitted with special bolt carrier, adjustable match trigger. Designed as Match grade rifle.

EXC.	V.G.	GOOD
800	700	600

◆ HAR-15A2 Bull Gun
This model is fitted with a 1-inch stainless steel barrel with special front sight base.

EXC.	V.G.	GOOD
650	600	550

◆ HAR-15A2 Dispatcher
Fitted with a 16-inch barrel with full-length handguard.

EXC.	V.G.	GOOD
600	550	500

◆ HAR-15A2 Carbine
Fitted with a 16-inch heavy barrel and a non-collapsing stock with short handguard.

EXC.	V.G.	GOOD
500	475	450

◆ M14-H Standard Rifle
This is a semi-automatic version of the M14 rifle chambered for the .308 cartridge. It is fitted with a new receiver, walnut stock or synthetic stock. Each rifle is sold with a sling, annual, and 10 round magazine and an extra original M145 stock.

EXC.	V.G.	GOOD
800	700	600

◆ M14-H Brush Rifle
This model has the same features as the standard rifle but with an 18-inch barrel.

EXC.	V.G.	GOOD
800	700	600

■ MODEL 47 RIFLE
This is a copy of the AK-47 and it is chambered for the 7.63x39 cartridge. It is also available in .223 caliber.

EXC.	V.G.	GOOD
450	400	350

HIGH STANDARD MANUFACTURING CO.
Houston, Texas

Website: www.highstandard.com

This company offers the Mil-Spec series of AR-type rifles.

■ HSA-15 RIFLE A2

Military pattern A2 style. Chambered in 5.56mm/.223. 20inch barrel. Fixed carry handle. Fixed stock. Has a flash hider and bayonet lug.

MSRP	EXC.	V.G.	GOOD
905	750	675	600

■ HSA-15 CARBINE A2

Ar-type rifle with CAR-15 style handguard. 16-inch barrel. Fixed carry handle. Six-position telescoping buttstock.

MSRP	EXC.	V.G.	GOOD
895	750	675	600

■ HSA-15 FLAT TOP RIFLE

Flat top receiver for scope mounting or adjustable sight. Carry handle; standard front sight. 20-inch barrel. Has a flash hider and bayonet lug.

MSRP	EXC.	V.G.	GOOD
905	800	700	600

■ HSA-15 FLAT TOP CARBINE

AR-type rifle with A2-style flat top receiver for scope mounting or adjustable sight carry handle. Standard front sight. 16-inch barrel. Has a flash hider and bayonet lug. Six-position telescoping buttstock.

MSRP	EXC.	V.G.	GOOD
905	800	700	600

■ HSA-15 NATIONAL MATCH RIFLE

A2 receiver, National match sights, 20-inch stainless steel free float barrel, two stage trigger, A2 stock.

MSRP	EXC.	V.G.	GOOD
1250	900	800	700

■ HSA-15 LONG RANGE RIFLE

Flat top receiver, 24-inch fluted heavy barrel, two stage trigger, A2 stock.

MSRP	EXC.	V.G.	GOOD
1250	900	800	700

■ HSA M4 9MM CARBINE A2

A2-style receiver. Cal. 9mm with a 16-inch barrel. Six-position telescoping buttstock.

MSRP	EXC.	V.G.	GOOD
1025	850	750	650

■ HSA M4 9MM FLAT TOP CARBINE

Flat top receiver. Cal. 9mm with a 16-inch barrel. Six-position telescoping buttstock.

MSRP	EXC.	V.G.	GOOD
985	800	700	600

HI-POINT FIREARMS
Dayton, Ohio

Website: www.hi-pointfirearms.com

■ MODEL 995 CARBINE

Introduced in 1996, this economy priced semi-automatic rifle is available in 9mm or .40 S&W. It has a 16-1/2-inch barrel and an overall length of 32-1/2 inches. Weight is 7 lbs. Features include an all-weather black or camo polymer stock. Grip mounted magazine release, quick on/off thumb safety, fully adjustable sights with "Ghost Ring" rear sight and front post. Scope base to allow mounting of a regular rifle scope or red dot scope. 10 round magazines.

MSRP	EXC.	V.G.	GOOD
250	200	175 1	50

■ MODEL 995 TACTICAL

The new version of the Model 995 features picatinny rails on the top of receiver, underside of forearm and barrel. Skeletonized stock. 10 round magazines.

MSRP	EXC.	V.G.	GOOD
274	250	225	200

THE HI POINT MODEL 995 CARBINE IN VARIOUS CONFIGURATIONS

HOLLOWAY ARMS CO.
Ft. Worth, Texas

■ HAC-7

A 7.62mm semi-automatic rifle. An interesting design that has features adopted from the FN FAL, AKM and AR-10. It has a 20-inch barrel. Offered in right or left hand versions. Side folding stock. Uses modified Armalite AR-10 magazines. Approximately 350 were made 1984-85.

EXC.	V.G.	GOOD
3500	3000	2500

HOLLOWAY ARMS HAC-7 RIFLE CAL. .308

IMI
(ISRAEL MILITARY INDUSTRIES)
Israel

The small arms manufacturer for the Israeli military. They have also exported several models to the U.S. IMI products are imported by several companies including Action Arms, Springfield Armory and Magnum Research.

■ UZI CARBINE

A 9mm semi-automatic version of the legendary submachine gun. It has a 16-inch barrel and a collapsible steel stock. Sold with a dummy 10-inch barrel that simulates the appearance of the original SMG.

◆ Model A (Imported 1980-83)

EXC.	V.G.	GOOD
1400	1200	1000

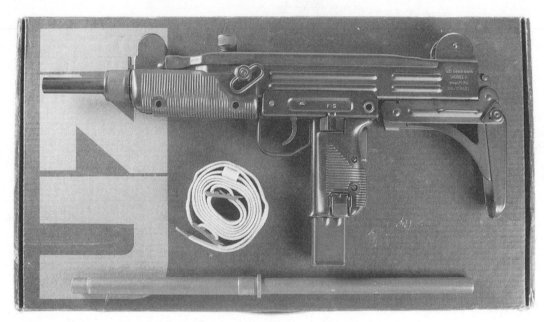

ISRAEL MILITARY INDUSTRIES UZI 9MM CARBINE

◆ Model B

As above with minor internal changes due to BATFE requirements that it not accept the original UZI submachinegun bolt. Also offered in .45 ACP. Imported 1983-89.

EXC.	V.G.	GOOD
1250	1100	950

■ UZI CONVERSION KIT FOR .22LR

With one 12 round magazine. Installs on the B model.

EXC.	V.G.	GOOD
400	325	275

Note: Also see UZI listings under Norinco and Vector Arms.

■ UZI MINI CARBINE

A scaled down version of the Uzi Carbine. 19-3/4-inch barrel. Steel stock folds to the side. Imported 1988-89.

EXC.	V.G.	GOOD
2000	1750	1500

■ UZI PISTOL

A 9mm or .45 ACP pistol that resembles the micro UZI submachine gun. 4-1/2-inch barrel.

EXC.	V.G.	GOOD
1000	800	650

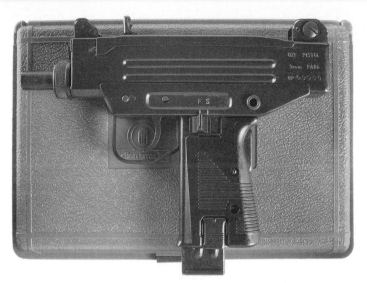

UZI 9MM PISTOL

■ GALIL

An Israeli designed rifle using a refined Kalishnikov (AK-47) action.

◆ Galil Model 386 AR 5.56mm
16-1/8-inch barrel. Side folding stock. 35 round magazine. Importation discontinued in 1989.

EXC.	V.G.	GOOD
2500	2100	1750

IMI GALIL RIFLE, IMPORTED BY SPRINGFIELD ARMORY

◆ Galil Model 329 AR 7.62mm
19-inch barrel. Side folding stock. 12 and 25 round magazines. Importation discontinued in 1989.

EXC.	V.G.	GOOD
2600	2200	1850

◆ Galil Model 372 ARM 5.56mm
Heavier version of the AR with a folding bipod.

EXC.	V.G.	GOOD
2750	2500	2200

◆ Galil Model 332 ARM 7.62mm
.308/7.62 NATO version of the AR with a folding bipod.

EXC.	V.G.	GOOD
2700	2550	2300

◆ Hadar II SA 7.62mm
Sporter version of the Galil AR featuring a walnut stock with thumbhole pistol grip. Imported in 1989-90.

EXC.	V.G.	GOOD
1400	1150	850

IMI

IMI HADAR RIFLE 7.62MM

NOTE: *Also see Galil entries under Ohio Rapid Fire and Elite Firearms.*

INTERDYNAMICS OF AMERICA
Miami, Florida

■ KG-9

A 9mm semiautomatic handgun with a machine pistol appearance. It has a 5-inch barrel protected by a perforated steel shroud. The muzzle is threaded. 32 round magazine. Fires from an open bolt. The BATFE ruled this model to be illegal to manufacture because it was too easy to modify to full automatic. Manufactured 1981-83.

EXC.	V.G.	GOOD
1000	750	600

■ KG-99

A redesigned version of the KG-9. Striker fired from a closed bolt. Also was available in stainless steel. Manufactured in 1984.

EXC.	V.G.	GOOD
500	425	350

■ KG-9 MINI

As above but has a 3-inch barrel. The muzzle is threaded. Made without the barrel shroud.

EXC.	V.G.	GOOD
500	425	350

INTRATEC
Miami, Florida

This was Interdynamics reorganized under a new name. They were forced out of business in the late 1990s after lawsuits over misuse of their products.

■ TEC-9 OR TEC-DC9

A 9mm semiautomatic handgun with a machine pistol appearance. It has a 5-inch barrel protected by a perforated steel shroud. The muzzle is threaded. 32 round magazine. Matte black or stainless steel finish. Manufactured 1985-94.

EXC.	V.G.	GOOD
500	425	350

INTERDYNAMICS KG-9,
99 INTRATEC TEC-9 PISTOL

TEC-9 MINI

As above but has a 3-inch barrel. The muzzle is threaded. Made without the barrel shroud.

EXC.	V.G.	GOOD
500	425	350

TEC-22 OR SKORPION

A 22LR semi-automatic pistol similar to the Tec-9. 4-inch barrel with threaded muzzle. Does not have the barrel shroud. 30 round magazine. This pistol uses a magazine that is interchangeable with that of the Ruger 10-22 rifle. Manufactured 1988-94.

EXC.	V.G.	GOOD
350	300	250

AB-10

This is simply a post-ban Tec-9 Mini without the threaded muzzle. Shipped with a 10 round magazine, but also accepts the earlier 32 round version.

EXC.	V.G.	GOOD
300	250	200

SPORT-22

Post-ban version of the Tec-22 without the threaded muzzle. Sold with a 10 round rotary magazine but also accepts the earlier high-capacity versions.

EXC.	V.G.	GOOD
275	250	200

I.O. INC.

Monroe, NC.

Website: www.ioinc.us

Manufacturer and importer of AK type rifles. Formerly known as Inter-Ordnance.

STG-2000

Cal. 7.62x39mm with a 16.25-inch barrel with A2 type flash hider. An AK-47 variation designed in East Germany. Made in the U.S.A. with new made and new import parts. Choice of black, dark earth tone or pink polymer stock. Uses any AK pattern 7.62x39mm magazines. Weight: 7.0 lbs.

MSRP	EXC.	V.G.	GOOD
685	525	475	425

IO STG-2000 RIFLE

AK-47

Cal. 7.62x39mm with a 16.25-inch barrel. Classic AK design. Made In the U.S.A. with new made and new import parts. Russian type laminated stocks. Weight: 7.0 lbs

MSRP	EXC.	V.G.	GOOD
500	475	425	375

PPS-43 PISTOL

A 7.62x25mm semi automatic handgun based on the Russian PPS-43 sub-machine gun. Made in Radom, Poland by Pioneer for IO. Features a 10 inch barrel. Has the metal stock welded in the closed position thus making this a legal pistol. Uses original 35 round PPS-43 magazines.

NIB	EXC.	V.G.	GOOD
550	450	425	400

IO PPS-43 PISTOL

■ AK-47C

Cal. 7.62x39mm with a 16.25-inch barrel. An AK variation with STG-2000 stock and a tactical handguard with picitinny rail. Made In the U.S.A. with new made and new import parts. Choice of black, dark earth tone or pink polymer stock. Weight: 7.0 lbs

MSRP	EXC.	V.G.	GOOD
500	475	425	375

■ CALIFORNIA LEGAL AK

Non-pistol grip configuration.

MSRP	EXC.	V.G.	GOOD
409	350	300	275

■ SSG-97

Romanian SVD sniper rifle design in Cal. 7.62x54Rmm with a 26.75-inch barrel with flash hider. Iron sights. Picatinny scope rail on left side of receiver, instead of the Soviet pattern mount system. No optics included. Made in the U.S.A. with new made and new import parts. Laminated furniture. 10 round detachable magazine. Weight: 9.0 lbs

MSRP	EXC.	V.G.	GOOD
1100	950	825	700

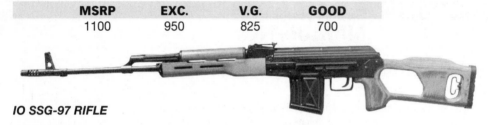

IO SSG-97 RIFLE

■ SSG-2000

SVD sniper rifle design in cal. 7.62x54Rmm with a 26.75-inch barrel with flash hider. Iron sights. Picatinny scope rail on Left side of receiver, instead of the Soviet pattern mount system. No optics included. Made in the U.S.A. with new made and new import parts. Black polymer furniture. 10 round detachable magazine. Weight: 9.0 lbs

MSRP	EXC.	V.G.	GOOD
1100	950	850	750

J AND R ENGINEERING
South El Monte, California

■ MODEL 68

A 9mm semi-automatic rifle. It has a 16-1/4-inch barrel that ends with a cone shaped flash hider. Wood buttstock and forearm. 31 round magazine. This design first appeared in the 1960's. It was later manufactured by Wilkinson Arms as the Terry carbine.

EXC.	V.G.	GOOD
450	400	350

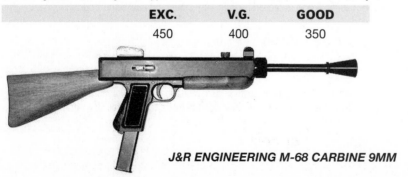

J&R ENGINEERING M-68 CARBINE 9MM

KEL-TEC CNC INDUSTRIES
Cocoa, Florida
Website: www.kel-tec-cnc.com

■ SUB-2000 RIFLE

A 9mm or .40 S&W semi-automatic rifle. It has a 16-1/8-inch barrel. The rifle can be folded closed with a length of 16 inches. They offer different grip assemblies that can use different magazines. The standard one takes S&W type magazines. Other grip options include Glock, SIG or Beretta. Introduced 2001.

MSRP	EXC.	V.G.	GOOD
409	350	300	275

KEL TEC SUB 2000 RIFLE 9MM & .40 CAL.

SUB 2000 RIFLE FOLDED

■ SU-16A

A semi-automatic rifle in 5.56mm. 18-inch barrel. Picatinny rail for sight mounting. The nylon forearm splits open and folds down to become a bi-pod. The stock can be rotated for storage. Two 10 round or one 30 round magazine can be stored in the buttstock. Accepts AR-15/M-16 series magazines.

MSRP	EXC.	V.G.	GOOD
665	600	500	400

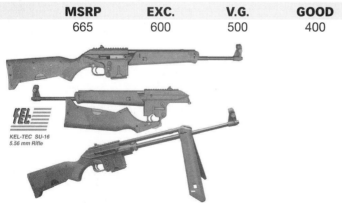

KEL-TEC SU-16A OPEN (TOP), FOLDED (MIDDLE) AND WITH BIPOD EXTENDED (BOTTOM)

■ SU-16 B

The "B" model retains all the features of the original SU-16, such as integrated bipod, picatinny rail, and rotating stock with magazine storage. 16-inch barrel. The rear sight is hard coat anodized aluminum and adjustable for windage. The front sight, also aluminum, is removable and accepts standard M-16 posts. Note: The "B" type sights can be purchased as a retrofit for SU-16 owners preferring the M-16 system.

MSRP	EXC.	V.G.	GOOD
718	625	550	475

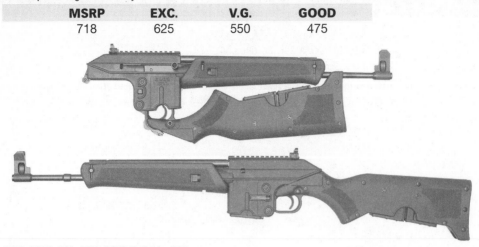

KEL TEC SU-16B RIFLE CAL .223

◼ SU-16C

Retains most features of the original SU-16, such as integrated bipod, picatinny rail, and M-16 magazine compatibility. The sights are similar to the "B" model, but with the front sight integrated into the gas block. The SU-16C has a true folding stock and can be fired with the stock folded. A reciprocating dust cover and a case deflecting operating handle are also integrated into the rifle. The barrel is 16 inches long and of medium weight. The muzzle is threaded 1/2x28 to accept standard attachments.

NIB	EXC.	V.G.	GOOD
770	650	575	500

KEL-TEC SU-16C OPEN WITH BIPOD EXTENDED (TOP) AND FOLDED (BOTTOM)

◼ SU-16 CA

The SU-16CA is a hybrid of the SU-16C and SU-16A rifles. The receiver, 16-inch barrel with 1/2-28 threads, bolt carrier, dust cover, sights, and case deflecting operating handle of the C model are combined with the stock of the A model. The SU-16CA comes with two 10 round magazines that store in the stock just like the A model and has all the same parkerized parts as the C model. Just like the A model the SU-16CA can be folded for storage and it will not fire in the folded position. This allows for it to be purchased in most states that still have an "assault weapons ban."

MSRP	EXC.	V.G.	GOOD
770	650	575	500

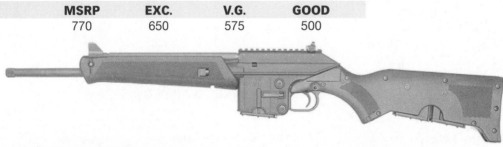

KEL TEC SU-16 CA RIFLE CAL .223

■ PLR-16

A gas operated, semi-automatic pistol chambered in 5.56mm NATO caliber. The PLR-16 has a conventional gas piston operation and utilizes the proven M-16 breech locking system. The rear sight is adjustable for windage. The front sight is of M-16 type. An integrated MIL-STD-1913 picatinny rail will accept a multitude of standard accessories. The muzzle end of the barrel is threaded to accept standard attachments such as a muzzle brake. Except for the barrel, bolt, sights, and mechanism, the PLR-16 pistol is made entirely of high-impact glass fiber reinforced polymer.

MSRP	EXC.	V.G.	GOOD
665	575	500	425

KEL TEC PLR-16 PISTOL, CAL. 5.56

■ PLR-22

A .22LR blowback operated pistol based on the PLR-16. It has a 10-inch barrel. The total length is 18-1/2 inches. Weight is 2-3/4 lbs. Accepts many of the accessories for the PLR-16 and SU-16 series. 27 round magazine. Also accepts Atchison M-16 22LR conversion magazines.

MSRP	EXC.	V.G.	GOOD
390	325	300	275

KEL TEC PLR-22 PISTOL, CAL. .22LR

■ SU-22

Based on the popular SU-16 series. .22LR blowback operated. 16.1-inch barrel with threaded muzzle. Total length is 40 inches. Fixed stock. Weight is 4 lbs. 27 round magazine. Also accepts Atchison M-16 .22LR conversion magazines.

MSRP	EXC.	V.G.	GOOD
440	400	350	300

■ PMR-30

A .22 Magnum semi automatic pistol with a 30 round magazine. 4.3-inch barrel. Polymer construction. A new version of the Grendel P-30. New for 2010.

MSRP	EXC.	V.G.	GOOD
415	375	N/A	N/A

■ RFB RIFLE

This bullpup design was introduced at the 2007 SHOT show as the SRT-8 (Sniper Rifle Tactical). The name has been changed to RFB

(Rifle Forward ejection Bullpup) The RFB is a short-stroke gas piston operated semi-automatic rifle in 7.62mm NATO caliber. It accepts standard metric FAL type magazines which work "drop free" and do not need to be tilted in. Barrels on current models are 18 inches long, with a chrome lined bore and chamber. A Mil-Spec picatinny rail is attached rigidly to the barrrel. Longer barrel lengths of 24, 26 and 32 inches will be available in the future.

MSRP	EXC.	V.G.	GOOD
1880	1800	1650	1350

KEL TEC RFB .308 RIFLE

KIMEL INDUSTRIES
Matthews, North Carolina

■ AP-9 PISTOL

A 9mm semi-automatic pistol with a machine pistol look. Five-inch barrel with vented shroud. Magazine inserts in front of trigger guard. Black matte finish. Manufactured 1989-94.

EXC.	V.G.	GOOD
400	350	300

KIMEL INDUSTRIES AP-9 PISTOL

■ MINI AP-9

As above except with a 3-inch barrel without shroud. Made with a matte black or nickel finish.

EXC.	V.G.	GOOD
425	375	325

Knight's Manufacturing Co.
Vero Beach, Florida

Website: www.knightarmco.com

This company was established in 1993 by Reed Knight. AR-15 inventor Eugene Stoner was involved in the early design of their products. As of mid-2010, some models have limited availability due to government contracts.

■ STONER SR-15 RIFLE

A 5.56mm/.223 flat top rifle with a 20-inch standard weight barrel. Two stage target trigger. Front and rear folding sights. RAS (rail accessory system) hand guard has accessory rails on four sides. SOCOM type adjustable stock.

NIB	EXC.	V.G.	GOOD
1700	1400	1200	1000

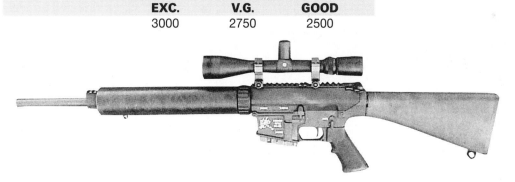

KNIGHT'S MANUFACTURING SR-15 RIFLE

■ STONER SR-15 M-4 CARBINE

As above with a 16-inch barrel. Flip up rear sight included. RAS hand guard. Choice of fixed or collapsible buttstock.

NIB	EXC.	V.G.	GOOD
1750	1400	1200	1000

■ STONER SR-25 SPORTER

A modernized version of the AR-10 rifle chambered in 7.62mm/.308. It has a flat top receiver with removable carry handle. 20-inch light-weight barrel. Round hand guard. 5, 10, or 20 round magazines. Manufactured 1993-97.

EXC.	V.G.	GOOD
3000	2750	2500

KNIGHT'S STONER SR-25 SPORTER

■ STONER SR-25 CARBINE (OLD VERSION)

As above but with a 16-inch free floating barrel. Flat top receiver with a removable carry handle. Fixed stock. Introduced in 1995. Discontinued.

EXC.	V.G.	GOOD
3000	2750	2500

■ STONER SR-25 ENHANCED MATCH RIFLE

Features a flat top receiver including flip sight. 20-inch free float barrel and URX hand guard with quad accessory rails. Two stage match trigger. A2 or Collapsible buttstock.

NIB	EXC.	V.G.	GOOD
3700	3250	2750	2200

■ STONER SR-25 ENHANCED MATCH CARBINE

Features a flat top receiver including flip sight. 16-inch free float barrel and URX hand guard with accessory rails. Two stage match trigger. Fixed or collapsible buttstock.

NIB	EXC.	V.G.	GOOD
3700	3250	2750	2200

■ STONER SR-25 MATCH RIFLE

Flat top receiver shipped without any sights. Fitted with a 24-inch target contour free floating barrel. Round hand guard with folding bi-pod. Fixed buttstock. Mfg: 1993-2008

EXC.	V.G.	GOOD
3200	3000	2750

■ STONER SR-25 MK-11 MOD 0

This is a version of the SR-25 that has been adopted as a sniper rifle by the U.S. Marine Corp and the U.S. Army. It features a flat top receiver, 20-inch free float barrel and URX hand guard with accessory rails. Fixed buttstock. Civilian sales have been suspended. Current production goes to fill government orders.

EXC.	V.G.	GOOD
6500	5000	4000

A USMC GENERAL TRIES OUT THE STONER SR-25

■ M110 SASS

The Semi Automatic Sniper rifle System is a version of the SR-25 that has been designed as a sniper rifle. It features a flat top receiver, 20-inch free float barrel, full length quad rail handguard with folding bi-pod. A2 contour buttstock with adjustable butt-plate.

MSRP	EXC.	V.G.	GOOD
14450	12000	10000	8000

KNIGHT SEMI AUTO SNIPER SYSTEM

GALLERY OF
TACTICAL RIFLES

DEL-TON M-4 CARBINE -
WITH A TRIJICON REFLEX SIGHT,
COMMAND ARMS COLLAPSIBLE STOCK
AND PISTOL GRIP, AND MAGPUL P-MAG

BARRETT MODEL 98B -
.338 LAPUA MAGNUM 27" BARREL- BLACK

ARMALITE AR-10 A4 -
7.62 X 51MM NATO / .308
WITH FOWARD ASSIST,
20" BARREL- GREEN,
LEOPOLD SCOPE

ARMALITE M-15 A4 CARBINE -
5.56 X 45MM NATO / .223
16" BARREL - GREEN,
EOTECH SIGHT

ARMALITE AR-10T -
.338 FEDERAL SST
22" BARREL- BLACK,
LEOPOLD SCOPE

ARMALITE AR-10
SUPER S.A.S.S -
7.62 X 51MM NATO / .308
WITH FOWARD ASSIST,
20" BARREL- BLACK,
LEOPOLD SCOPE

BARRETT MODEL 99 - .416 BARRETT OR .50 BMG, 32" BARREL- TAN

ABOVE AND RIGHT - ARMALITE AR-50A1 - .50 BMG, 30" BARREL

BARRETT MODEL 82A1 - .416 BARRETT OR .50 BMG, 29" BARREL- BLACK

KRISS SUPER V VECTOR
CRB/SO .45 ACP
CIVILIAN CARBINE

made in Israel
by Tdi-arms

Kestrel 4000

NK
NIELSEN-KELLERMAN

**BARRETT MODEL REC7 -
5.56 NATO & 6.8 SPC,
BARREL LENGTH VARIES**

**AK-47 RLS-
7.62 X 39MM NATO,
CUSTOM STOCK,WITH RLS
LASERLYTE SYSTEM**

**SPRINGFIELD AA9126
M1A SCOUT SQUAD-
7.62 X 51MM NATO / .308 WIN.,
18" BARREL - BLACK,
AIMPOINT COMPML2 SIGHT**

**ABOVE: SPRINGFIELD AA9124
M1A SCOUT SQUAD-
7.62 X 51MM NATO / .308 WIN.,
18" BARREL - MOSSY OAK STOCK,
BUSHNELL HOLO SIGHT**

**BELOW: SPRINGFIELD MA9102
STANDARD M1A-
7.62 X 51MM NATO / .308 WIN.,
22" BARREL - WALNUT STOCK**

SABRE DEFENCE PMR -
(PRECISION MARKSMAN RIFLE)
5.56, .223 & 6.5 GRENDEL,
20" & 24" BARRELS

FNH SCAR 17S -
7.62 X 51MM NATO/.308 WIN,
16.25" BARREL- TAN

SIG SAUER SIG516 PATROL -
5.56 X .45MM NATO, 16" BARREL

TOP: SIG SAUER SIG556 CLASSIC SWAT -
5.56 X .45MM NATO, 16" BARREL

BOTTOM: SIG SAUER SIG556 CLASSIC -
5.56 X .45MM NATO, 16" BARREL

**ABOVE: ROCK RIVER ARMS
MODEL LAR-15 - 5.56 X 45MM NATO / .223,
YANKEE HILL FRONT SIGHT &
COMMAND ARMS LIGHTED
VERTICAL FOREGRIP**

SPRINGFIELD AA9126 LOADED M1A-
7.62 X 51MM NATO / .308 WIN., 22" STAINLESS BARREL, SUREFIRE SCOUT LIGHT

LEFT: ROCK RIVER ARMS MODEL A4-
5.56 X 45MM NATO / .223, 18" HEAVY STAINLESS BARREL, HOUGE GRIP & BUSHNELL ELITE SCOPE

SPRINGFIELD AA9626 M1A SOCOM 16-
7.62 X 51MM NATO / .308 WIN., 16.25" BARREL - BLACK, TRIJICON SIGHT

109

**FNH FN TACTICAL
P90 TR LASER VISIBLE-
5.7 X 28MM, 10.39" BARREL**

110

FNH FS2000 TACTICAL CARBINE-
5.56 X 45MM NATO / .223 REM.,
17.44" BARREL, OD GREEN

SPRINGFIELD AA9628
M1A SOCOM II-
7.62 X 51MM NATO / .308 WIN.,
16.25" BARREL - URBAN CAMO

BENELLI MR1 -
5.56 X 44MM NATO, SYNTHETIC TACTICAL
PISTOL GRIP, 16" BARREL

LANCASTER ARMS

Goodyear, Arizona

Website: www.lancasterarms.com

This company produces a series of AK-type rifles and pistols. These are built with a U.S.-made receiver and the required number of U.S. made parts combined with original AK parts.

■ AK-47 STAMPED RECEIVER RIFLE

Cal. 7.62x39mm. Basic AK-M type rifle with 1mm thick stamped receiver. 16-inch barrel. Offered with several stock options, including Russian Laminate, blond hardwood, Russian red plastic, Bulgarian black plastic.

MSRP	EXC.	V.G.	GOOD
599	500	450	400

■ AK-47 STAMPED RIFLE W/ FOLDING STOCK

As above with Polish manufactured underfolding stock.

MSRP	EXC.	V.G.	GOOD
749	650	550	475

■ AK-47 STAMPED RIFLE W/ SIDE FOLDING STOCK

AK-47 stamped receiver with a Russian side folding stock.

MSRP	EXC.	V.G.	GOOD
899	500	450	400

■ AK- 47T TACTICAL

Stamped receiver AK-47 fitted with a quad rail fore-arm and a six-position sliding CAR style stock.

NIB	EXC.	V.G.	GOOD
699	600	550	500

■ AK-47 MILLED RECEIVER RIFLE

Cal. 7.62x39mm. Basic AK-47 type rifle with milled steel receiver. 16-inch barrel. Blond wood stocks.

NIB	EXC.	V.G.	GOOD
799	700	625	550

■ AK-47 MILLED RIFLE W/ FOLDING STOCK

Milled receiver AK-44 rifle with an underfolding stock and Red Russian plastic forearm. .

NIB	EXC.	V.G.	GOOD
929	750	675	600

■ AK-47 MILLED RIFLE W/SIDE FOLDING STOCK

Milled receiver AK-47 fitted with a side folding stock. Red Russian plastic forearm.

NIB	EXC.	V.G.	GOOD
899	800	700	600

■ POLISH TANTAL

AK-74 type rifle in 5.45x39mm. Fixed stock. Choice of blond or red wood. Discontinued.

EXC.	V.G.	GOOD
700	625	550

■ POLISH TANTAL W/ FOLDING STOCK

As above with underfolding stock. Choice of synthetic or wood forearm. Discontinued.

EXC.	V.G.	GOOD
725	650	575

■ POLISH TANTAL W/ SIDE FOLDING STOCK

Cal 5.45x39mm. Side folding stock. Synthetic forearm. Wood available at higher cost. Discontinued.

EXC.	V.G.	GOOD
700	625	550

■ AK PISTOL

7.62x39mm, 9-1/2-inch or 11.5-inch barrel. Blond wood or red synthetic pistol grip and forearm. .

MSRP	EXC.	V.G.	GOOD
679	600	625	575

◼ AK TACTICAL PISTOL

7.62x39mm, 9-1/2-inch or 11.5 inch barrel. Fitted with a quad rail forearm.

MSRP	EXC.	V.G.	GOOD
679	600	625	575

◼ AK MILLED RECEIVER PISTOL

7.62x39mm, 9-1/2-inch or 11.5-inch barrel. Blond wood or red synthetic pistol grip and forearm. .

MSRP	EXC.	V.G.	GOOD
829	750	675	550

LEADER DYNAMICS
Tasmania, Australia

Imported by World Public Safety of Culver City, California.

◼ MODEL T2 MK. 5

A 5.56mm/.223 semi-automatic rifle. Many action parts are made from stamped steel. Similar to the Armalite AR-180. 16-1/4-inch barrel. Synthetic stocks. A small quantity was imported 1986-89.

EXC.	V.G.	GOOD
1250	1100	950

LEADER DYNAMICS T2 MK 5 RIFLE

◼ SAP PISTOL

A handgun using the same action as the Leader rifle. It has a 10-1/2-inch barrel.

EXC.	V.G.	GOOD
1250	1100	950

LEINAD

Another name for the maker of the M-11 semi-automatic pistol series. Pricing on all these is about the same. See: SWD.

LES BAER CUSTOM
Hillsdale, Illinois

Website: www.lesbaer.com

This company is a well regarded maker of precision 1911-A1 type pistols as well as their line of AR-15 type rifles.

◼ ULTIMATE AR.223 SUPER VARMINT MODEL

AR-type rifle with LBC forged and precision machined upper and lower receivers (available with or without forward assist upper), picatinny style flat top rail, LBC ultimate national match carrier (chromed), LBC ultimate bolt (chromed), LBC ultimate extractor (chromed), Jewell two-stage trigger group, LBC precision machined adjustable free float handguard with locking ring,

LBC aluminum gas block with picatinny rail top, LBC bench rest 416 R stainless steel barrel with precision cut rifling (1:9 twist standard, optional twists available including 1:12, 1:8, 1:7) 20-inch length standard (18-inch, 22-inch and 24-inch optional), newly designed LBC custom grip with extra material under the trigger guard corner, Versa Pod, 20 round magazine, LBC ultimate AR .223 rifle soft case, stainless steel barrel, coated on request.

MSRP	EXC.	V.G.	GOOD
2290	1900	1700	1500

■ ULTIMATE AR SUPER VARMINT .204 RUGER

As above but chambered in .204 Ruger.

MSRP	EXC.	V.G.	GOOD
2520	2250	2050	1850

■ ULTIMATE AR.223 SUPER MATCH MODEL

Features include LBC forged and precision machined upper and lower receivers (available with or without forward assist upper), picatinny style flat top rail, LBC ultimate national match carrier (chromed), LBC ultimate bolt (chromed), LBC ultimate extractor (chromed), Jewell two-stage trigger group, four-position free float handguard with integral picatinny rail system, LBC aluminum gas block, LBC bench rest 416 R stainless steel barrel with precision cut rifling (1:9 twist standard, optional twists available including 1:12, 1:8, 1:7) 20-inch length standard (18-inch, 22-inch and 24-inch optional), newly designed LBC custom grip with extra material under the trigger guard corner, Versa Pod Installed, 20 round magazine, LBC ultimate AR .223 rifle soft case, stainless steel barrel, coated on request.

MSRP	EXC.	V.G.	GOOD
2390	2100	1850	1600

LES BAER ULTIMATE AR.223 SUPER MATCH MODEL

■ ULTIMATE AR SUPER MATCH .204 RUGER

As above, but chambered in .204 Ruger.

MSRP	EXC.	V.G.	GOOD
2590	2200	2000	1750

■ ULTIMATE AR.223 M-4 FLAT TOP MODEL

Features include LBC forged and precision machined upper and lower receivers (available with or without forward assist upper), picatinny style flat top rail, LBC ultimate national match carrier (chromed), LBC ultimate bolt (chromed), LBC ultimate extractor (chromed), LBC bench rest 416 R stainless steel barrel with precision cut rifling (1:9 twist standard, optional twists available including 1:12 or 1:8) 16-inch length standard, four-position free float handguard with locking ring and with integral picatinny rail system (12 inch standard) with aluminum gas block covered by rail system, Versa-Pod installed, 20 round magazine, LBC ultimate AR .223 rifle soft case, stainless steel barrel, coated on request.

MSRP	EXC.	V.G.	GOOD
2240	1900	1750	1550

LES BAER ULTIMATE AR.223 M-4 FLAT TOP MODEL

LES BAER CUSTOM

◼ ULTIMATE AR.223 IPSC ACTION MODEL

Features include LBC forged and precision machined upper and lower receivers with or without provision for forward assist, picatinny style flat top rail, LBC ultimate national match carrier (chromed), LBC ultimate bolt (chromed), LBC ultimate extractor (chromed), LBC bench rest 416 R stainless steel barrel with precision cut rifling (1:9 twist standard, optional twists available including 1:12, 1:8, 1:7) 20-inch length standard, Jewell two-stage trigger standard (ultra single stage trigger substituted on request), LBC precision machined aluminum free floating handguard with locking ring, LBC aluminum gas block, Versa-Pod installed, 20 round magazine, LBC ultimate ar .223 rifle soft case.

MSRP	EXC.	V.G.	GOOD
2540	2200	1850	1700

LES BAER ULTIMATE AR.223 IPSC ACTION MODEL

◼ THUNDER RANCH RIFLE

Features include: LBC forged and precision machined upper and lower receivers, picatinny style flat top rail, A2 style detachable carry handle, LBC ultimate national match carrier (chromed), LBC ultimate bolt (chromed), LBC ultimate extractor, Les Baer custom bench rest 16-inch barrel of 416 R stainless steel with precision cut bench rest rifling and 1:8 twist, barrel is precision fluted in front of gas block for better heat dissipation, Jewell two-stage trigger tuned to 4-1/2-pound pull (total pull weight), special thunder ranch free float handguard with locking ring, sling stud mounted front of free float handguard, nylon weather proof sling and lockable front sling swivel. Discontinued.

EXC.	V.G.	GOOD
2200	2000	1800

LES BAER THUNDER RANCH RIFLE

◼ ULTIMATE CMP COMPETITION RIFLE

CMP legal for service rifle matches. Features LBC forged and precision machined upper and lower receivers, National Match rear sights with hooded aperture, 1/4-minute clicks both windage and elevation, LBC national match carrier (chromed), LBC bolt carrier, LBC extractor, 20-inch LBC precision cut bench rest style 416 R stainless steel barrel, 1:8 twist, Jewell two-stage trigger set at 4-1/2 lbs., special DCM/CMP style free float tube, precision machined front sight housing (drilled and tapped for barrel clamping), lead weight in both stock and forend (total weight is 17 lbs. with lead added), 2 20 round magazines.

MSRP	EXC.	V.G.	GOOD
3200	2750	2400	2200

◼ ULTIMATE NRA MATCH RIFLE

Features include LBC forged and precision machined upper and lower (available with or without forward assist upper), picatinny style flat top rail, LBC ultimate national match carrier (chromed), LBC ultimate bolt (chromed), LBC ultimate extractor (chromed), Jewell two-stage trigger group, LBC precision machined adjustable free float handguard with locking ring, hand stop with sling swivel, LBC aluminum gas block, LBC bench rest 416 R stainless steel barrel with precision cut rifling (1:8 twist standard, optional twists available including 1:7) 30-inch length standard (18-inch, 20-inch, 22-inch and 24-inch optional), newly designed LBC custom grip with extra material under the trigger guard, LBC ultimate AR .223 rifle soft case, one 20 round magazine. Sold without sights.

MSRP	EXC.	V.G.	GOOD
2600	2250	2000	1750

LES BAER ULTIMATE NRA MATCH RIFLE

■ ULTIMATE AR .264LBC OR 6X45 M4 STYLE

Except for being chambered in .264 LBC or 6x47mm, this model is essentially the same as the .223 caliber, medium weight M4 described above, excep that it has the same handguard as the Thunder Ranch model and its gas block will include a rail on top to allow mounting add-on sights.

MSRP	EXC.	V.G.	GOOD
2240	2100	1900	1700

■ ULTIMATE AR .264 LBC OR 6X45 SUPER VARMINT MODEL

Similar to the Ultimate .223 model described above but chambered in .264 LBC or 6x45mm.

MSRP	EXC.	V.G.	GOOD
2290	1950	1750	1550

■ AR STYLE RIFLE WITH PISTON SYSTEM

AR style rifle with a Baer designed gas piston system. Availible with a 9-inch or 11-inch piston. Cal. 5.56mm. Flat top upper receiver, quad rail free float handguard (short for 9 inch, long for 11 inch), ATI 6 position collapsible stock.

MSRP	EXC.	V.G.	GOOD
1890	1750	1650	1500

LMT-LEWIS MACHINE & TOOL
Milan, Ill.

Website: www.lewismachine.net

This company produces a series of AR type rifles. The basic models are listed here. Numerous other options are offered.

■ .308 MODULAR WEAPON SYSTEM

AR style .308 rifle with a 16-inch stainless steel barrel. Flat top upper receiver, Monolithic Rail Platform handguard , SOPMOD collapsible stock.

MSRP	EXC.	V.G.	GOOD
2797	2500	2100	1750

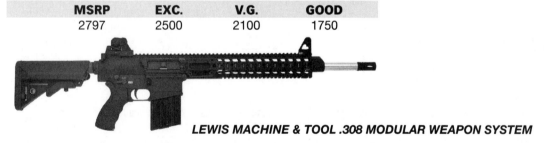

LEWIS MACHINE & TOOL .308 MODULAR WEAPON SYSTEM

■ CQB MRP DEFENDER MODEL PISTON 16

5.56mm AR-style rifle with a LMT designed gas piston system. Features a 16-inch barrel, flat top upper with receiver sight, Monolithic Rail Platform handguard, SOPMOD collapsible stock.

MSRP	EXC.	V.G.	GOOD
2055	1850	1650	1500

LMT DEFENDER PISTON 16 RIFLE

■ CQB DEFENDER MRP DEFENDER MODEL 16

AR style .223 rifle with a 16-inch barrel. Flat top upper receiver, tactical rear sight, Monolithic Rail Platform handguard, SOP-MOD collapsible stock.

Note: *Also offered in a "compliant" version with pinned stock and no flash hider.*

MSRP	EXC.	V.G.	GOOD
1829	1700	1450	1250

■ 6.8 SPC CQB RIFLE WITH SOPMOD STOCK

As above with a 16-inch 6.8 SPC barrel.

MSRP	EXC.	V.G.	GOOD
2030	1750	1650	1500

■ DEFENDER STANDARD MODEL W/ SOPMOD STOCK

Features a 16-inch M4 contour barrel, flat top receiver, tactical rear sight, Standard CAR handguard, SOPMOD collapsible stock.

MSRP	EXC.	V.G.	GOOD
1288	1000	850	700

■ DEFENDER STANDARD PATROL MODEL 16

As above but fitted with a traditional CAR style collapsible stock.

MSRP	EXC.	V.G.	GOOD
1272	975	825	675

LWRC INTERNATIONAL
Cambridge, Maryland
Website: www.lwrci.com

This company produces a series of AR type rifles. All feature the LWRCI patented short stroke gas piston system. The basic models are listed here. Numerous other options are offered.

■ M6 RIFLE

Cal. 5.56mm or 6.8 SPC 16-inch barrel. Flat top receiver with detachable rear sight, CAR hand guard. Magpul MOE adjustable stock.

MSRP	EXC	V.G.	GOOD
1610	1500	1250	1000

■ M6A1 RIFLE

As above with a quad rail free float handguard.

MSRP	EXC	V.G.	GOOD
1990	1800	1650	1500

■ M6A2 RIFLE

Cal. 5.56mm or 6.8 SPC 16-inch barrel. Flat top receiver with folding front and rear sights, mid length quad rail handguard. VLTOr EMod adjustable stock.

MSRP	EXC	V.G.	GOOD
2100	1850	1750	1650

LWRC M6A2 RIFLE

■ M6A2 PISTOL

Cal. 5.56mm with an 8-inch barrel. Shortened buffer tube. Flat top receiver. Quad rail handguard.

MSRP	EXC	V.G.	GOOD
2170	1850	1750	1650

■ M6A3 RIFLE

The same as the M6A2 with a four-position adjustable gas system.

MSRP	EXC	V.G.	GOOD
2250	2000	1850	1700

■ R.E.P.R. (RAPID ENGAGEMENT PRECISION RIFLE)

Rapid Engagement Precision Rifle, Cal. 7.62 NATO. Optional. 16-, 18-, or 20-inch barrel. Flat top receiver with folding BUIS front and rear sights, full length quad rail handguard. Magpul PRS adjustable stock. Weight: 11.5 lbs with 20-inch barrel shown.

MSRP	EXC	V.G.	GOOD
3725	3400	3000	2500

LWRC RAPID ENGAGEMENT PRECISION RIFLE

MARLIN FIREARMS CO.
New Haven, Connecticut

This old-line gun maker has discontinued production of the two models they offered that loosely fit the criteria set forth in these pages. Despite the fact that they were sold with traditional looking wood stocks, the Camp 9 and Camp 45 are included due to the fact that they accept high capacity magazines. Additionally, there are some tactical type stocks available from other manufacturers; these have pistol grips and folding stocks.

■ CAMP 9

A semi-automatic rifle in 9mm. Simple blowback operation. 16-1/2 inch barrel. Open sights. Receiver is drilled to allow scope mounting. Marlin made magazines in 4-, 10- and 12 round capacity. The rifle also accepts S&W 59 series magazines.

EXC.	V.G.	GOOD
450	400	350

MARLIN CAMP 9 CARBINE

■ CAMP 45

As above but chambered in .45 ACP. Uses 1911-A1 type magazines.

EXC.	V.G.	GOOD
650	575	500

MASTERPIECE ARMS
Carrolton, Ga.
Website: www.masterpiecearms.com

Manufacturer of improved versions of the MAC/Cobray, SWD type pistols.

■ 22LR MINI PISTOL, TOP COCKING

5-inch threaded barrel. 30 round magazine.

MSRP	EXC	V.G.	GOOD
440	350	300	250

MPA 22LR PISTOL

■ 22LR MINI PISTOL, SIDE COCKING
5-inch threaded barrel. Picatinny rail top.

MSRP	EXC	V.G.	GOOD
525	450	375	300

■ 45 ACP PISTOL, TOP COCKING
6-inch threaded barrel. Uses original M3 Grease gun 30 round magazines.

MSRP	EXC	V.G.	GOOD
489	400	350	325

■ 45 ACP PISTOL, SIDE COCKING
6-inch threaded barrel. Picatinny rail top.

MSRP	EXC	V.G.	GOOD
570	475	400	350

■ 9MM PISTOL, TOP COCKING
6-inch threaded barrel. 35 round polymer magazine.

MSRP	EXC	V.G.	GOOD
489	400	350	325

■ 9MM PISTOL, SIDE COCKING
5-inch threaded barrel. Picatinny rail top.

MSRP	EXC	V.G.	GOOD
570	475	400	350

MPA 9MM PISTOL WITH TACTICAL RAIL

■ 9MM MINI PISTOL, TOP COCKING
3.25-inch threaded barrel. 30 round magazine.

MSRP	EXC	V.G.	GOOD
489	400	350	325

MASTERPIECE ARMS MINI 9MM PISTOL

■ 9MM RIFLE, SIDE COCKING

16-inch threaded barrel with flash hider. Picatinny rail top. CAR handguard. Fixed stock.

MSRP	EXC	V.G.	GOOD
717	600	500	400

■ 45ACP RIFLE, SIDE COCKING

16-inch threaded barrel with flash hider. Picatinny rail top. CAR handguard. Fixed stock.

MSRP	EXC	V.G.	GOOD
717	600	500	400

MICROTECH SMALL ARMS RESEARCH
Bradford, Pennsylvania
Website: www.msarinc.com

Manufacturer of a improved version of the Steyr AUG Rifle.

■ STG-556 SPORTING MODEL

Cal. 5.56mm/.223. Gas-operated semi-automatic bullpup rifle featuring a quick interchangeable barrel available in 14-, 16- and 20-inch lengths. The sporting model features either a 1.5x integral sight, like the original AUG system, or an elevated picatinny rail. The weight is 7-1/2 lbs. Available with black or green stock. Uses AUG pattern 10, 20, 30 and 42 round magazines.

MSRP	EXC	V.G.	GOOD
2100	1650	1450	1250

MICROTECH SMALL ARMS STG 556 RIFLE

MITCHELL ARMS INC.
Santa Ana, California

Note: Mitchell Arms imported a series of .22LR semi-automatic copies of assault rifles. These were made in Italy by Armi Jager or Adler. See Armi Jager. Mitchell Arms also imported some Zastava-made Kalashnikov rifles from Yugoslavia in the late 1989. Importation was banned in 1989.

■ AK-47

Typical pattern. Cal. 7.62x39mm. 16-1/2-inch barrel. Wood stocks. Imported 1989 only. The single shipment of these AKs was held in customs for over a year due to the just-enacted import ban. BATFE required the bayonet lug be removed and the muzzle cap be welded in place before they were released.

EXC.	V.G.	GOOD
1250	1000	900

MITCHELL ZASTAVA AK-47 RIFLE

■ AK-47 WITH FOLDING STOCK

As with the standard AK-47 above, the folding stock version was also held up by U.S. customs. Mitchell Arms was forced to have a plastic thumbhole stock made for these. The original folding stock was left intact but was welded in the closed position. It was common for these stocks to be restored to functional condition by subsequent owners. Such a restoration would be a violation of 922r regulations unless enough U.S. made parts were added to the rifle.

EXC.	V.G.	GOOD
1350	1150	950

■ AK-47 IN 7.62X51MM/.308

Similar to above. Fixed stock only. 20 round magazine. Scarce.

EXC.	V.G.	GOOD
1750	1500	1250

NOTE: *add $200 for each additional 20 round magazine.*

■ M-76 SNIPER RIFLE

A Kalashnikov rifle chambered in 8x57mm Mauser. Side rail scope mount. 10 round magazine.

EXC.	V.G.	GOOD
2000	1750	1500

■ RPK

Patterned after the Soviet RPK light machine gun. Chambered in 7.62x39mm or 7.62x51/.308. Heavy barrel with cooling fins. Folding bi-pod. Scarce.

EXC.	V.G.	GOOD
2500	2000	1750

MITCHELL ZASTAVA RPK RIFLE CAL .308

NATIONAL ORDNANCE

El Monte, California

In the 1970s this company manufactured new M-1 carbine receivers and assembled complete rifles with USGI parts.

■ M-1 CARBINE

A basic pattern M-1 carbine. Will be seen with a variety of stock configurations. Caliber .30 M-1.

EXC.	V.G.	GOOD
450	400	350

NORINCO

China

This is a commercial front for the Chinese military arms production factories. The first Norinco products were imported in the mid 1980s. They offered semi-automatic variations of AKM rifles as well as the SKS. These were imported by several companies. Importer names observed include B-West, Clayco, CSI, KSI, Labanu, and Sile.

After the 1989 ban on imported "assault weapons" the Norinco product line was altered to comply with "sporting use" criteria in the GCA 1968. This was when the thumbhole stocks appeared on AK type rifles. In 1994, President Clinton banned further import of Norinco produced firearms with rifled barrels. Some sporting shotguns are still imported.

NORINCO AKM VARIATIONS

Pre-1989 imports. Rifles with stamped sheet steel receivers were usually made at Factory 66. The factory mark is a triangle with 66 in the center. There were a few model markings found on these. The following entries indicate models observed. There were probably more models imported.

■ AKS

The earliest Norinco AKS were imported by Clayco Sports in 1984. Caliber 7.62x39mm. They have red synthetic stocks. Originally boxed with three 30 round magazines and a bayonet.

EXC.	V.G.	GOOD
1200	1000	750

■ AKM/47S, TYPE 56S

As above. Later import. Light colored wood stocks.

EXC.	V.G.	GOOD
1100	950	700

NORINCO AKS RIFLE

◆ Type 56S-1

As above but with a underfolding stock.

EXC.	V.G.	GOOD
1150	950	750

◆ Type 84S

An AKS chambered in 5.56mm/.223.

EXC.	V.G.	GOOD
1050	900	750

◆ Type 84S-1
As above, with an under folding stock.

EXC.	V.G.	GOOD
1100	900	800

◆ Type 84S 5
As above with a sidefolding stock. Black synthetic forearm. Imported in 1989 only.

EXC.	V.G.	GOOD
1250	1050	850

◆ Type 86S
A 7.62x39mm AKS in bullpup configuration. Imported in 1989. Only one shipment came in before the ban. Fewer than 2000 imported.

EXC.	V.G.	GOOD
1500	1250	1000

NORINCO TYPE 86 BULLPUP RIFLE

POST 1989 IMPORT BAN AK MODELS

The 1989 ban on imported "assault rifles" caught several importers unprepared. There had been little discussion of such an executive action before it occurred. Some shipments were stuck in customs warehouses while others were on ships that had to be turned back to China. A few importers were allowed to modify rifles already paid for to remove offending characteristics such as the bayonet lug and threaded muzzles. This was when they came up with the thumbhole stocks that eliminate the separate pistol grip. There were even some folding stock versions that had the stock welded in the closed position and a thumbhole stock installed behind it. Others had the folding stock removed, leaving the hole in the receiver where it was.

It did not take long before Norinco began producing rifles that complied with the characteristics imposed by the ban. Model names found on the thumbhole stocked models include MAK-90, NHM-90 or 91. The name "Sporter" will also appear on these.

Warning: It is common to encounter a post-1989 imported Norinco AK type rifle that has had a standard pistol grip stock set installed. If you are examining a AK type gun that is marked MAK-90, BWK-90, NHM-91, or Sporter be aware that it might be an illegal rifle. According to BATFE regulations, it is not legal to modify an imported rifle to a configuration that cannot be imported, unless enough U.S. made parts are installed. This is a very confusing law.

■ MAK-90
Standard AKM type rifle in 7.62x39mm with a thumbhole stock.

EXC.	V.G.	GOOD
500	425	350

NORINCO AK SPORTER

BWK-90

As above but in 5.56mm with a thumbhole stock.

EXC.	V.G.	GOOD
500	425	350

NHM-90

7.62x39mm with a 16-3/4 inch barrel. Thumbhole stock.

EXC.	V.G.	GOOD
500	425	350

NHM-91

AK type rifle in 7.62x39mm with a 23-1/4-inch barrel and a folding bipod. Thumbhole stock.

EXC.	V.G.	GOOD
550	475	400

AK HUNTER

An AKM action with a traditional sporting type stock installed. 7.62x39mm. 19-inch barrel.

EXC.	V.G.	GOOD
400	325	275

NDM86

A copy of the Soviet SVD "Dragonov" sniper rifle. Chambered for 7.62x54Rmm or 7.62x51mm/.308. 24-inch barrel. Skeletonized stock made from laminated wood. 10 round magazine.

EXC.	V.G.	GOOD
1500	1200	900

MODEL 320

A semi-automatic copy of the Israeli UZI submachine gun. Cal 9mm. 16-inch barrel. The only shipment of Model 320s was stopped by the 1989 import ban. The folding metal stocks were replaced with a thumbhole stock and the barrel nut was welded so the barrel could not be removed.

EXC.	V.G.	GOOD
750	600	500

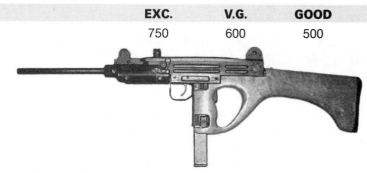

NORINCO UZI SPORTER RIFLE

M-14

A copy of the U.S. M-14 service rifle. Chambered for 7.62mm/.308. No flash hider. Rubber recoil pad. These have become popular for receivers to build into M1-A type rifles.

EXC.	V.G.	GOOD
850	750	600

NORINCO SKS WITH DETACHABLE MAGAZINE

SKS rifle re-designed to feed from AK-47 type detachable magazines. There are three variants. The first was a standard pattern SKS with a 16-inch barrel, with or without the bayonet. Import was banned in 1991.

EXC.	V.G.	GOOD
700	600	500

NORINCO SKS M "SPORTER"

After the ban on importation of "assault rifles," the Norinco SKS was made in a "sporter" configuration called the model M. One variation has a Monte Carlo stock; the other has a thumbhole stock. There is no provision for a bayonet. Values tend to be the same for both stock configurations.

EXC.	V.G.	GOOD
550	475	400

NORINCO SKS DETACHABLE MAGAZINE RIFLE WITH THUMBHOLE STOCK

OHIO ORDNANCE WORKS
Chardon, Ohio
Website: www.ohioordnance.com

This manufacturer builds semi-automatic versions of famous machine guns. Other models are available on a build basis with customers parts kit.

■ BAR MODEL 1918A3 SELF LOADING RIFLE

A semi-automatic version of the legendary Browning Automatic Rifle. Caliber .30-06. 20 round magazines. Introduced in 1996. Offered with walnut or synthetic stock.

MSRP	EXC.	V.G.	GOOD
3800	3000	2500	2000

OHIO ORDNANCE M1918A3 BROWNING AUTOMATIC RIFLE SEMI-AUTO

■ COLT BROWNING MODEL 1917 WATER COOLED MACHINE GUN

A semi-automatic version of the famous belt-fed machine gun. Offered in .30-06, 7.65mm or .308. Parkerized finish. Sold with a tri-pod, wooded ammo box, water can and hose and one 250 round cloth belt. Introduced in 2001.

MSRP	EXC.	V.G.	GOOD
5000	4700	4200	3500

Note: *The .308 version is worth approximately $250 more.*

■ M240 SLR

This is a semi-automatic version of the FN MAG M240 machine gun currently used by the U.S. military. Cal. 7.62mm/.308. Uses disintegrating metal links. Introduced in 2007. Limited production. Weight: 24 lbs.

MSRP	EXC.	V.G.	GOOD
13,500	12,000	10,000	8500

■ VZ-2000

A semi-automatic version of the Czechoslovakian Vz-58 rifle. Caliber 7.62x39mm. Synthetic stocks. Shipped with four 30 round magazines, bayonet, sling, cleaning kit, manual and extra folding stock.

MSRP	EXC.	V.G.	GOOD
995	900	800	700

OLYMPIC ARMS

Olympia, Washington

Website: www.olyarms.com

This company manufactures several versions of AR-15 type firearms. Numerous options are availible at additional cost.

24- AND 20-INCH MODELS

■ K4B

The same dimensions as the U.S. Military M-16-A2. Semi-automatic. Cal 5.56mm/.223. 20-inch barrel. A2 upper receiver with adjustable sight. Fixed stock.

MSRP	EXC.	V.G.	GOOD
970	750	700	650

■ K4B-A4

An AR-15 model with a 20-inch barrel, flat top upper receiver, FIRSH quad rail free floating handguard and fixed A2 buttstock. Discontinued.

EXC.	V.G.	GOOD
850	775	700

■ K8 TARGETMATCH

This Targetmatch model features a flat top upper receiver and gas block with picatinny rails. 20-inch stainless steel bull barrel with satin bead blast finish. Aluminum free floating handguard with knurled surface. Fixed A2 stock.

MSRP	EXC.	V.G.	GOOD
908	750	700	650

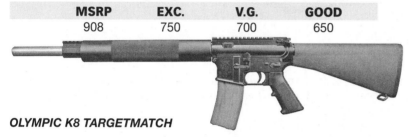

OLYMPIC K8 TARGETMATCH

■ K8-MAG TARGETMATCH MAGNUM

The Targetmatch Magnum is chambered for Winchester .223, 243 or 25 Super Short Magnum (WSSM) cartridges. Features a flat top upper receiver and gas block that have picatinny rails. 24-inch bull barrel. Aluminum free floating handguard with knurled surface. Fixed A2 stock.

MSRP	EXC.	V.G.	GOOD
1364	1200	1000	800

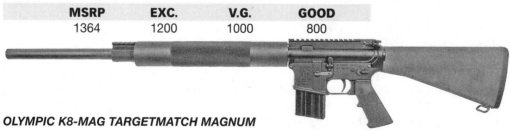

OLYMPIC K8-MAG TARGETMATCH MAGNUM

■ PLINKER PLUS 20

This model is an entry level AR-15 rifle. 20-inch standard weight barrel. All of the same features as Olympic's other AR-15 models but the rear sight is changed to an A1 type. Also offered in a 16-inch barrel version. Same price.

MSRP	EXC.	V.G.	GOOD
844	700	650	600

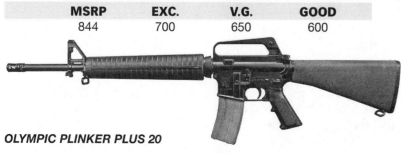

OLYMPIC PLINKER PLUS 20

■ SM-1 SERVICEMATCH

A2 upper and lower receiver are premium quality. 20-inch stainless steel barrel. Free floating handguard.

MSRP	EXC.	V.G.	GOOD
1273	1050	900	750

OLYMPIC SM-1 SERVICEMATCH

■ SM-1P SERVICEMATCH PREMIUM

As above but with AC4 pneumatic recoil buffer, Bob Jones interchangeable sight system. Two-stage match trigger. Front sight post is attached using set screws.

MSRP	EXC.	V.G.	GOOD
1728	1500	1250	1000

OLYMPIC SM-1P SERVICEMATCH PREMIUM

■ UM-1 ULTRAMATCH

20-inch Ultramatch broach-cut bull barrel coupled with a free floating handguard and forged receiver for target and competition shooting. Flat top upper receiver and gas block that have picatinny rails. Aluminum free floating handguard with knurled surface.

MSRP	EXC.	V.G.	GOOD
1329	1150	1000	800

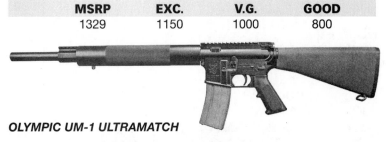

OLYMPIC UM-1 ULTRAMATCH

■ UM-1P ULTRAMATCH PREMIUM

High-end target shooting model. 24-inch free floating bull barrel. Pneumatic recoil buffer. Williams set trigger. Harris S series bipod installed.

MSRP	EXC.	V.G	GOOD
1623	1300	1050	900

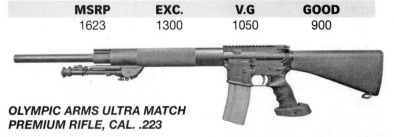

OLYMPIC ARMS ULTRA MATCH PREMIUM RIFLE, CAL. .223

■ GAMESTALKER

Choice of .223, .243, or 25 Winchester Super Short Magnum. 22-inch stainless steel barrel. flat top receiver, no sights, free float aluminum tubulat handguard, Ace FX fixed stock. Camouflage finish. Weight: 7.5 lbs.

MSRP	EXC.	V.G.	GOOD
1359	1150	1000	850

16-INCH BARREL MODELS

◆ GI-16

Otherwise identical to the Plinker Plus model. The GI-16 features an A2 forged upper with A1 rear sight, 16-inch button rifled barrel and M4 collapsible stock.

MSRP	EXC.	V.G.	GOOD
857	700	625	575

OLYMPIC GI-16

◆ K10 Pistol Cal. 10mm

10mm in an AR-15 platform with a 16-inch barrel. Uses standard AR-15 lower receivers that accept modified pistol caliber magazines. CAR type collapsible buttstock.

MSRP	EXC.	V.G.	GOOD
1007	800	725	650

◆ K16

Features a 16-inch bull barrel, flat top upper, free floating handguard, rail gas block and fixed A2 buttstock.

MSRP	EXC.	V.G.	GOOD
830	675	625	575

◆ K30R 7.62x39mm

Cal. 7.62x39mm, 16-inch barrel. AR-15 platform. A2 upper receiver with adjustable sight. Six-position collapsible buttstock.

MSRP	EXC.	V.G.	GOOD
930	800	750	700

◆ K3B

Base model AR-15 carbine. 16-inch barrel, A2 upper receiver, CAR handguard, Fiberite six position stock.

MSRP	EXC.	V.G.	GOOD
815	750	700	650

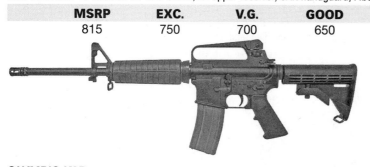

OLYMPIC K3B

■ K3B-CAR

This K3B variant has an 11.5-inch barrel with a permanently attached 5.5-inch flash suppressor.

MSRP	EXC.	V.G.	GOOD
969	800	750	700

OLYMPIC K3B-CAR

■ K3B-FAR FEATHERWEIGHT CARBINE

As above but with the Featherweight (FAR) barrel which lightens the weight of the carbine significantly without compromising accuracy or quality.

MSRP	EXC.	V.G.	GOOD
1006	800	750	700

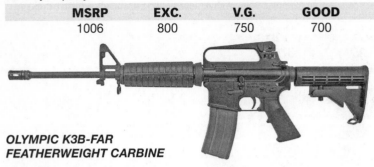

OLYMPIC K3B-FAR
FEATHERWEIGHT CARBINE

■ K3B M-4

Variant of the K3B model and features an M4 contoured barrel and M4 handguards.

MSRP	EXC.	V.G.	GOOD
1039	825	775	725

OLYMPIC K3B M-4

■ K3B M-4 A3-TC

16-inch M-4 contour barrel, flat top receiver with detachable A2 carry handle and rear sight, FIRSH quad rail free floating handguard.

MSRP	EXC.	V.G.	GOOD
1247	1000	900	800

■ K40

Pistol caliber .40 S&W in an AR-15 platform with a 16-inch barrel. Olympic Arms pistol caliber models use standard AR-15 lower receivers that accept modified pistol cal magazines. CAR type collapsible buttstock.

MSRP	EXC.	V.G.	GOOD
1006	800	750	700

OLYMPIC K40

■ K40GL

Pistol caliber .40 S&W in an AR-15 platform with a purpose-made lower receiver that uses Glock˝ magazines. CAR type collapsible buttstock.

MSRP	EXC.	V.G.	GOOD
1092	800	750	700

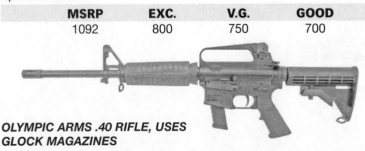

OLYMPIC ARMS .40 RIFLE, USES
GLOCK MAGAZINES

■ K45
Pistol caliber 45 ACP in an AR-15 platform with a 16-inch barrel. Olympic Arms pistol cal models use standard AR-15 lower receivers that accept modified pistol cal magazines. CAR type collapsible buttstock.

MSRP	EXC.	V.G.	GOOD
1006	800	750	700

■ K68
Cal. 6.8 Remington SPC, 16-inch M-4 contour barrel, A2 upper receiver, six-position telescoping stock.

MSRP	EXC.	V.G.	GOOD
1039	825	775	725

■ K7 ELIMINATOR
Cal. 5.56mm, 16-inch barrel, A2 upper receiver and rear sight, rifle length gas system and round handguard, A2 stock.

MSRP	EXC.	V.G.	GOOD
973	800	750	700

■ K74 5.45X39MM
Cal. 5.45x39mm with a 16-inch barrel, A2 upper receiver and rear sight, CAR handguard, six-position collapsible stock.

MSRP	EXC.	V.G.	GOOD
917	850	750	650

■ K7-ORT ELIMINATOR
Cal. 5.56mm, 16-inch barrel, flat top receiver, no sights, mid-length gas system, quad rail free float handguard, CAR six-position telescoping stock.

MSRP	EXC.	V.G.	GOOD
973	900	800	700

■ K9 GL
Pistol caliber 9mm in an AR-15 platform with a purpose-made lower receiver that uses Glock˜ magazines. CAR type collapsible buttstock.

MSRP	EXC.	V.G.	GOOD
1092	875	825	775

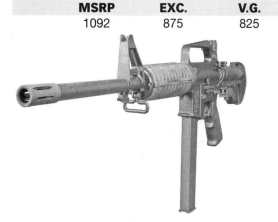

OLYMPIC K9 GL

■ LIGHTWEIGHT TACTICAL FLUTED
The LTF model has fluting along the full length of the barrel increasing heat dissipation. Other options are also included standard: Flat top upper receiver and gas block with picatinny rail. FIRSH quad rail free floating handguard. ACE FX Skeleton stock.

MSRP	EXC.	V.G.	GOOD
1240	1075	950	825

OLYMPIC ARMS LIGHTWEIGHT TACTICAL FLUTED CARBINE

■ LIGHTWEIGHT TACTICAL M4

The LT-M4 model has an M4 barrel. Other options are also included standard: Flat top upper receiver and gas block with picatinny rail. FIRSH quad rail free floating handguard. ACE FX Skeleton stock.

MSRP	EXC.	V.G.	GOOD
1142	1000	900	800

■ MULTIMATCH ML-1

The Multimatch model ML-1 is basically an enhanced standard AR-15 with an Ultramatch barrel, free floating aluminum handguard and M4 collapsible stock.

MSRP	EXC.	V.G.	GOOD
1188	950	900	800

OLYMPIC MULTIMATCH ML-1

■ MULTIMATCH ML-2

The Ultramatch features flat top upper receiver and gas block with picatinny rail. Bull barrel, free floating aluminum handguard and an A2 trapdoor buttstock put the ML-2 model in a class above standard AR-15 carbines.

MSRP	EXC.	V.G.	GOOD
1188	950	900	800

OLYMPIC MULTIMATCH ML-2

■ OA-93-CAR

This AR-15 model features the OA Operations System upper receiver which incorporates a gas piston recoil system into a flat top upper. This allows us to add an aluminum side-folding stock. Discontinued as of September of 2007.

EXC.	V.G.	GOOD
1150	1050	950

OLYMPIC ARMS OA 93 CARBINE

■ OA-93-PT

Using the OA Operations System upper receiver incorporates the recoil system into a flat top upper allowing the OA-93-PT model to have a detachable aluminum stock. Discontinued as of September of 2007.

EXC.	V.G.	GOOD
1150	1050	950

AR-15 PISTOLS

■ K23 P

AR-15 pistol model featuring a 6.5-inch barrel, no buttstock and a padded receiver extension tube.

MSRP	EXC.	V.G.	GOOD
974	800	750	700

OLYMPIC K23 P

■ K23P 9MM

K23 pistol with a 6.5-inch 9mm barrel.

MSRP	EXC.	V.G.	GOOD
929	800	725	650

■ K23P-AT-3C TACTICAL PISTOL

AR-15 pistol model featuring a 6.5-inch barrel, no buttstock and a padded receiver extension tube. The A3-TC variant adds a flat top upper with detachable carry handle and FIRSH quad rail free floating handguard.

MSRP	EXC.	V.G.	GOOD
1188	975	875	775

OLYMPIC ARMS K23P-AT-3C TACTICAL PISTOL

■ K22 P

.22LR semi-automatic. 7.5-inch barrel, flat top receiver, no sights, aluminum tubular handguard.

MSRP	EXC.	V.G.	GOOD
895	800	700	575

■ OA-93

Unique to Olympic Arms, the OA Operations System incorporates the recoil system into a flat top upper receiver eliminating the need for a buttstock. The OA-93 was the first AR-15 pistol on the market.

MSRP	EXC.	V.G.	GOOD
1202	1000	900	800

OLYMPIC ARMS OA-93 .223 PISTOL

■ OA-98

A skeletonized, extremely lightweight version of the OA-93. Discontinued as of September of 2007.

EXC.	V.G.	GOOD
950	875	800

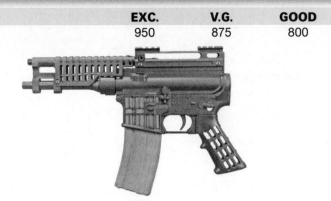

OLYMPIC ARMS OA-98 PISTOL

P.A.W.S. INC
Salem, Oregon

This company manufactured some copies of the English Sterling sub-machine gun in the 1990's.

■ ZX6 CARBINE

A semi-automatic carbine chambered for 9mm or .45 ACP. It has a 16-inch barrel. Folding metal stock. Matte black finish. 10 and 32 round magazines. Introduced in 1989.

EXC.	V.G.	GOOD
900	750	600

■ PAWS PISTOL

A short version of the ZX6 without the stock. 4- or 6-inch barrel.

EXC.	V.G.	GOOD
900	750	600

PATRIOT ORDNANCE FACTORY
Phoenix, Arizona

Website: www.pof-usa.com

POF manufactures a line of AR-15 type rifles that uses their "Regulated Short Stroke Gas Piston Weapon System."

■ P-415 SPECIAL PURPOSE RIFLE

Cal. .223. Features an 18-inch heavy contour barrel, fluted to reduce weight and heat. 11SX M.R.R. (Modular Rail Receiver) upper. Gas piston operated, rotating bolt (short stroke system). Reversible piston/gas trap design (adjustable: two modes of fire). C.R.O.S. (corrosion resistant operating system); chrome plated barrel, gas block/tube, gas plug, gas piston, bolt carrier assembly, NP3 coated upper receiver and charging handle. POF Modular Rail Receiver free float rail system handguard. Timney drop-in 4-lb. single stage trigger group. Ergo pistol grip. Vltor EMOD buttstock. Weight is 8.2 lbs.

MSRP	EXC.	V.G.	GOOD
1975	1850	1700	1550

PATRIOT ORDNANCE P-415 SPECIAL PURPOSE RIFLE

P-415 RECON RIFLE

Cal. .223. Features a 16-inch heavy contour barrel, fluted to reduce weight and heat. 9SX M.R.R. (Modular Rail Receiver) upper. Gas piston operated, rotating bolt (short stroke system). Reversible piston/gas trap design (adjustable: two modes of fire). C.R.O.S. (corrosion resistant operating system) chrome plated: barrel, gas block/tube, gas plug, gas piston, bolt carrier assembly, NP3 coated upper receiver and charging handle. POF Modular Rail Receiver free float rail system handguard. Timney drop-in 4-lb. single stage trigger group. Ergo pistol grip. VLTOR six-position buttstock with mil-spec tube. Weight is 7.8 Lbs.

MSRP	EXC.	V.G.	GOOD
1975	1800	1650	1500

PATRIOT ORDNANCE FACTORY MODEL 415 RECON RIFLE

P-415 CARBINE

Cal. .223. Features a 14.5-inch heavy contour barrel with permanent muzzle brake. 9SX M.R.R. (Modular Rail Receiver) upper. Gas piston operated, rotating bolt (short stroke system). Reversible piston/gas trap design (adjustable: two modes of fire). C.R.O.S. (corrosion resistant operating system) chrome plated: barrel, gas block/tube, gas plug, gas piston, bolt carrier assembly, NP3 coated upper receiver and charging handle. POF Modular Rail Receiver free float rail system handguard. Timney drop-in 4-lb. single stage trigger group. Ergo pistol grip. VLTOR six-position buttstock with mil-spec tube. Weight is 7.8 Lbs.

MSRP	EXC.	V.G.	GOOD
1975	1800	1650	1500

P-415 CARBINE, M-4 TYPE

Cal. .223. Features a 16-inch heavy contour barrel, fluted to reduce weight and heat. A3 flattop upper receiver, forged 7075-t6 aircraft aluminum alloy. Gas piston operated, rotating bolt (short stroke system). Reversible piston/gas trap design (adjustable: two modes of fire). C.R.O.S. (corrosion resistant operating system) chrome plated: barrel, gas block/tube, gas plug, gas piston, bolt carrier assembly, silicone nickel plated A3 flattop upper receiver and charging handle. CAR handguard. Mil-spec semi-auto trigger. Mil-spec six-position retractable stock. Tango Down battle grip. Weight is 6.9 lbs.

MSRP	EXC.	V.G.	GOOD
1650	1450	1300	1150

PATRIOT ORDNANCE FACTORY MODEL 415 M-4 CARBINE

P-308 SPECIAL PURPOSE RIFLE

Cal. .308. Features an 18-inch barrel. M.R.R. (Modular Rail Receiver) upper. Gas piston operated, rotating bolt (short stroke system). Reversible piston/gas trap design (adjustable: two modes of fire). C.R.O.S. (corrosion resistant operating system); chrome plated barrel, gas block/tube, gas plug, gas piston, bolt carrier assembly, NP3 coated upper receiver and charging handle. POF Modular Rail Receiver free float rail system handguard. Timney drop-in 4-lb. single stage trigger group. Ergo pistol grip. VLTOR six position buttstock. Uses DPMS, Knight Armament, or original AR-10 "waffle" magazines. Weight is 8.2 lbs.

MSRP	EXC.	V.G.	GOOD
2600	2250	2000	1700

P-308 RECON RIFLE

Cal. .308. Features a 16-inch barrel, M.R.R. (Modular Rail Receiver) upper. Gas piston operated, rotating bolt (short stroke system). Reversible piston/gas trap design (adjustable: two modes of fire). C.R.O.S. (corrosion resistant operating system) chrome plated barrel, gas block/tube, gas plug, gas piston, bolt carrier assembly, NP3 coated upper receiver and charging handle. POF Modular Rail Receiver free float rail system handguard. Timney drop-in 4-lb. single stage trigger group. Ergo pistol grip. VLTOR six position buttstock with mil-spec tube. Uses DPMS, Knight Armament, or original AR-10 "waffle" magazines. Weight is 7.8 Lbs.

MSRP	EXC.	V.G.	GOOD
2600	2250	2000	1700

PATRIOT ORDNANCE FACTORY RECON CARBINE

■ P-308 CARBINE

Cal. .308. Features a 14.5-inch heavy contour barrel with permanent muzzle brake. M.R.R. (Modular Rail Receiver) upper. Gas piston operated, rotating bolt (short stroke system). Reversible piston/gas trap design (adjustable: two modes of fire). C.R.O.S. (corrosion resistant operating system) chrome plated: barrel, gas block/tube, gas plug, gas piston, bolt carrier assembly, NP3 coated upper receiver and charging handle. POF Modular Rail Receiver free float rail system handguard. Timney drop-in 4-lb. single stage trigger group. Ergo pistol grip. VLTOR six position buttstock with mil-spec tube. Uses DPMS, Knight Armament, or original AR-10 "waffle" magazines. Weight is 7.8 Lbs.

MSRP	EXC.	V.G.	GOOD
2600	2250	2000	1700

PIETTA

Brescia, Italy

Website: www.pietta.us/categories/index.html

Full name: F. Lli Pietta. This Italian manufacturer of replica black powder firearms also makes some .22LR look alike firearms. They have been imported by a few different importers since the 1980's.

■ PPS-50

Cal. .22LR semi-automatic rifle that looks similar to the Russian PPSh sub-machine gun. They were first imported in the mid 1980's. Re-introduced to the American market in 2009. The new versions have wood or black synthetic stocks. 50 round drum and 30 or 10 round stick magazines are availible.

Note: add $50-100 for each functional 50 round drum magazine.

MSRP	EXC.	V.G.	GOOD
600	500	425	350

PIETTA PPS-50 RIFLE, CAL. .22LR

■ MK 85

A .22LR pistol that resembles a British Sterling sub-machine gun. Announcd at the 2010 SHOT show. No pricing information yet established.

PIETTA MK 85 STERLING PISTOL .22LR

PLAINFIELD MACHINE CO.
Dunnelein, New Jersey

A maker of new production M-1 carbines. No longer in business.

■ SUPER ENFORCER

A handgun based on the M-1 carbine action. 12-inch barrel. Caliber .30M-1. Blued finish with a walnut stock.

EXC.	V.G.	GOOD
550	450	350

■ M-1 CARBINE

EXC.	V.G.	GOOD
475	400	375

■ M-1 PARATROOPER CARBINE

As above with a telescoping wire buttstock

EXC.	V.G.	GOOD
500	450	400

POLY TECHNOLOGIES (POLYTECH)
Beijing, China

This is another name used by the Chinese arms production network. It might have been a separate branch from Norinco. Poly Tech produced variations of the AK series as well as an M-14 type rifle. Imported by Kengs Firearms Specialists (KFS) of Atlanta, Georgia.

■ AKS

This is a standard AKM rifle chambered in 7.62x39mm and it was made with a stamped receiver. It has a folding bayonet and is the same configuration of the Chinese military issue Type 56.

EXC.	V.G.	GOOD
1250	1100	950

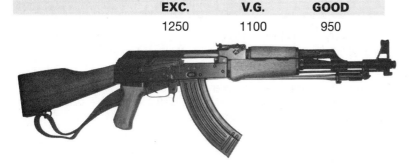

POLY TECHNOLOGIES AKS RIFLE 7.62X39MM W/ FOLDING BAYONET

■ AKS SIDE FOLDING STOCK

This version takes a standard blade bayonet. Stocks are made from red plastic or light colored wood. It features a side folding stock.

EXC.	V.G.	GOOD
1400	1250	1000

POLY TECHNOLOGIES AKS FOLDING STOCK RIFLE. COURTESY ROCK ISLAND AUCTIONS.

■ LEGEND SERIES MODEL AK-47/S

This is the closest copy of the original AK-47 that was imported. It has a milled steel receiver, instead of the stamped receiver found on the later AKM. Poly Tech made two versions.

◆ Fixed Stock

EXC.	V.G.	GOOD
1400	1175	1050

◆ Under Folding Stock

EXC.	V.G.	GOOD
1500	1250	1100

◆ Post Import Ban Legend

KFS had some rifles caught in customs when the import ban was imposed. These were fitted with a thumbhole stock and the bayonet lug and barrel threads were removed. Later, there were some Poly Tech made milled receiver sporter rifles imported that had the name MAK-90 added to them.

EXC.	V.G.	GOOD
750	625	500

POLY TECH LEGEND SPORTER RIFLE

■ M-14/S

This is a copy of the U.S. M-14 rifle. Chambered in 7.62 NATO/.308. Wood stock. It has a cosmetic flash hider that was made without venting slots. No bayonet mount.

EXC.	V.G.	GOOD
850	750	650

PROFESSIONAL ORDNANCE, INC.
Ontario, California

This Company was purchased by Bushmaster in 2003, who added the Carbon 15 to their product line.

■ CARBON-15 PISTOL—TYPE 97

Introduced in 1996 this semi-automatic pistol is built on a carbon fiber upper and lower receiver. Chambered for the 5.56 cartridge it has a 7.25-inch fluted stainless steel barrel. Ghost ring sights are standard. Magazine is AR-15 compatible. Quick detach compensator. Furnished with a 10 round magazine. Weight is approximately 46 oz.

Note: This pistol has several options which will affect value.

EXC.	V.G.	GOOD
600	500	400

■ CARBON-15 RIFLE—TYPE 97

Similar to the above model but fitted with a 16-inch barrel, quick detachable buttstock, quick detach compensator, Weaver type mounting base. Overall length is 35 inches. Weight is about 3.9 lbs.

EXC.	V.G.	GOOD
750	650	500

■ CARBON-15 RIFLE—TYPE 97S

Introduced in 2000, this rifle incorporated several new features. Its foregrip is double walled and insulated with a sheet of ultra-lightweight amumina silica ceramic fiber. The recoil buffer has been increased in size by 30 percent for less recoil. A new ambidextrous safety has been added, and a new multi-carry silent sling with Hogue grip is standard. Weight is approximately 4.3 lbs.

EXC.	V.G.	GOOD
850	700	550

■ CARBON-15 PISTOL—TYPE 21

Introduced in 1999 this model features a light profile stainless steel 7.25-inch barrel. Ghost ring sights are standard. Optional recoil compensator. A 30 round magazine is standard. Weight is about 40 oz.

EXC.	V.G.	GOOD
650	550	450

■ CARBON-15 RIFLE—TYPE 21

This model is fitted with a 16-inch light profile stainless steel barrel. Quick detachable stock, Weaver mounting base. Introduced in 1999. Weight is approximately 3.9 lbs.

EXC.	V.G.	GOOD
800	700	550

■ CARBON-15 RIFLE—CAL. .22LR

A Carbon 15 rifle chambered in .22LR. Flat top rail. Fixed stock. 10 or 20 round magazine.

EXC.	V.G.	GOOD
500	450	400

PTR 91 INC.
Unionville, CT
Website: www.ptr91.com

This company makes a series of rifles based on the HK-91 Rifle.

■ PTR 91 F

Basic rifle with a 18-inch .308 caliber barrel. Features a machined aluminum handguard, HK navy type polymer trigger housing, black synthetic stock. Uses HK-91 magazines.

MSRP	EXC.	V.G.	GOOD
1295	1200	1100	1000

■ PTR 91 KF

As above, with a 16-inch barrel.

MSRP	EXC.	V.G.	GOOD
1295	1200	1100	1000

■ PTR 91 SC

The Squad Carbine features a 16-inch fluted target barrel, machined aluminum handguard with 3-6.5 Inch rails, HK navy type polymer trigger housing. Weight: 9.8 lbs.

MSRP	EXC.	V.G.	GOOD
1580	1500	1350	1200

■ PTR 91 KFM4

As above with a five-position M-4 type collapsible stock. Weight: 9.8 lbs.

MSRP	EXC.	V.G.	GOOD
1435	1350	1225	1100

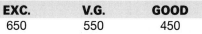

PTR 91 KFM4 RIFLE IN 7.62NATO/.308. COURTESY ROCK ISLAND AUCTIONS.

■ PTR-MSG 91

Cal. .308 with an 18-inch fluted barrel, machined aluminum handguard with a single rail on the underside, Harris Bipod, HK navy-type polymer trigger housing, tactical stock with adjustable length and height.

MSRP	EXC.	V.G.	GOOD
2125	1900	1750	1600

■ PTR 32 KF

A 7.62x39 version of the HK-91. Features a 16-inch barrel, machined aluminum handguard, HK navy style polymer trigger housing. Uses AK type magazines.

MSRP	EXC.	V.G.	GOOD
1365	1250	1150	1050

PTR 32 KFM4

As above, fitted with a five-position CAR type stock.

MSRP	EXC.	V.G.	GOOD
1435	1325	1200	1100

PTR 44

A new-made semi-automatic version or the German WWII MP-44 "Sturmgewehr" in 8x33mm Kurz. It is made In Germany by Sport System Dittrich. All dimensions duplicate the original MP-44. New for 2010. No sold examples found at time of printing.

MSRP	EXC.	V.G.	GOOD
5500	N/A	N/A	N/A

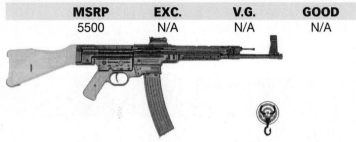

PTR 44, NEW GERMAN MANUFACTURE MP-44 IN 8X33 KURZ

RED ROCK ARMS
(FORMERLY BOBCAT ARMS)
Mesa, Arizona
Website: www.redrockarms.com

ATR-1

Based on the FN FAL platform. 16-1/4-inch barrel. Caliber 5.56/.223 1:9 twist. Weight is 8 lbs. Aircraft grade, 7075 T6 aluminum receiver is machined from a solid bar to exacting specifications in the U.S. Design specifically to accept AR-15 (M-16) magazines. Last round hold open and paddle magazine release. Original FN FAL gas operated piston breech block unlocking system, proven, reliable field history in Military and Law enforcement applications. Buttstock, forend and grip molded from glass filled nylon for added impact strength and thermal stability. The lower, including the fire control mechanism and all components thereof, are original FN FAL components. Semi-automatic ONLY. The receiver is NOT slotted to accept an auto sear. All primary exterior metal surfaces, except the magazine, are painted with Duracoat brand coatings. Minor parts are finished in black oxide.

MSRP	EXC.	V.G.	GOOD
1400	1250	1175	1100

BW5 FSA RIFLE

Based on the H&K MP-5 SMG. Caliber 9mm. Features: High-grade steel receiver is stamped, formed and welded to exacting specifications in the U.S. Paddle magazine release. Delayed blowback operated, roller lock bolt system has a proven, reliable field history in military and law enforcement applications. Button rifled, stainless steel, 9 inches, 3-lug barrel, rifled with 1:10 twist rate and fluted chamber. Billet machined, aluminum, permanently attached, fake suppressor is black anodized and extends the barrel length to 16.5 inches (rifle only). Fixed buttstock and forend molded from glass filled nylon for added impact strength and thermal stability. Pistol polymer buttcap w/ D-ring. The fire control mechanism is housed in a polymer Navy/FBI style lower/grip and has ambidextrous selection for safe and semi-automatic fire. All exterior metal surfaces, except the magazine, are epoxy coated for exceptional durability and finish. Discontinued.

EXC.	V.G.	GOOD
1500	1400	1300

BW5 FSA PISTOL

Based on the H&K MP-5 SMG. Caliber 9mm. Features include: High-grade steel receiver is stamped, formed and welded to exacting specifications in the U.S. Paddle magazine release. Delayed blowback operated, roller lock bolt system has a proven, reliable field history in Military and Law Enforcement applications. Button rifled, stainless steel, 9 inches, 3-lug barrel, rifled with 1:10 twist rate and fluted chamber. Forend molded from glass filled nylon for added impact strength and thermal stability. Pistol polymer buttcap w/ D-ring. The fire control mechanism is housed in a polymer Navy/FBI style lower/grip and has ambidextrous selection for safe and semi-automatic fire. All exterior metal surfaces, except the magazine, are epoxy coated for exceptional durability and finish. Discontinued.

EXC.	V.G.	GOOD
1500	1400	1300

REMINGTON ARMS CO.
Madison, North Carolina
Website: www.remington.com

In 2008, this old line manufacturer of sporting arms added a few AR-15 based rifles. Remington is currently owned by Cerberus.

■ R-15 VTR PREDATOR RIFLE CAL. 223

AR-15-style rifle developed with the predator hunter in mind. It features a 22-inch free-floating button-rifled 0.680-inch muzzle OD ChroMoly barrel with recessed hunting crown for superior accuracy. The fluted barrel design reduces weight and promotes rapid barrel cooling. Clean-breaking single-stage hunting trigger. Receiver-length picatinny rail for adding optics. Ergonomic pistol grip. Fore-end tube drilled and tapped for accessory rails. Full Advantage" MAX-1 HDTM camouflage coverage. Includes a 5 round magazine. Legal for hunting in most states. Compatible with aftermarket AR-15 magazines.

MSRP	EXC.	V.G.	GOOD
1225	1000	850	700

REMINGTON R-15 PREDATOR .223 RIFLE

■ R-15 VTR PREDATOR RIFLE CAL. .204 RUGER

As above but chambered in .204 Ruger.

MSRP	EXC.	V.G.	GOOD
1225	1000	850	700

■ R-15 VTR SS VARMINT

An R-15 rifle fitted with a 24-inch stainless steel barrel.

MSRP	EXC.	V.G.	GOOD
1412	1200	1050	900

■ R-15 VTR THUMBHOLE

As above with a Thumbhole type buttstock.

MSRP	EXC.	V.G.	GOOD
1412	1200	1050	900

REMINGTON R-15 PREDATOR CARBINE WITH COLLAPSIBLE STOCK

■ R-15 VTR PREDATOR CARBINE CAL. .223

As above with an 18-inch barrel.

MSRP	EXC.	V.G.	GOOD
1225	1000	850	700

■ R-15 VTR PREDATOR CARBINE CAL. .204 RUGER

As above chambered for .204 Ruger. Discontinued.

EXC.	V.G.	GOOD
1000	850	700

■ R-15 VTR PREDATOR CARBINE CS CAL. .223

A Predator carbine featuring a CAR style collapsible stock.

MSRP	EXC.	V.G.	GOOD
1225	1050	900	750

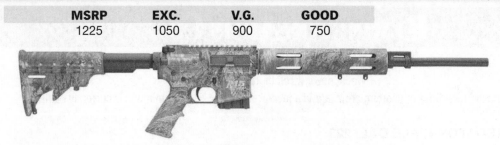

REMINGTON R-15 PREDATOR CARBINE WITH COLLAPSIBLE STOCK

■ R-15 VTR PREDATOR CARBINE CS CALIBER .204 RUGER

As above but chambered in .204 Ruger. Discontinued.

EXC.	V.G.	GOOD
850	775	700

■ R-15 VTR BYRON SOUTH SIGNATURE EDITION

R-15 rifle with a 18-inch barrel. Receiver-length picatinny rail for adding optics, ergonomic pistol grip, fore-end tube drilled and tapped for accessory rails, full Advantage® MAX-1 HD camo coverage. Includes 5-round magazine.

MSRP	EXC.	V.G	GOOD
1775	1500	1250	1000

■ R-15 .450 BUSHMASTER

R-15 rifle with a 18-inch barrel chambered in .450 Bushmaster. Finished in Mossy Oak New Break Up camo.

MSRP	EXC.	V.G.	GOOD
1225	1100	1000	900

■ R-25 RIFLE

The R-25 is an AR-10 type rifle. Offered in .243 Win, 7mm-08 and .308 Win. It features Receiver-length Picatinny rail for adding optics and accessories, 20-inch free-floated chromoly barrels with recessed hunting crown, fluted barrel, single-stage hunting trigger (factory set to 4.5-5 lbs.), full Mossy Oak Treestand coverage. The Remington R-25 is compatible with aftermarket DPMS 308 Win. magazines. Weight: 8 lbs.

MSRP	EXC.	V.G.	GOOD
1567	1300	1150	1000

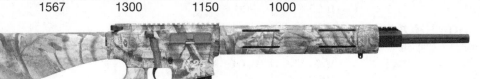

REMINGTON R-25 RIFLE, CAL. 308

ROBINSON ARMAMENT
Salt Lake City, Utah
Website: www.robarm.com

■ XCR SERIES

The XCR was originally designed for military trials in the SOCOM program. Civilian sales began in 2006. The XCR employs a Kalashnikov type gas system. The rifle uses an upper and lower receiver. The upper receiver features picatinny rails on all four sides. The top rail is 17 inches long, providing ample room for any available sighting system. Many features of the XCR can be special ordered. Consult a factory catalog to see the numerous options. The XCR is a multi-caliber weapon system. The base platform is chambered in 5.56 NATO. Other caliber offerings include 6.8SPC, 6.5 Grendel, 7.62x39. The conversions are easily achieved by changing to the appropriately chambered barrel and bolt. Conversions can be done in two-three minutes.

■ XCR-L STANDARD

The base model rifle in 5.56mm/.226 has a barrel length of 16 inches. Side folding or fixed stock. The weight is 7-1/2 lbs. The XCR uses M-16 series magazines.

MSRP	EXC.	V.G.	GOOD
1500	1350	1200	1100

Note: *For XCR in calibers other than .223 add 200 to MSRP.*

ROBINSON ARMAMENT XCR RIFLE

■ XCR-L MICRO PISTOL

A pistol using the XCR operating system. 7-1/2-inch barrel. It Is available In .223, 6.8mm, or 7.62x39mm. Weight: 5.2 lbs.

MSRP	EXC.	V.G.	GOOD
1500	1350	1200	1100

■ M96 EXPEDITIONARY RIFLE

The M96 is based on the Stoner 63 Weapon System designed by Eugene Stoner and used by the U.S Navy Seals in Vietnam. The Stoner "63" receiver, using a variety of modular components, could be configured as a rifle, carbine, a top fed light machine gun, a belt fed squad automatic weapon, or a vehicle mounted weapon. The M96 has been designed with similar modularity in mind but has been simplified for easier maintenance. It is chambered for 5.56mm/.223. The barrel is 20 inches long and included a built-in muzzle brake. The barrel can be quickly changed. Total length is 40 inches. The weight is 8-1/2 lbs. The action is piston driven gas operation. Stainless steel receiver with a matte black finish. Picatinny rails can be added on top of receiver and sides of fore-arm. Front and rear sights are adjustable for windage and elevation. Black, green or tan synthetic stock and forearm. Uses M-16 magazines and drums.

MSRP	EXC.	V.G.	GOOD
1599	1350	1200	1050

**ROBINSON ARMAMENT M-96
EXPEDITIONARY RIFLE, CAL. .223**

■ M96 RECON CARBINE

As above with a 16-inch barrel.

MSRP	EXC.	V.G.	GOOD
1599	1350	1200	1050

■ M96 RECON CARBINE WITH TOP FEED

A M96 carbine that features a top feed or "BREN" type magazine system. The top cover features an offset rear sight.

MSRP	EXC.	V.G.	GOOD
1899	1600	1400	1200

■ VEPR SERIES

These Russian made rifles were imported by Robinson Armament. The line has been discontinued. The VEPR Rifles and Carbines are sporting arms based on the famous Soviet designed RPK machine gun. VEPR rifles are manufactured in Russia at the historic Vyatskie Polyany Machine Building Plant (a.k.a. "MOLOT").

■ VEPR II

A 7.63x39mm rifle with a 20-1/2-inch barrel. The total length is 39-3/4 inches. Weight is 9 lbs. Open sights. Russian type scope mount on Left side of receiver. Synthetic stocks. Accepts AK magazines and drums.

EXC.	V.G.	GOOD
1000	850	700

Note: *add $50 for muzzle brake.*

■ VEPR II .223

As above but chambered for 5.56mm/.223.

EXC.	V.G.	GOOD
1000	850	700

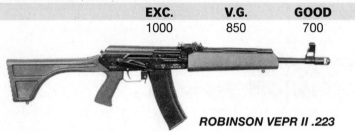

ROBINSON VEPR II .223

■ VEPR II .308

A VEPR rifle chambered in 7.62mm/.308. It has a 20-1/2-inch barrel. Available magazines hold 5 or 10 rounds.

EXC.	V.G.	GOOD
1100	975	850

■ VEPR K 7.62X39MM, 223 OR 5.45X39MM

A VEPR II with a 16-1/2-inch barrel. Other features are the same as listed above.

EXC.	V.G.	GOOD
1000	850	700

■ SUPER VEPR .308

A deluxe version of the original VEPR rifle. It has a 21-1/2-inch barrel. Total length is 41 inches. It weighs 8-1/2 lbs. One piece walnut stock with ambidextrous grip and recoil pad. Adjustable sights as well as Weaver Rail. 5 and 10 round magazines.

EXC.	V.G.	GOOD
1250	1100	950

■ VEPR .308 RIFLE

This rifle features a 23-1/4-inch barrel. Total length is 39-3/4 inches. The rifle weighs 8.3 lbs. Checkered walnut stock and forearm. 5 and 10 round magazines.

EXC.	V.G.	GOOD
1100	975	850

■ VEPR .308 CARBINE

This rifle features a 20-1/2-inch barrel. Total length is 39-3/4 inches. The rifle weighs 8.3 lbs. Checkered walnut stock and forearm. 5 and 10 round magazines.

EXC.	V.G.	GOOD
1100	975	850

VEPR .308 RIFLE, AS IMPORTED BY ROBINSON ARMS

ROCK RIVER ARMS, INC.
Colona, Illinois
Website: www.rockriverarms.com

RRA makes a variety of AR-15 type rifles and pistols. The basic models are listed. All can be factory ordered to be assembled with different options. Price will be based on options selected. They also offer lower and upper receiver assemblies.

■ PPS RIFLE

RRA Performance Piston System. Caliber 5.56mm. 16 inch barrel. Full length top mounting rail, injection molded handguard, RRA side folding tactical CAR stock. Weight: 7.5 lbs. New in 2010.

MSRP	EXC.	V.G.	GOOD
1685	1500	1350	1100

■ LAR-15 .223/5.56MM RIFLES

◆ CAR A2

This is an AR-15-style rifle chambered for the .223 cartridge. Fitted with a 16-inch barrel with CAR handguards. Two stage trigger. Choice of A2 or RRA Tactical CAR collapsible buttstock. Choice of black or green furniture. Weight is about 7 lbs.

MSR	EXC.	V.G.	GOOD
975	800	700	650

◆ CAR A2M

Same as above but with mid-length handguard.

MSR	EXC.	V.G.	GOOD
975	800	700	650

◆ CAR A4

Similar to the models above but with flattop receiver and CAR handguard.

MSR	EXC.	V.G.	GOOD
940	800	725	650

ROCK RIVER CAR A4M

◆ CAR A4M

Flattop receiver with mid-length handguard.

MSR	EXC.	V.G.	GOOD
940	800	725	650

◆ Standard A2

The AR-15-style rifle is fitted with a 20-inch barrel and chambered for the .223 cartridge. Two stage trigger. Fixed stock and full-length handguard. Weight is about 8.2 lbs.

MSR	EXC.	V.G.	GOOD
980	750	700	650

◆ Standard A4 Flattop

Same as Standard A2 but with flattop receiver.

MSR	EXC.	V.G.	GOOD
940	725	700	650

◆ National Match A2

This model features a .22 Wylde chamber with a 20-inch Wilson air-gauged match stainless steel barrel. A2 receiver. Two stage trigger. Free float high temperature thermo mold handguard. Match sights. Weight is about 9.7 lbs.

MSR	EXC.	V.G.	GOOD
1215	1000	900	800

◆ National Match A4

As above but with a flat top receiver and removable carry handle with national match sight.

MSR	EXC.	V.G.	GOOD
1310	1200	1050	950

◆ Varmint Rifle A4

This flattop model is fitted with a 16-, 18-, 20- or 24-inch stainless Wilson steel barrel without sights. Fixed stock. Two-stage trigger. Weight is about 9.5 lbs.

MSR	EXC.	V.G.	GOOD
1105	900	825	750

Note: Add $10 for each barrel length from 16 inch.

◆ Varmint EOP (Elevated Optical Platform)

Chambered for the .223 with a Wylde chamber and fitted with a Wilson air-gauged bull stainless steel barrel. Choice of 16-, 18-, 20- or 24-inch barrel length. Free float aluminum handguard. National Match two stage trigger. Weight is about 8.2 lbs. with 16-inch barrel and 10 lbs. with 24-inch barrel.

MSR	EXC.	V.G.	GOOD
1140	950	875	800

Note: *Add $10 for each barrel length from 16 inches.*

◆ Predator Pursuit

Flat top receiver, 20-inch stainless steel match barrel, RRA aluminum free float handguard. Weight: 8.1 lbs.

MSR	EXC.	V.G.	GOOD
1125	950	875	800

◆ Coyote Rifle

Flat top receiver, 20-inch heavy barrel with Smith Vortex flash hider, Hogue Overmolded free float rifle length handguard, RRA Operator A2 stock.

MSR	EXC.	V.G.	GOOD
1205	1000	900	800

RRA LAR-15 COYOTE RIFLE

● Coyote Carbine

As above but fitted with a 16-inch heavy barrel. CAR length Hogue overmolded handguard.

MSR	EXC.	V.G.	GOOD
1190	1000	900 800	

◆ Pro Series Government Model

Chambered for the .223 cartridge and fitted with a 16-inch Wilson chrome barrel with A2 flash hider. National Match two stage trigger. A4 upper receiver. Flip-up rear sight. EOTech M951 light system. Surefire M73 Quad Rail handguard, and 6 position tactical CAR stock. Weight is about 8.2 lbs.

MSR	EXC.	V.G.	GOOD
2350	2050	1850	1700

ROCK RIVER PRO SERIES GOVERNMENT MODEL

◆ Pro Series Elite

A3 flat top receiver, 16-inch chrome lined barrel, Daniel Defense quad rail handguard, Aimpoint Comp M2 sight with QRP mount and spacer, A.R.M.S. flip sight, Surefire 910A foregrip weapon light, RRA Operator CAR stock. Weight: 9.5 lbs.

MSR	EXC.	V.G.	GOOD
2950	2500	2250	1900

◆ Elite Comp

A3 Flat top receiver, 16-inch barrel, A.R.M.S. flip sight, RRA 1/2 quad full top rail handguard, RRA Operator CAR stock. Weight: 8.4 lbs.

MSR	EXC.	V.G.	GOOD
1450	1250	1000	850

◆ Tactical CAR A4

This .223 caliber rifle has a 16-inch Wilson chrome barrel with A2 flash hider. A4 upper receiver with detachable carry handle. Two stage National Match trigger. R-4 handguard. Six-position tactical CAR stock. Weight is about 7.5 lbs.

MSR	EXC.	V.G.	GOOD
995	900 850	750	

◆ Elite CAR A4

As above but with mid-length handguard. Weight is about 7.7 lbs.

MSR	EXC.	V.G.	GOOD
995	900	850	750

◆ Tactical CAR UTE (Universal Tactical Entry) 2

This .223 caliber rifle has a 16-inch Wilson chrome barrel with A2 flash hider. It has a R-2 handguard. The upper receiver is a UTE2 with standard A4 rail height. Two stage trigger and six-position CAR tactical stock. Weight is about 7.5 lbs.

MSR	EXC.	V.G.	GOOD
1060	900	850	750

ROCK RIVER TACTICAL CAR UTE (UNIVERSAL TACTICAL ENTRY) 2

◆ Elite CAR UTE 2

As above but with mid-length handguard. Weight is about 7.7 lbs.

MSR	EXC.	V.G.	GOOD
1060	900	850	750

◆ Entry Operator

Flat top receiver, Optional A2 carry handle, 16-inch R-4 contour barrel, RRA Operator CAR stock. Weight: 7.2 lbs.

MSR	EXC.	V.G.	GOOD
1080	900	800	700

ROCK RIVER ARMS ENTRY OPERATOR

◆ Tactical Operator

As above but fitted with a 16-inch standard barrel.

MSR	EXC.	V.G.	GOOD
1080	900	800	700

◆ Elite Operator

As above but fitted with a 16-inch standard barrel and RRA half-quad mid-length handguard.

MSR	EXC.	V.G.	GOOD
1200	1000	900	800

◆ Entry Tactical

This .223 model features a 16-inch Wilson chrome barrel with a R-4 profile. A4 upper receiver with detachable carry handle. National Match two stage trigger. Six-position tactical CAR stock. R-4 handguard. Weight is about 7.5 lbs.

MSR	EXC.	V.G.	GOOD
995	900	800	700

◆ TASC Rifle

This rifle features a 16-inch Wilson chrome barrel with A2 flash hider. A2 upper receiver with windage and elevation rear sight. R-4 handguard. A2 buttstock. Weight is about 7.5 lbs. Discontinued.

EXC.	V.G.	GOOD
850	775	700

ROCK RIVER TASC RIFLE

■ 9MM & .40 RIFLES

◆ 9mm CAR A2

These are AR-15-style rifles chambered for the 9x19mm cartridge. 16-inch barrel with optional CAR length or mid-length handguard. Two stage trigger. Choice of A2 or non-collapsible buttstock. Weight is about 7 lbs.

MSR	EXC.	V.G.	GOOD
1110	975	900	825

ROCK RIVER 9MM CAR A2

◆ 9mm CAR A4

As above with a flat top receiver.

MSR	EXC.	V.G.	GOOD
1085	975	900	825

ROCK RIVER 9MM CAR A4

◆ 40 S&W CAR A2

Chambered for the .40 S&W cartridge. 16-inch barrel with optional CAR length or mid-length handguard. Two stage trigger. Choice of A2 or non-collapsible buttstock. Weight is about 7 lbs.

MSR	EXC.	V.G.	GOOD
1150	1000	925	850

◆ 40 S&W CAR A4

As above with a flat top receiver.

MSR	EXC.	V.G.	GOOD
1125	1000	925	850

■ 6.8MM REMINGTON SPC RIFLES

◆ AR 6.8 SPC CAR A2

Fitted with a 16-inch barrel with CAR handguards. Also available with mid-length handguards. Two stage trigger. Choice of A2 or non-collapsible buttstock. Weight is about 7 lbs.

MSR	EXC.	V.G.	GOOD
985	825	775	700

ROCK RIVER LAR 6.8 SPC CAR A4

◆ AR 6.8 SPC CAR A4

As above with a flat top receiver.

MSR	EXC.	V.G.	GOOD
950	825	775	700

◆ 6.8 Coyote Carbine

A4 flat top. 16-inch heavy barrel. CAR length Hogue Overmolded handguard. RRA operator A2 stock

MSR	EXC.	V.G.	GOOD
1190	1000	900 800	

■ .458 SOCOM RIFLES

◆ LAR-458 CAR A4

Fitted with a 16-inch barrel with free float aluminum handguards. Two stage trigger. Choice of A2 or CAR buttstock. Weight is about 7 lbs.

MSR	EXC.	V.G.	GOOD
1150	1050	950	850

ROCK RIVER LAR-458 CAR A4

◆ LAR-458 CAR A4 Operator

As above with RRA Quad rail free float handguard, Smith Vortex flash hider, RRA Operator CAR stock.

MSR	EXC.	V.G.	GOOD
1420	1200	1100	1000

◆ LAR-458 Mid-Length A4

16-inch barrel, RRA free float handguard, mid-length gas system, Two stage trigger. Choice of A2 or CAR buttstock. Weight is about 7.8 lbs.

MSR	EXC.	V.G.	GOOD
1150	1050	950	850

◆ LAR-458 Mid-Length A4 Operator

As above with RRA half quad/full top handguard, Smith Vortex flash hider, RRA Operator CAR stock.

MSR	EXC.	V.G.	GOOD
1445	1250	1150	1050

■ .308 / 7.62 NATO RIFLES

◆ LAR-8 Mid-Length A4

Fitted with a 16-inch barrel. Two stage trigger. RRA Tactical CAR stock. Weight: 8.1 lbs.

MSR	EXC.	V.G.	GOOD
1265	1150	1000	900

ROCK RIVER LAR-8 A4 RIFLE

◆ LAR-8 Elite Operator

Fitted with a 16-inch barrel with Smith Vortex flash hider, Flip front sight gas block, RRA Advanced Half Quad handguard, Operator buttstock.

MSR	EXC.	V.G.	GOOD
1655	1400	1250	1100

◆ LAR-8 A4 Rifle

Flat top receiver. 20-inch barrel, A2 handguard, A2 buttstock. Weight: 9.0 lbs.

MSR	EXC.	V.G.	GOOD
1300	1100	1000	900

◆ LAR-8 Standard Operator

As above with Smith Vortex flash hider, RRA Advanced Half Quad handguard, flip front sight block, RRA Operator A2 stock.

MSR	EXC.	V.G.	GOOD
1705	1500	1300	1100

RRA LAR-8 OPERATOR

◆ LAR-8 Varmint A4

Fitted with a 20- or 26-inch Wilson stainless steel bull barrel. Free float aluminum handguard. Match trigger. A2 buttstock. Uses FAL metric or inch magazines.

MSR	EXC.	V.G.	GOOD
1500	1300	1150	1000

ROCK RIVER LAR-8 VARMINT A4

◆ LAR-8 Predator HP

Flat top receiver, 20-inch bead blasted lightweight stainless steel barrel, A2 buttstock. Weight: 8.6 lbs.

MSR	EXC.	V.G.	GOOD
1535	1300	1150	1000

◆ LAR-8 A2 Rifle

Fitted with a 20-inch Wilson barrel. Mid-length handguards. A2 type upper receiver. Two stage trigger. A2 stock. Uses FAL metric or inch magazines. Discontinued.

	EXC.	V.G.	GOOD
	1150	1000	950

■ PPS PISTOL

Performance Piston System. Caliber 5.56mm. 8-inch barrel. Full top rail receiver. Weight: 5 lbs. New in 2010.

MSR	EXC.	V.G.	GOOD
1335	1200	1050	900

ROCK RIVER LAR-15 A2 AND LAR-15 A4 PISTOLS

■ LAR PISTOLS

Rock River Arms pistols can be ordered with standard round, aluminum free float round, or quad rail free float handguard. Prices vary based on configuration.

◆ LAR-15 A2 Pistol .223/5.56

Offered with a Wilson 7- or 10-1/2-inch barrel. A2 rear sight. Standard front sight. Weight: 5.0 lbs.

MSR	EXC.	V.G.	GOOD
955	850	775	700

◆ LAR-15 A4 Pistol

As above with a flat top receiver. Gas block sight base.

MSR	EXC.	V.G.	GOOD
990	850	775	700

◆ LAR-9 / LAR-40 A2

9mm or .40 S&W. Offered with a 7- or 10-1/2-inch barrel.

MSR	EXC.	V.G.	GOOD
1150	1000	925	850

◆ LAR-9 / LAR-40 A4 Pistol 9mm

As above with a flat top receiver.

MSR	EXC.	V.G.	GOOD
1150	1000	925	850

RUGER
Southport, Connecticut

■ MINI-14

A 5.56mm/.223 semi-automatic carbine. Basically a scaled-down M-14 rifle. 18-1/2 inch barrel. Blued or Stainless steel. Introduced in 1975. Now discontinued. Originally sold with a birch stock and handguard. Handguard was later changed to a synthetic material with steel liner. 5, 10, 20 or 30 round magazine. Original model without scope bases has been discontinued.

◆ Blued

EXC.	V.G.	GOOD
550	475	400

◆ Stainless Steel

EXC.	V.G.	GOOD
625	525	450

■ MINI-14 GB MODEL

This is a Mini-14 shipped from the factory with a all steel side folding stock with pistol grip. Barrel has a flash hider and bayonet mount. There are also restricted, by Ruger, to law enforcement sales only. Many have filtered onto the civilian market.

EXC.	V.G.	GOOD
1100	950	800

Note: *The folding stocks will be seen on standard Mini-14's as well. Add $200 for any Ruger Mini-14 with a factory folding stock.*

■ MINI-14 TACTICAL RIFLE

A Mini-14 with a 16-inch barrel with flash hider. Blued steel finish, Black synthetic stock.

MSRP	EXC.	V.G.	GOOD
921	700	600	500

■ MINI-14 ATI

A Mini-14 with a 16-inch barrel with flash hider. Blued Steel finish. ATI stock features multiple rails and side folding CAR type six-position collapsible stock.

MSRP	EXC.	V.G.	GOOD
921	700	600	500

RUGER TACTICAL RIFLE W/ ATI STOCK. COURTESY ROCK ISLAND AUCTIONS.

■ MINI-14 RANCH RIFLE

A Mini-14 with scope mounting bases machined into the receiver. Birch stock. Ruger 1-inch rings are included.

◆ Blued

MSRP	EXC.	V.G.	GOOD
881	600	500	400

RUGER MINI-14 RANCH RIFLE, CURRENT PRODUCTION

◆ Stainless

As above, but also offered as the All Weather model with a black synthetic stock.

MSRP	EXC.	V.G.	GOOD
966	650	575	500

■ MINI-14 TARGET RIFLE-HOGUE

Mini-14 Ranch Rifle with a 22 inch barrel. Black Hogue overmolded stock. Weight: 8.5 lbs.

MSRP	EXC.	V.G.	GOOD
1098	875	750	600

■ MINI-14 TARGET RIFLE

Introduced in 2008 this Mini 14 has a 22-inch barrel. Laminated thumbhole stock. Comes with Ruger rings.

MSRP	EXC.	V.G.	GOOD
1098	875	750	600

RUGER MINI-14 TARGET RIFLE

■ MINI-30

A Mini-14 Ranch rifle chambered in 7.62x39mm. 18-1/2-inch barrel. Sold with Ruger rings. Introduced in 1987. Blued model is discontinued.

◆ Blue

EXC.	V.G.	GOOD
600	525	450

Stainless, with black synthetic All Weather stock

MSRP	EXC.	V.G.	GOOD
949	775	625	525

■ MINI 6.8

A Mini-14 Ranch rifle chambered in 6.8mm Remington SPC. Black All Weather stock.

MSRP	EXC.	V.G.	GOOD
949	775	625	525

■ SR-556

Rugers' version of the AR type rifle features a gas piston operation system. Caliber 5.56mm 16-inch barrel, flat top receiver, folding battle sights, quad rail handguard, CAR telescoping stock. Weight 8 lbs.

MSRP	EXC.	V.G.	GOOD
1995	1650	1400	1250

RUGER SR556 RIFLE

■ SR-22

Ruger 10-22 action. 16-inch barrel with flash hider, AR pistol grip, rail top, tubular handguard, CAR telescoping stock.

MSRP	EXC.	V.G.	GOOD
625 500	425	350	

■ POLICE CARBINE

A 9mm or .40S&W semi-automatic rifle. 16-1/4-inch barrel. Synthetic black stock. 10 and 15 round magazines. Introduced 1998. Discontinued.

EXC.	V.G.	GOOD
550	475	400

RUSSIAN AMERICAN ARMORY CO.
Scottsburg, Indiana
Website: www.raac.com

This company is the current importer for the Saiga series of rifles and shotguns. These are based on the Kalashnikov design and are the only Russian made AK's currently imported. They are made in Russia by Izhmash.

EAA and others have imported these as well. Pricing is the same.

■ SAIGA .308

A semi-automatic rifle based on the Kalishnikov design. Caliber .308. Barrel length is 16.3 or 21.8 inches. Total length is 37-1/4 or 43-1/4 inches. The weight is 8.5 lbs. Black synthetic stocks. Magazines hold 8 rounds.

NIB	EXC.	V.G.	GOOD
500	450	400	350

SAIGA .308 RIFLE, IMPORTED BY RUSSIAN AMERICAN ARMORY

■ SAIGA .308 VER 2.1

As above fitted with a wooden thumbhole type stock. 21-3/4-inch barrel.

NIB	EXC.	V.G.	GOOD
600	525	450	400

■ SAIGA 100

A semi-automatic hunting rifle in .308 or .30-06. 21.8-inch barrel. Adjustable sights. Black synthetic stock. 3 round magazine. Weight: 8.3 lbs.

NIB	EXC.	V.G.	GOOD
600	525	450	400

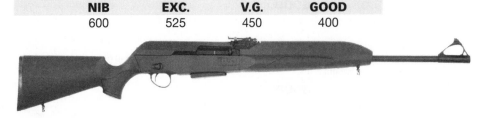

SAIGA 100

■ SAIGA RIFLE

Available as a rifle with 20-1/2 inch barrel or a carbine with 16-1/4-inch barrel. Offered in 5.56mm/.223, 5.45x39mm and 7.62x39mm. Black synthetic stocks. Factory magazine capacity is five and ten rounds. Higher capacity magazines are available. The importer has added thumbhole type stocks to the available options for the Saiga. Price for base model rifle in 7.62x39mm.

NIB	EXC.	V.G.	GOOD
400	375	325	275

SAIGA RIFLE CAL. 223, 5.45X39MM OR 7.62X39MM

SABRE DEFENCE INDUSTRIES
Nashville, Tennessee

Website: www.sabredefence.com

Sabre manufacturers a line of AR-15 type rifles.

■ COMPETITION DELUXE PISTON

Sabre A3 upper, mid-length gas piston operating system, Magpul CTR stock, free-float quadrail handguards, ergo grip, match trigger. Available with a fluted 16-, 18- or 20-inch barrel. Chambered in 5.56. Weight: 7.8 lbs.

MSRP	EXC.	V.G.	GOOD
2599	2250	2000	1750

■ M4 TACTICAL GAS PISTON CARBINE

Cal. 5.56mm Features a 14.5- or 16-inch M4 contour barrel. Sabre A3 upper and matched lower, Carbine length gas piston operating system, Magpul CTR stock, free float quadrail handguards, ergo grip, match trigger.

MSRP	EXC.	V.G.	GOOD
2499	2200	1950	1750

■ M5 TACTICAL PISTON CARBINE

As above with a mid-length gas piston operating system and quad rail handguards.

MSRP	EXC.	V.G.	GOOD
2499	2200	1950	1750

■ A2 NATIONAL MATCH

Sabre A3 upper and matched lower CNC machined from 7075-T6 forgings, cal. 5.56mm/.223. 20-inch barrel. A2 stock, National Match handguards, A2 grip, two-stage match trigger, forged front sights/NM rear sight. Discontinued.

EXC.	V.G.	GOOD
1400	1200	1000

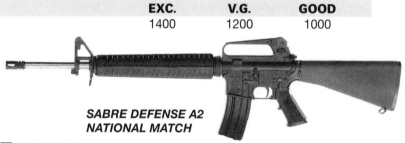

SABRE DEFENSE A2 NATIONAL MATCH

■ A4 RIFLE

As above with a flat top upper receiver.

MSRP	EXC.	V.G.	GOOD
1418	1100	950	800

■ COMPETITION DELUXE

Sabre A3 upper and matched lower CNC machined from 7075-T6 forgings, Magpul collapsible stock, quad rail handguards, ergo grip, match trigger, flip-up sights, Sabre competition gill-brake. Available with a fluted 16-, 18- or 20-inch barrel. Chambered in 5.56 or 6.5 Grendel (add $200).

MSRP	EXC.	V.G.	GOOD
2299	2000	1850	1700

SABRE COMPETITION DELUXE RIFLE

■ COMPETITION EXTREME

Sabre A3 upper and matched lower CNC machined from 7075-T6 forgings, Magpul CTR stock, tubular free-float handguards, ergo grip, match trigger, 45 degree flip-up sights. Cal. 5.56mm. Available with a fluted 16-, 18- or 20-inch barrel.

MSRP	EXC.	V.G.	GOOD
2189	1850	1750	1600

COMPETITION SPECIAL

Sabre A3 upper and matched lower CNC machined from 7075-T6 forgings, A2 stock, tubular free-float handguards, ergo grip, match trigger, gas block. Available with a fluted 16-, 18- or 20-inch barrel. Chambered in 5.56 or 6.5 Grendel (add $200).

MSRP	EXC.	V.G.	GOOD
1899	1650	1500	1350

FLAT TOP CARBINE

Sabre A3 upper and matched lower CNC machined from 7075-T6 forgings. 16-inch barrel. CAR round handguards, flip-up sights, ergo grip, single stage mil trigger, six-position collapsible stock.

MSRP	EXC.	V.G.	GOOD
1319	1200	1100	1000

HEAVY BENCH TARGET

Sabre A3 upper and matched lower CNC Machined from 7075-T6 forgings, tubular free-float handguards, flip-up sights, ergo grip, single stage adjustable trigger, A2 stock, sling swivel stud and bipod. Fitted with a 24-inch 410 stainless steel fluted match-grade heavy barrel, 11-degree target crown. Calibers: 5.56, .204 Ruger or 6.5 Grendel.

MSRP	EXC.	V.G.	GOOD
1889	1700	1550	1400

SABRE DEFENSE HEAVY BENCH TARGET

M4 CARBINE

Sabre flat top A3 upper and matched lower CNC machined from 7075-T6 forgings, M4 oval handguards, forged front sights, A2 grip, single stage mil trigger, CAR collapsible stock. 16-inch M4 contour barrel. Cal. 5.56mm, or 6.5 Grendel (add $200).

MSRP	EXC.	V.G.	GOOD
1377	1100	950	800

M5 CARBINE

As above with mid-length gas system and oval handguard.

MSRP	EXC.	V.G.	GOOD
1377	1100	950	800

M4 FLAT TOP

An M4 carbine fitted with flip-up front and rear sights.

MSRP	EXC.	V.G.	GOOD
1541	1200	1050	900

SABRE M4 FLAT TOP CARBINE

M5 FLAT TOP

As above with mid-length gas system and handguard.

MSRP	EXC.	V.G.	GOOD
1537	1200	1050	900

M4 TACTICAL

Sabre A3 upper and matched lower CNC machined from 7075-T6 forgings, quad rail handguards, Magpull CTR stock, flip-up sights, ergo grip, single stage mil trigger. 16-inch or 14-1/2-inch barrel with permanent A2 flash hider. Available in 5.56mm or 6.5 Grendel (add $200).

MSRP	EXC.	V.G.	GOOD
2042	1750	1550	1300

■ M5 TACTICAL

As above with mid-length gas system and quad rail handguard.

MSRP	EXC.	V.G.	GOOD
2117	1850	1600	1500

SABRE M5 TACTICAL RIFLE

■ PRECISION MARKSMAN RIFLE

Sabre A3 upper and matched lower CNC machined from 7075-T6 forgings. Fluted 20- or 24-inch barrel. Cal. 5.56mm. Mid-length gas system, rail handguards, ergo tactical deluxe grip with palm rest, match trigger, Magpul PRS stock. Add $200 for 6.5 Grendel.

MSRP	EXC.	V.G.	GOOD
2499	2200	2000	1750

SABRE PRECISION MARKSMAN RIFLE

■ SPR

Sabre A3 upper and matched lower CNC machined from 7075-T6 forgings, 16- or 18-inch fluted barrel. Magpul CTR stock, quad rail handguard, ergo grip, match trigger, flip-up sights, bipods. Add $200 for 6.5 Grendel.

MSRP	EXC.	V.G.	GOOD
2499	2250	2000	1750

SABRE SPECIAL PURPOSE RIFLE

■ VARMINT

Sabre A3 upper and matched lower CNC machined from 7075-T6 forgings, 20-inch fluted barrel, tubular free float handguards, ergo grip, match trigger, A2 stock, sling swivel stud.

MSRP	EXC.	V.G.	GOOD
1709	1550	1400	1250

■ LIGHT SABRE

16-inch barrel, Sabre A3 upper receiver, one-piece polymer lower assembly, mid-length CAR handguard. Weight: 5.9 lbs

MSRP	EXC.	V.G.	GOOD
1229	1000	850	700

SAIGA
Izhmash, Russia

See Russian American Armory.

SIG ARMS AG
Neuhausen, Switzerland

■ PE-57

A semi-automatic version of the Stgw57 Swiss service rifle. Chambered in 7.5x55mm. 18-3/4-inch barrel. Folding bipod. Wood stock. Approximately 4000 were produced. Discontinued in 1988.

EXC.	V.G.	GOOD
5000	4500	4000

■ SIG AMT

A version of the PE-57 but chambered in 7.62mm/.308. Fewer than 3000 were produced. Discontinued in 1988.

EXC.	V.G.	GOOD
6000	5250	4500

SIG AMT

■ SIG 550

A semi-automatic version of the current Swiss service rifle. The 550 has an 18-inch barrel. Synthetic side-folding stock and forearm. One small lot was imported in 1988, just before the import ban.

EXC.	V.G.	GOOD
8500	7500	6500

■ SIG 551

A semi-automatic version of current Swiss service rifle. The 551 has an 16-inch barrel. Synthetic side folding stock and forearm. One small lot was imported in 1988, just before the import ban.

EXC.	V.G.	GOOD
10,000	8500	7500

SIG SAUER
Exeter, N.H.

■ SIG556

A U.S. produced version of the SIG 550, chambered for 5.56mm/.223. It has a 16-inch barrel. Gas piston operation. Flat top receiver with picatinney rail and flip-up sights. Magpul CAR-15 type sliding buttstock. Uses AR-15/M-16 series magazines. Discontinued.

EXC.	V.G.	GOOD
1250	1100	975

■ SIG556 SWAT

As above with a quad rail forearm. Magpul sliding stock. Discontinued.

EXC.	V.G.	GOOD
1250	1100	975

SIG-SAUER 556 SWAT RIFLE

■ SIG 556 CLASSIC

A new model that more closely copies the Swiss military issue SIG 550. The Classic name is based on the rifle's Swiss heritage. The adjustable stock snaps and securely locks into a folded position with a length-of-pull that can be preset by the user. The clean tapered forend styling allows for a firmer grip and better control. The redesigned trigger housing improves access to functional controls while improving the overall ergonomics of the rifle. The SIG556 operating system is topped off with a red dot and a rotary diopter sighting system that ensures quick target acquisition. Weight: 8.2 lbs.

MSR	EXC.	V.G.	GOOD
2250	1800	1500	1150

SIG 556 CLASSIC RIFLE

■ SIG 556 CLASSIC SWAT

Features include an aluminum quad-rail handguard that is ideally suited for mounting tactical accessories. The stock is a hinged folding Swiss-style that is able to collapse for ease of transportation or use in tight quarters. This feature is made possible by a new stock interface into the trigger casing. The adjustable stock snaps and securely locks into a folded position with a length-of-pull that can be preset by the user. Obtaining a sight picture with the SIG556 SWAT model now takes place using a new rear rotary diopter sight, utilizing aperture calibrations from close quarter ranges out to 100m, 200m, and 300m.

MSR	EXC.	V.G.	GOOD
2400	1850	1600	1250

■ SIG 556 DMR

Features include a 21-inch military grade cold hammer-forged heavy contour barrel. The rifle is chambered in 5.56mm NATO, with a twist rate of 1:10. The match grade heavy barrel features a target crown and matte black nitride finish for the ultimate in corrosion resistance. The forearm, housing the gas operating system, is a vented non-slip polymer featuring the SIG TriRai design with three integrated Picatinny rails for mounting a bipod and other accessories. The Picatinny rail equipped receiver is made of high strength steel with a durable wear-resistant Nitron-X finish. The trigger housing is machined from an aircraft grade aluminum alloy forging with a hard-coat anodized finish designed to survive extreme conditions. The rifle comes equipped with an enhanced single stage target trigger, ambidextrous safety and is designed to accept standard AR magazines. The ergonomically designed pistol grip features an integrated storage compartment.

MSR	EXC.	V.G.	GOOD
2400	1850	1600	1250

■ SIG 556 SCM

Designed especially for sportsman, the SCM is compliant in most states and features a fixed A2-style stock, a 16-inch barrel with crowned muzzle, and ships with a standard 10-round magazine.

MSR	EXC.	V.G.	GOOD
1839	1600	1300	1000

■ SIG 556 PATROL RIFLE

Features include a 16-inch barrel with the maneuverability and quick pointing ergonomics of the SIG556 Short in a compact package. The reduced length gas system and Swiss style forearms provide the ideal combination of functionality and light weight.

MSR	EXC.	V.G.	GOOD
2000	1700	1400	1100

SIG 556 SWAT PATROL RIFLE

s above with a quad rail forearm.

MSR	EXC.	V.G.	GOOD
2143	1800	1500	1200

SIG 556 SWAT PATROL RIFLE

SIG 522 CLASSIC

The look and feel of the classic SIG556 ™ in .22 Long Rifle featuring SIG556 parts including a Swiss type folding stock and polymer forend on a durable metal receiver with integral Picatinny rail. The SIG522 provides the avid sport shooter plenty of action on a classic military style platform that give the look, feel and dependability of the full size SIG556. 10 or 25 round magazines.

MSR	EXC.	V.G.	GOOD
572	500	450	400

.22LR SIG 522 RIFLE

SIG 522 SWAT

As above with a quad rail forearm. 10 or 25 round magazines.

MSR	EXC.	V.G.	GOOD
686	600	500	450

SMITH & WESSON
Springfield, Massachusetts

In 2006 S&W entered the paramilitary rifle market with the release of the Military and Police (M&P) line. These are based on the AR-15 pattern.

website: www.smith-wesson.com

M&P 15 RIFLE

Cal. 5.56mm/.223. 16-inch M4 contour barrel. flat top upper receiver with removable A2 carry handle and rear sight. CAR type six-position telescoping buttstock.

NIB	EXC.	V.G.	GOOD
1406	1000	925	850

S&W M&P 15 RIFLE

■ M&P 15A RIFLE

As above with a flat top receiver. Rear folding sight.

NIB	EXC.	V.G.	GOOD
1422	1000	925	850

■ M&P 15T TACTICAL RIFLE

Flat top receiver. Folding rear sight. Quad rail free float handguard Six-position collapsible stock. M15FT version has the stock fixed in the extended position, to comply with some state laws.

NIB	EXC.	V.G.	GOOD
1888	1250	1100	950

S&W M&P 15T TACTICAL RIFLE/M&P M15FT WITH FIXED STOCK

■ M&P 15PC RIFLE

Cal. 5.56/.223. 20-inch heavy barrel. Free float round handguard. Flat top receiver. A2 stock.

NIB	EXC.	V.G.	GOOD
1967	1850	1675	1500

S&W M&P 15PC RIFLE

■ M&P 15VTAC RIFLE

16-inch barrel with Sure Fire flash hider, flat top receiver, Viking Tactical JP handguard with three adjustable rails, G-2 light with mount, six-position CAR stock.

NIB	EXC.	V.G.	GOOD
2196	1850	1600	1350

■ M&P 15 MOE

Magpul Original Equipment. M&P15 rifle featuring Magpul MBUS rear sight, handguard, MOE stock and grip. Weight: 6.5 lbs. New in 2010.

NIB	EXC.	V.G.	GOOD
1375	1250	1050	850

■ M&P 15 PS

New S&W designed Piston Operating System. Flat top receiver, no sights, CAR handguard and six-position CAR stock.

NIB	EXC.	V.G.	GOOD
1531	1400	1200	1000

■ M&P 15 PSX

As above with a Troy Modular Quad Rail Handguard.

NIB	EXC.	V.G.	GOOD
1422	1000	925	850

■ M&P 15X

The M&P15X is designed with a new four-rail drop-in tactical handguard for easy accessory insertion and removal. The black anodized rifle measures 35 inches in length when fully extended and measures a compact 32 inches with the stock collapsed. The rifle is standard with an A2 post front sight, a rear Troy folding battle sight, and a 30 round detachable magazine.

NIB	EXC.	V.G.	GOOD
1525	1250	1075	900

■ M&P 15 OR

The M&P15OR (Optics Ready) rifle features a gas block with integral picatinny-style rail for additional sight mounting. The rifle is without standard sights, providing users with a broad platform for additional optics, lights or other aiming devices. The black anodized rifle measures 35 inches in length when fully extended and measures a compact 32 inches with the stock collapsed. The M&P15OR is standard with a 30 round detachable magazine.

NIB	EXC.	V.G.	GOOD
1209	975	900	800

■ M&P 15 FT

The M&P15FT (Fixed Tactical) features a fixed-position stock and a 10 round detachable magazine making it compliant for sale in Connecticut, Massachusetts, Maryland, New Jersey and New York. The rifle is standard with a front and rear Troy folding battle sight.

NIB	EXC.	V.G.	GOOD
1888	1000	925	850

■ M&P 15-22

.22LR version of the M&P 15 featuring 16-inch barrel, flat top receiver, removable adjustable rear sight, quad rail handguard, six position CAR stock. 10 or 25 round polymer magazine. Weight: 5.5 lbs.

NIB	EXC.	V.G.	GOOD
569	475	400	350

■ M&P 15-22 MOE

As above with Magpul Original Equipment sights, stock and grip.

NIB	EXC.	V.G.	GOOD
687	575	500	425

SPITFIRE MFG. CO
Phoenix, Arizona

■ SPITFIRE CARBINE

This was probably the first .45-caliber semi-automatic rifle made to look like a sub-machinegun. It resembles the Model 1928 Thompson. It fires from an open bolt, just like real SMGs. In fact, it was so easy to convert these to full-automatic that in 1968 the BATFE ruled that they were machine guns. This means that they had to be registered just like a machine gun. If a Spitfire was not registered by the close of the 1968 amnesty it is considered "contraband" today. There is currently no way to register one. Values below are for registered examples.

EXC.	V.G.	GOOD
9000	7000	5000

SPITFIRE CARBINE, .45 CAL., RULED A MACHINEGUN BY BATFE

SPRINGFIELD ARMORY USA
Geneseo, Illinois

Note: In January of 1993, Springfield Inc. purchased the inventory, name, patents, trademarks, and logo of the Springfield Armory Inc. Products, services, and distribution patterns remain unchanged. They are currently using the name Springfield Armory U.S.A.

■ M1A BASIC RIFLE

Chambered for .308 Win. and fitted with a painted black fiberglass stock. Barrel length is 22 inches without flash suppressor. Front sights are military square post and rear military aperture (battle sights). Magazine is a 5, 10, or 20 round box. Rifle weighs 9 lbs.

NIB	EXC.	V.G.	GOOD
1250	1050	900	800

SPRINGFIELD ARMORY M1A BASIC RIFLE

■ M1A STANDARD RIFLE

This model is chambered for the .308 Win. or .243 cartridge. Also fitted with a 22-inch barrel but with adjustable rear sight. Fitted with a walnut stock with fiberglass handguard, it comes equipped with a 20 round box magazine. Weight 9 lbs.

NIB	EXC.	V.G.	GOOD
1500	1250	1050	900

A 1975-VINTAGE SPRINGFIELD ARMORY M1-A RIFLE

■ M1A-A1 BUSH RIFLE

Chambered for .308 or .243 cartridge with choice of walnut stock, black fiberglass, or folding stock (no longer produced). Fitted with 18.25-inch barrel. Rifle weighs 8.75 lbs.

NIB	EXC.	V.G.	GOOD
1400	1200	1000	900

Note: Add $250 for folding stock.

■ M1A SCOUT SQUAD RIFLE

This .308 model is fitted with an 18-inch barrel and a choice of fiberglass or walnut stock. Military sights. Supplied with 10 round magazine. Weight with fiberglass stock is about 9 lbs., with walnut stock about 9.3 pounds. Camo finish.

NIB	EXC.	V.G.	GOOD
1600	1350	1200	1000

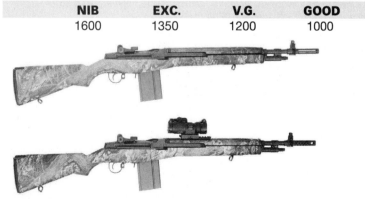

SPRINGFIELD ARMORY M1-A SCOUT RIFLE

M1A NATIONAL MATCH

Chambered for .308 as standard or choice of .243 cartridge. Fitted with a medium weight National Match 22-inch glass bedded barrel and walnut stock. Special rear sight adjustable to half minute of angle clicks. Weighs 10.06 lbs.

NIB	EXC.	V.G.	GOOD
2050	1750	1400	1250

SPRINGFIELD ARMORY M1A NATIONAL MATCH

M1A SUPER MATCH

This is Springfield's best match grade rifle. Chambered for .308 as standard and also .243 cartridge. Fitted with special over-size heavy walnut stock, heavy Douglas match glass bedded barrel, and special rear lugged receiver. Special rear adjustable sight. Weighs 10.125 lbs.

NIB	EXC.	V.G.	GOOD
2500	2000	1750	1500

Note: *For walnut stock and Douglas barrel add $165. For black McMillan stock and Douglas stainless steel barrel add $600. For Marine Corp. camo stock and Douglas stainless steel barrel add $600. For adjustable walnut stock and Douglas barrel add $535. For adjustable walnut stock and Krieger barrel add $900.*

SPRINGFIELD M1A SUPER MATCH

M1A MODEL 25 CARLOS HATHCOCK

Introduced in 2001 this model features a match trigger, stainless steel heavy match barrel, McMillan synthetic stock with adjustable cheek pad, Harris bipod, and other special features. Chambered for the .308 cartridge. Weight is about 12.75 lbs. A special logo bears his signature.

NIB	EXC.	V.G.	GOOD
4650	3500	2800	2200

M21 LAW ENFORCEMENT/TACTICAL RIFLE

Similar to the Super Match with the addition of a special stock with rubber recoil pad and height adjustable cheekpiece. Available as a special order only. Weighs 11.875 lbs.

NIB	EXC.	V.G.	GOOD
2400	1750	1350	900

M1A SOCOM 16

This M1A1 rifle features a 16.25-inch barrel with muzzlebrake. Black fiberglass stock with steel buttplate. Forward scout-style scope mount. Front sight post has tritium insert. Weight is about 9 lbs. Introduced in 2004.

NIB	EXC.	V.G.	GOOD
1525	1250	1100	1000

SPRINGFIELD ARMORY M1A SOCOM 16

M1A SOCOM II

Introduced in 2005 this model features a full length top rail and short bottom rail for accessories. Weight is about 11 lbs.

NIB	EXC.	V.G.	GOOD
1700	1450	1250	1100

M1A SOCOM URBAN RIFLE
Similar to the SOCOM but with black and white camo stock. Introduced in 2005.

NIB	EXC.	V.G.	GOOD
1725	1475	1250	1100

SAR-48
This is a semi-automatic copy of the FN-FAL rifle. Chambered for the .308 Win. cartridge. It is fitted with a 21-inch barrel and has a fully adjustable rear sight. Weight is approximately 9.5 lbs. Made in Brazil by Imbel. Import stopped by the 1989 ban.

EXC.	V.G.	GOOD
1400	1250	1000

SAR-48 HEAVY BARREL
As above with a heavier barrel and folding bipod. Based on an Israeli pattern FAL light machine gun.

EXC.	V.G.	GOOD
1750	1400	1150

SAR-4800 SPORTER
This is a post ban version of the SAR-48 with a thumbhole stock. Made in Brazil by Imbel. Imported by Springfield Armory.

EXC.	V.G.	GOOD
1100	900	750

SAR-4800 MATCH 5.56 SPORTER
A version of the FAL chambered in 5.56mm/.223. Made in Brazil, by Imbel. Imported briefly in the 1990s.

EXC.	V.G.	GOOD
1400	1200	1000

SAR- 3
Caliber .308 copy of the HK 91 rifle made in Greece. Imported by Springfield Armory in the late 1980's.

EXC.	V.G.	GOOD
1500	1300	1100

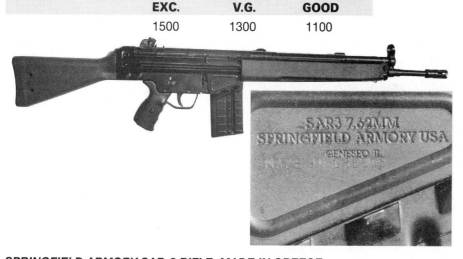

SPRINGFIELD ARMORY SAR-3 RIFLE, MADE IN GREECE

SAR-8
This semi-automatic rifle is similar in appearance to the HK-91. It is chambered for the .308 Winchester and is of the recoil operated delayed roller-lock design. It was assembled by Springfield Armory using a cast aluminum receiver made by DC Industries in Bloomington, Minnesota. Barrel length is 18 inches and the rear sight is fully adjustable. Weight is about 8.7 lbs.

EXC.	V.G.	GOOD
900	750	600

SAR-8 SPORTER
This is a copy of the HK G-3 that uses a stamped steel receiver, as found on the original HK made guns. Manufactured in Greece by EBO and imported by Springfield Armory. Synthetic thumbhole stock.

EXC.	V.G.	GOOD
1200	1000	800

■ SAR-8 TACTICAL

Similar to the above model but fitted with a heavy barrel. Synthetic Dragunov type stock with adjustable cheek rest. Round handguard with folding bipod. Fewer than 100 imported into US.

EXC.	V.G.	GOOD
1350	1100	900

■ M-60 SA 1 SEMI-AUTOMATIC

A semiautomatic version of the M-60 machine gun. Cal 7.62 NATO. Belt fed. Limited production in the late 1980s.

EXC.	V.G.	GOOD
7500	6000	4500

STAG ARMS
New Britain, Connecticut
Website: www.stagarms.com

Note: *All Stag rifles are available in left hand configuration. The prices are approximately $25-$40 higher than the right handed models listed here.*

■ STAG-15 MODEL 1

Basic M-4 Carbine pattern. Cal. 5.56mm/.223. 16-inch M-4 barrel with flash hider and bayonet lug. Flat top receiver with a detachable A2 carry handle and rear sight. Six-position collapsible buttstock.

MSRP	EXC.	V.G.	GOOD
949	875	825	750

■ STAG-15 MODEL 2

As above but with a flat top upper receiver. Includes Midwest flip type rear sight assembly.

MSRP	EXC.	V.G.	GOOD
940	850	800	750

STAG ARMS MODEL 2 RIFLE

■ STAG-15 MODEL 2T

As above but with a A.R.M.S. sight system and Samson Star C Quad rail handguard.

MSRP	EXC.	V.G.	GOOD
1130	950	875	800

■ STAG-15 MODEL 3

M-4 type carbine featuring a flat top receiver and gas block. No sights. Six-position collapsible buttstock.

MSRP	EXC.	V.G.	GOOD
895	825	775	725

■ STAG-15 MODEL 4

20-inch barrel. Flat top receiver with detachable A2 carry handle and rear sight. A2 stock.

MSRP	EXC	V.G.	GOOD
1015	875	800	725

STAG ARMS MODEL 4 RIFLE, LEFT HAND VERSION

■ STAG-15 MODEL 5 6.8SPC
Cal. 6.8 SPC. 16 inch barrel. Flat top receiver. Six-position collapsible buttstock. 25 round magazine.

MSRP	EXC.	V.G.	GOOD
1045	900	825	750

■ STAG-15 MODEL 6 6.8 SUPER VARMITER
6.8mm SPC. 24-inch heavy barrel. No flash hider. Flat top receiver. No sights. Two stage trigger. Free float round handguard. A2 type fixed stock.

MSRP	EXC.	V.G.	GOOD
1055	950	875	800

■ STAG-15 MODEL 7 6.8SPC HUNTER
As above with a 20.7-inch barrel

MSRP	EXC.	V.G.	GOOD
1055	900	825	750

■ STAG-15 MODEL 8 PISTON
Cal. 5.56mm. 16 inch M4 contour barrel, Stag Arms piston system. Flat top receiver with Midwest Industries front and rear flip sights, CAR stock and handguard.

MSRP	EXC.	V.G.	GOOD
1145	1000	900	800

STAG ARMS PISTON RIFLE

STERLING ARMAMENT LTD.
Dagenham, England

■ MARK VI CARBINE
A 9mm semi-automatic carbine based on the Sterling sub-machinegun. 16-inch barrel. Folding stock. 10 and 32 round magazines. Limited importation until 1989, when it ceased altogether.

EXC.	V.G.	GOOD
2500	2200	1700

STERLING ARMAMENT MARK VI 9MM CARBINE

■ PARAPISTOL MK7

A pistol version of the Sterling SMG. It was made with a 4- or 9-inch barrel. No stock. 10 and 32 round magazines. Limited importation until 1989.

EXC.	V.G.	GOOD
1500	1200	900

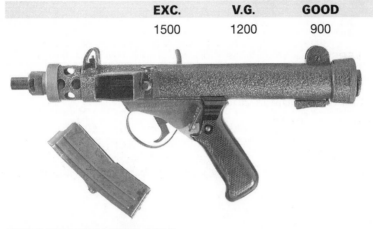

STERLING PARAPISTOL MK 7

STEYR
Austria

■ AUG

A 5.56mm semi-automatic rifle. Bullpup configuration, with magazine located in front of hand grip. 20-inch barrel. Integral Swarovski 1.5x scope. Green composite stock. Import discontinued in 1989.

EXC.	V.G.	GOOD
3500	3000	2500

STEYR AUG RIFLE CAL. 5.56MM/.223

■ AUG POLICE MODEL

A shipment of AUGs with a 16-inch barrel and black stock was stopped by the 1989 import ban. The importer, Sports South, was eventually allowed to sell them to law enforcement officers only. Many have found their way into civilian hands.

EXC.	V.G.	GOOD
4000	3500	3000

■ AUG USR

A post-1989 import ban version of the AUG. The only difference from the original AUG is a stock piece behind the pistol grip as well as in front, and the 20-inch barrel has no flash suppressor. About 3000 were imported in the early 1990s.

EXC.	V.G.	GOOD
2750	2250	1800

■ AUG/A3 SA USA

A new version of the Steyr AUG rifle. Features a 16-inch quick change barrel with flash hider. Picatinny rail top. No sights. Weight: 8.1 lbs. Made for Steyr by Sabre Defense. New for 2010 .

MSRP	EXC.	V.G.	GOOD
1800	1700	1500	1300

THE NEW STEYR AUG/A3 RIFLE

S.W.D. INC.
Atlanta, Georgia

■ COBRAY M/11

A 9mm pistol based on the MAC-10 SMG pattern. Sheet metal construction. Parkerized finish. Pistols made before 1994 have a threaded muzzle. Three round synthetic magazine.

NIB	EXC.	V.G.	GOOD
375	300	250	200

■ M/11 CARBINE

As above with a 16-1/4-inch barrel. Removable steel stock. Discontinued in 1995.

EXC.	V.G.	GOOD
450	375	300

■ COBRAY M/12

A .380 version of the M/11.

	EXC.	V.G.	GOOD
350	300	250	

SUPERIOR ARMS
Wapello, Iowa
Website: www.superiorarms.com

Manufacturer of AR-15 Type Rifles

■ S-15 16-INCH M-4

Flat top receiver, no sights, Cal. .223 with a 16-inch M-4 contour barrel. CAR handguard. CAR six-position telescoping stock.

MSRP	EXC.	V.G.	GOOD
905	750	700	650

■ S-15 16-INCH CARBINE

As above with a standard contour barrel.

MSRP	EXC.	V.G.	GOOD
905	750	700	650

■ S-15 16-INCH MID-LENGTH

As above with a mid-length gas system and handguard.

MSRP	EXC.	V.G.	GOOD
925	750	700	650

■ S-15 20-INCH H-BAR

Flat top receiver. No sights, 20-inch heavy barrel, A-2 round handguards, A2 stock.

MSRP	EXC.	V.G.	GOOD
985	800	725	650

■ S-15 20-INCH VARMINT

Flat top receiver, Montana Premium 20-inch stainless steel bull barrel, aluminum free float handguard, rail gas block, A2 stock.

MSRP	EXC.	V.G.	GOOD
1075	850	775	700

TENNESSEE GUNS
Louisville, Tennessee

■ SKORPION VZ-61

A semi-automatic copy of the Czechoslovakian Vz-61 machine pistol. Caliber 7.65mm/.32 automatic. It has a 4-1/2-inch barrel, with a total length of 10-1/2 inches. Unloaded weight is under 2-1/2 pounds. 10- and 20 round magazines. Made in the Czech Republic. Imported by TN Guns. Discontinued. See listing in CZ section.

EXC.	V.G.	GOOD
650	550	450

TENNESSEE GUNS CZECH VZ-61 SKORPION 7.65MM/.32 AUTO

TNW FIREARMS
Vernonia, Oregon
Website: www.tnwfirearms.com

This company manufactures semi-automatic versions of famous machine guns. Distributed through Atlantic Firearms, Military Gun Supply, Centerfire Systems and others.

■ SEMI-AUTO M2HB

Based on the legendary Browning M-2 machinegun in .50 caliber. The modified original Browning M2 heavy-barrel has been remanufactured using genuine G.I. parts. Specs and design of this remanufactured weapon are very close to the original. Intended for sharpshooters, re-enactors or military vehicle enthusiasts. Fires commercial ammunition or blanks. All components internal and external are finished with a gray military type parkerization process. The M3 tripod is finished in current mil spec coating. Each M2HB includes an original IM2 training manual, headspacing gauge, 200 .50-caliber links, left and right hand feed mechanism and ATF approval letter. Several mounting and barrel configurations are available. Introduced in 1997.

NIB	EXC.	V.G.	GOOD
7000	6500	6000	5500

TNW SEMI-AUTO M2HB

■ SEMI-AUTO MG-34

This modified original German MG34 has been remanufactured using genuine parts to shoot semi-auto only and cannot be converted to full auto. It shoots closed bolt. Fires commercial 8mm ammunition. Includes belts and BATF approval letter.

NIB	EXC	V.G.	GOOD
3800	3600	3400	3200

TNW FIREARMS MG-34 SEMI-AUTOMATIC

■ BROWNING 1919 SEMI-AUTO

The Browning Model 1919 was the workhorse of the U.S. and allied armies. They were used in aircraft, tanks and front line infantry and saw action from WWII through Vietnam. This modified original Browning 1919-A4 has been remanufactured using genuine G.I. parts to shoot semi-auto only and cannot be converted to full-auto. This firearm is BATF approved and may be legally owned like any other rifle and in all fifty states. Fires commercial ammunition or blanks. All components internal and external are finished with a gray military type parkerization process. The tripod is finished in current milspec coating. Each 1919 comes with 250 links, a training manual and BATF approval letter. 30-06 or .308 caliber. Also offered in 1919A6 configuration with shoulder stock and bipod. Discontinued.

EXC.	V.G.	GOOD
1750	1600	1450

TNW FIREARMS BROWNING M1919 SEMI-AUTO

■ SEMI-AUTO PPSH-41

Made from original communist-manufactured parts sets with a new 16-inch barrel. Barrel cover has been extended to fit the longer barrel. Caliber 7.62x25mm. Action design fires from a closed bolt. Uses original PPSH 30 round stick and 50 round drum magazines. Extra magazines might need some fitting to feed properly.

NIB	EXC	V.G.	GOOD
795	700	600	500

■ SEMI-AUTO SUOMI M-31

Made with original Finnish Suomi parts. Cal. 9mm. New 16-inch barrel. Extended barrel shroud. Uses Suomi 36, 50 or 71 round magazines.

NIB	EXC	V.G.	GOOD
699	600	550	450

AUTHOR SHOOTING TNW SUOMI SEMI-AUTO

TRANSFORMATIONAL DEFENCE INDUSTRIES INC. (T.D.I.)
Virginia Beach, Virginia

■ KRISS VECTOR CRB/SO

This new design is based on a .45 caliber sub-machine gun offered by the same company. Here is some text from the product announcement:

"The KRISS Vector CRB/SO is an ATF-approved, 38-State legal (folding stock), 16 inch barrel semi-auto version of the KRISS Vector SMG. The KRISS Vector CRB/SO shares the same milspec frame, Super V operating system, materials and rugged housing as the KRISS Vector SMG. Same light weight. Same maneuverability. Same simple and easy to maintain Super V mechanism that reduces felt recoil by more than 60% and reduces barrel elevation by more than 95%. Non-folding stock and California versions will follow in mid-2008. Offering the same acclaimed shootability of its fully-automatic SMG (sub-machine gun) sibling, the new KRISS Vector CRB/SO (Special Ops) is the only semi-automatic firearm that actually helps the operator dramatically improve accuracy in the field or on the range. By re-vectoring the forces of recoil and significantly reducing muzzle climb, the innovative KRISS Super V technology provides a more compact and lighter-weight operating system creating a firearm that can be handled more effectively, more accurately and for longer periods of time, allowing the operator to put more rounds on target more often."

.45 ACP caliber. 16-inch barrel. Total length is 34-3/4 inches with the stock in open position. Weight is 5.0 pounds. Picatinny accessory rail on top. Uses Glock 21 magazines with capacity of 10, 13 and 30 rounds.

NIB	EXC	V.G.	GOOD
2395	2000	1750	1500

T.D.I. KRISS VECTOR CARBINE, CAL. .45

UMAREX USA
Ft. Smith, Arkansas

This is the U.S. importer of Colt and Heckler & Koch licensed .22LR versions of the MP-5 sub-machine gun and the AR-15 rifle. The guns are made in Germany by Walther.

■ COLT M4 CARBINE .22 TACTICAL RIMFIRE

Features a 16-inch M4 contour barrel. Flat top receiver with removable A2 carry handle and rear sight. CAR handguards. CAR telescoping stock. .22LR 30 round magazine. Weight: 6 lbs.

MSRP	EXC.	V.G.	GOOD
599	525	450	375

UMAREX-COLT M4 CARBINE .22LR

■ COLT M4 OPS

Features a 16-inch M4 contour barrel. Flat top receiver with removable A2 rear sight, RIS Rail Interface System quad rail handguard, CAR telescoping stock.

MSRP	EXC.	V.G.	GOOD
640	550	475	400

UMAREX-COLT M4 OPS

■ COLT M16 RIFLE

.22LR version of the standard M-16A2 rifle. Features a 21-inch barrel. Flat top receiver with removable A2 carry handle/rear sight. Round handguards. A2 buttstock.

MSRP	EXC.	V.G.	GOOD
599	525	450	375

■ COLT M16 SPR

The M16 Special Purpose Rifle features a flat top receiver with rear andd front folding sights. Rifle length RIS quad rail handguard. A2 stock. Weight: 6.5 lbs.

MSRP	EXC.	V.G.	GOOD
670	600	500	400

UMAREX-COLT M16 SPECIAL PURPOSE RIFLE

■ MP5 A5

Features HK style a retractable stock, adjustable sights and forearm. 16-inch barrel is concealed inside a simulated suppressor. Cal. .22LR, 10 and 25 round magazines. Weight: 6.0 lbs.

MSRP	EXC.	V.G.	GOOD
905	825	775	725

UMAREX HK MP-5 RIFLE .22LR

■ MP5 SD

Features HK style a retractable stock, adjustable sights and forearm. 16-inch barrel is concealed inside a simulated Sound Dampener that matches the appearance of the original MP5SD. Cal. .22LR, 10 and 25 round magazines.

MSRP	EXC.	V.G.	GOOD
905	825	775	725

UMAREX HK MP-5SD RIFLE

■ HK 416

A copy of the AR-15. Features a flat top receiver with HK style sights, quad rail handguard, collapsible buttstock. .22LR, 16-inch barrel. 10 or 20 rd. magazines. Weight: 6.8 lbs.

MSRP	EXC.	V.G.	GOOD
905	825	775	725

UMAREX HK-416 RIFLE .22LR

◼ HK 416 PISTOL
A handgun with a 8.5-inch barrel. HK type adjustable sights. Quad rail handguard.

MSRP	EXC.	V.G.	GOOD
905	825	775	725

UMAREX HK416 PISTOL

UNIVERSAL FIREARMS
Hialeah, Florida/
Jacksonville, Arkansas

This company has manufactured a version of the U.S. Carbine Cal. .30 M-1 since the 1960s. The early guns consisted of a new receiver with USGI surplus parts. As the sources for original parts dried up they began manufacturing their own parts. At some point they re-engineered the receiver, trigger housing, and slide. The newer guns have only partial parts interchangeability with the G.I. M-1 Carbines. The factory model numbers are listed; however, these numbers do not always appear on the firearms. All can use U.S.G.I. M-1 carbine magazines.

◼ EARLY M-1 CARBINE
Assembled with a Universal receiver and all U.S.G.I. carbine parts.

EXC.	V.G.	GOOD
500	425	350

◼ MODEL 1000
The base model G.I. carbine copy. 18-inch barrel. Blue finish. Birch stock. Usually found with a steel handguard.

EXC.	V.G.	GOOD
400	350	300

◼ MODEL 1010
As above, but nickel plated.

EXC.	V.G.	GOOD
450	400	350

MODEL 1015

As above, but gold plated.

EXC.	V.G.	GOOD
500	425	350

MODEL 1005 DELUXE

M-1 carbine with a polished blue finish and Monte Carlo style stock.

EXC.	V.G.	GOOD
425	375	325

MODEL 1006 STAINLESS STEEL

M-1 carbine made from stainless steel.

EXC.	V.G.	GOOD
500	450	400

MODEL 1256 FERRET

M-1 carbine chambered for 256 Winchester Magnum.

EXC.	V.G.	GOOD
400	350	300

MODEL 5000 PARATROOPER

M-1 carbine with a folding or collapsible stock.

EXC.	V.G.	GOOD
475	425	375

MODEL 5006 PARATROOPER STAINLESS

As above, made from stainless steel.

EXC.	V.G.	GOOD
525	475	400

1981 COMMEMORATIVE CARBINE

Commemorates the 40th anniversary of WWII, 1941-81. A limited production carbine, sold in a case with accessories.

NIB	EXC.	V.G.	GOOD
600	400	350	300

MODEL 3000 ENFORCER PISTOL

A pistol version of the M-1 Carbine with an 11-1/4-inch barrel. Discontinued in 1983.

◆ Blued finish

EXC.	V.G.	GOOD
550	475	400

◆ Nickel finish

EXC.	V.G.	GOOD
600	550	500

UNIVERSAL FIREARMS ENFORCER PISTOL CAL .30M-1

◆ **Gold finish**

EXC.	V.G.	GOOD
700	600	500

◆ **Stainless Steel**

EXC.	V.G.	GOOD
650	550	450

U.S. ORDNANCE
Reno, Nevada

This company is the licensed U.S. manufacturer of M-60 series of machine guns for military and law enforcement sales. They also offer a line of semi-automatic versions of famous belt-fed machine guns. The semi-automatic models are distributed by Desert Ordnance.

website: www.desertord.com

■ M-60 STANDARD SEMI-AUTO

The M60 is a gas operated, disintegrating link, belt fed, air-cooled machine gun in semi-auto configuration. Chambered for 7.62mm NATO/ .308 Winchester. It fires from an closed bolt and features a 22-inch quick-change barrel. The barrel is Stellite-lined and chrome plated for long service. Each gun comes with 200 links, manual, cleaning kit, sling, and a one-year warranty. Discontinued.

EXC	V.G.	GOOD
10000	8000	6000

■ M-60 E4 MODEL 1 SEMI-AUTO

The M60E4/Mk43 Mod1 features a redesigned machined aluminum top cover with an integrated picatinny rail and an aluminum rail interface system handguard provides for mounting optics, infrared laser systems and other sensors giving the weapon 24 hour capability. Fail-safe reversible piston, positive-lock gas cylinder extension. Barrel changing handle eliminates need for heat mittens. Lightweight, one-hand operated receiver mounted bipod eliminates the weight of a bipod on the spare barrel. Lightweight forearm/pistol grip for improved control and protection during firing. Feed cover eliminates charging jams and improves operator safety. Lightweight trigger assembly with ambidextrous safety switch and winter trigger guard allows gun to be fired with winter gloves. New flat spring on trigger assembly prevents accidental detachment of the assembly. Lightweight buttstock with hinged shoulder rest and improved buffer attachment mechanism provides for fail-safe attachment of the buttstock to the receiver. Each gun comes in a custom Storm I3300 case with 200 links, manual, cleaning kit, sling, and a one-year warranty.

MSRP	EXC.	V.G.	GOOD
12000	10000	8000	6000

U.S. ORDNANCE M-60E4 SEMI AUTOMATIC 7.62MM/.308

■ M-60D ENHANCED SEMI-AUTO

The M60D is a gas operated, disintegrating link, belt fed, air-cooled semi-auto version of the machine gun. It fires from an closed bolt and features a quick-change barrel. The barrel is Stellite-lined and chrome plated for long service. Unlike the earlier version, the M60D Enhanced does not require a mitten to change barrels. The carrying handle is located on the barrel similar to the M60E3 and M60E4 versions to ease quick barrel changes. The M60D model differs from the standard M60 in that the buttstock and trigger grip assemblies are replaced with spade grips and a spade trigger assembly. The rear sight is replaced with a ring sight to assist in acquiring and tracking targets. This permits aimed fire from a pedestal or other similar mount. Other parts are required to adapt the gun to the ammunition feed system. The M60D Enhanced incorporates a bipod mounted on the front of the receiver instead of mounted on the barrel. The bipod is the same one used on the M60E4 therefore increasing interchangeability. The new bipod is lighter but just as strong as the original and reduces the weight and bulk of the spare barrels. The M60D Enhanced also incorporates some of trie features found on the M60E4 feedcover, which permits the user to load the weapon with the bolt in the closed position. Each gun comes with 200 links, manual, cleaning kit, sling, and a one-year warranty.

MSRP	EXC.	V.G.	GOOD
13000	10000	8500	7000

■ MODEL 1919

A semi-automatic version of the Browning Model 1919 machinegun. Manufactured in A4 or A6 configuration. Recoil operated, semi-auto. Gray parkerized finish. Caliber: 7.62x51mm NATO/.308 Winchester. Weight: A4 approximately 31 lbs., A6 approximately 32.5 lbs., Length: A4 approximately 41 inches, A6 approximately 53 inches. Barrel length approximately 24 inches. Sights: front flip-up blade, rear leaf adjustable. Stock: A6 Israeli marked metal detachable.; Handgrip: A6 Israeli marked, wood and metal detachable. Feed Device: Cloth or metal linked belts. Discontinued.

EXC.	V.G.	GOOD
1500	1250	950

VALKYRIE ARMS, LTD.
Olympia, Washington

This company manufactured semi-automatic versions of the Browning M1919 machine gun, M3A1 SMG and the Sten SMG. They filed for Chapter 13 bankruptcy in 2008 and are now operating under new management. Manufacture of the semi-auto guns has been discontinued.

■ U.S. M-3A1 GREASE GUN, PISTOL VERSION

.45 ACP semi-automatic. A faithful replica of this well-known U.S. submachine gun. 8-inch barrel. Uses original M-3 magazines.

EXC.	V.G.	GOOD
800	700	600

VALKYRIE ARMS M-3A1 PISTOL, .45 CALIBER

■ M-3 A1 CARBINE VERSION

As above but has a 16-1/2-inch barrel and a collapsible wire stock.

EXC.	V.G.	GOOD
850	750	650

VALKYRIE M-3 A1 CARBINE VERSION

■ M-3 A1 CARBINE OSS VERSION

As above but with simulated suppressor over the barrel.

EXC.	V.G.	GOOD
900	800	700

Note: *Valkyrie Arms discontinued its semi-automatic Browning M1919 belt fed replicas in January of 2008. No examples could be found to establish a price range.*

VALMET, INC.
Jyvaskyla, Finland

Valmet semi-automatic rifles were imported from 1968 until 1989. Importers include Stoeger, Interarms, and Odin International. Valmet rifles are all variations of the AKM, but their quality is considered to be superior to that of many other makers.

■ M-62S

A copy of the Finnish M-62 service rifle in 7.62x39mm. Milled receiver. 16-5/8-inch barrel with flash hider and bayonet mount. Manufactured with a walnut or tubular steel stock. 15 or 30 round magazines.

EXC.	V.G.	GOOD
2500	2200	1900

1970'S VALMET FIREARMS ADVERTISING

■ MODEL 71S

As above but chambered in 5.56mm/.223. 16-1/4-inch barrel with flash hider and bayonet mount. Walnut or synthetic stock. Synthetic forearm. 15-, 30- or 40-round magazines.

EXC.	V.G.	GOOD
1500	1350	1200

VALMET MODEL 71S

MODEL 76S 5.56

A 5.56mm/.223 AKM type rifle. 16-1/4-inch barrel with flash hider and bayonet mount. Synthetic stock and forearm.

EXC.	V.G.	GOOD
1500	1350	1200

VALMET M-76S RIFLE

MODEL 76 FS

As above, with a side-folding stock.

EXC.	V.G.	GOOD
1700	1500	1300

MODEL 76S 7.62

A 7.62mm/.308 AKM type rifle. Has a 20-1/2-inch barrel with flash hider and bayonet mount. Synthetic stock and forearm.

EXC.	V.G.	GOOD
1750	1500	1250

MODEL 78

Caliber 7.62 NATO/.308. 24-1/2-inch heavy barrel with folding bipod. Wood or synthetic stock and forearm. 20 round magazines.

EXC.	V.G.	GOOD
2000	1750	1500

Note: Add $100-200 for each original 20 round magazine.

MODEL 78 5.56MM

As above but chambered in 5.56mm/.223.

EXC.	V.G.	GOOD
2000	1750	1500

MODEL 82

A bullpup style semi-automatic rifle in 5.56mm/.223.

EXC.	V.G.	GOOD
1700	1450	1200

VECTOR ARMS
North Salt Lake, Utah

This company manufactured semi-automatic versions of the UZI, HK 51 & 53 and AK-47 from the mid 1990's until 2009. They ceased operations in 2009.

UZI BASED FIREARMS

UZGI CARBINE

This is a semi-auto 9mm version of the famous UZI rifle produced by IMI, using a U.S. made Group Industries receiver. Comes with an 16-inch barrel (an 18-inch barrel is available for Michigan residents). Comes with a folding stock and black furniture. Takes the standard UZI mags. Receiver is heat treated for durability. Parkerized finish. Comes with one 25 round mag.

EXC.	V.G.	GOOD
650	600	550

UZ FSP FULL SIZE PISTOL

This is a 9mm, semi-auto pistol version of the full size rifle. It has a 10-inch barrel and a sling loop on the butt instead of a stock. Parkerized finish. Comes with one 25 round mag.

EXC.	V.G.	GOOD
625	575	525

■ UZ GI GG GREASE GUN RIFLE

This is the .45 ACP version of the 9mm rifle above. Due to .45 UZI mags not being available any more, this model has a converted lower that allows this rifle to accept 30 round Grease Gun mags instead. This is a plus since the .45 UZI mags only held 16 rounds maximum and these hold 30 rounds.

Note: *This lower is designed for most grease gun mags although some mags might require tweaking to work in this gun.*

EXC.	V.G.	GOOD
675	625	600

■ UZGIFXW CARBINE WITH FIXED STOCK

Features include a 16-inch barrel with black grips and a parkerized finish. Choices of wood are walnut, gray laminate, and brown-stained poplar. These stocks can be removed with a screwdriver and a folding stock installed if wanted. Comes with one 25 round mag. Also available in .45 ACP for an $85 upcharge. Comes with one 30 round grease gun mag.

EXC.	V.G.	GOOD
650	600	550

■ UZMR MINI RIFLE

This custom order, 9mm mini carbine rifle is made from a U.S.-made Group Industries receiver, shortened to make it mini length. It is then heat treated for more strength. It comes with a side folding stock and a 16-inch barrel, black furniture and parkerized finish. It takes the standard UZI mags. Comes with one 25 round mag.

EXC.	V.G	GOOD
1000	850	700

■ UZMP MINI PISTOL

This custom order, 9mm mini is the pistol version of the mini carbine rifle. IMI did not make a mini pistol. The receiver is a U.S.-made, Group Industries receiver, shortened to mini length and then heat treated for durability. It comes with the full-auto length ported barrel (7.75 inch), and has a sling loop on the butt end. Comes with black furniture and a parkerized finish. It takes the standard UZI mags. One 25 round mag is included.

Note: *A stock cannot be legally added to this weapon without extending the barrel to 16 inches and welding a stock bracket on the back of the gun.*

EXC.	V.G.	GOOD
850	775	700

FIREARMS BASED ON HECKLER AND KOCH DESIGNS

■ V51 R RIFLE

Based on the H&K Model 51. Caliber .308. Barrel extension added to comply with 16-inch barrel laws. Comes with standard barrel thread, M15x1.0, MP5 replica handguard, SEF lower and full auto bolt carrier. One 20 round mag included.

EXC.	V.G.	GOOD
1000	925	850

■ V51LS

V51 Rifle with 16-inch barrel and fake suppressor. MP5 replica handguard, SEF lower and full auto bolt carrier. One 20 round mag included.

EXC.	V.G.	GOOD
1050	975	900

VECTOR ARMS V51LS

■ V51L

V51 Rifle w/16-inch barrel and flash hider. MP5 replica handguard, SEF lower and full auto bolt carrier. One 20 round mag included.

EXC.	V.G.	GOOD
1050	975	900

■ V51P V-51 PISTOL

Cal. 308 V51. Same specs as the V51 with no stock attachment provision. 8-1/2-inch barrel. MP5 replica handguard. SEF lower and full auto bolt carrier.

EXC.	V.G.	GOOD
1050	975	900

■ V53L

Based on the H&K 53. cal. .223. V-53. With a 16-inch barrel with standard flash hider.

EXC.	V.G.	GOOD
1300	1200	1100

VECTOR V53L

■ V53LS

The V-53LS is a V-53 with a 16-inch barrel and slip-on fake suppressor. The fake suppressor is a copy of the SOCOM suppressor made for the military. It screws on over the long barrel and has three set screws. Comes with standard barrel thread, M15x1.0, MP5 replica handguard. One 40 round magazine included.

EXC.	V.G.	GOOD
1400	1300	1200

■ V53NS

This version features a plastic "Navy lower" trigger housing, original paddle mag release and barrel extension to comply with the 16-inch barrel rule. Comes with standard barrel thread, M15x1.0, and MP5 replica handguard. Comes with a 40 round aluminum mag.

EXC.	V.G.	GOOD
1300	1200	1100

■ V53 PISTOL

Cal. .223. Same specs as the V53 but no stock attachment provision. 8-1/2-inch barrel. Comes with one 40 round aluminum magazine.

EXC.	V.G.	GOOD
1100	1000	900

VECTOR V53 PISTOL

AK-47 TYPE FIREARMS

■ AK 103

U.S. made on a DC Industies 7.62x39 receiver using the 103 style side-folding black polymer stock and Bulgarian parts kit. Blued finish. Comes with one 30 round mag.

EXC.	V.G.	GOOD
750	650	550

■ YUGO KRINKOV PISTOL

This pistol is made on a DC Industries or Global receiver using a Yugo 7.62x39 Krink parts kit. Finish is black Guncote paint. Blonde wood furniture.

EXC	V.G	GOOD
800	700	600

■ RPK-74

Vector 5.45x39 semi-auto RPK made with Bulgarian Parts kits and a 1.6mm NODAK Spud precision receiver. Black paint finish. Comes with bipod and flash hider on standard AK threads (M14x1.0 left-hand). Has laminated wood furniture and a 40 round magazine. This rifle does not accept bayonets. Also available with poly furniture which is in good, not excellent condition.

EXC.	V.G.	GOOD
900	800	700

VECTOR RPK-74

■ AKUP

This Vector AK47, in caliber 7.62x39, has an under-folder stock and comes with black poly furniture. Standard threads on barrel (M14x1.0 left-hand) and a slant brake. Parkerized finish. Accepts the older milled style bayonets, not the newer AKM style. Built from Polish, Hungarian, or Bulgarian parts kits. Comes with one 30 round magazine.

EXC.	V.G.	GOOD
700	650	600

■ AKUW

This Vector AK47, 7.62x39, has an under-folder stock and comes with medium blonde wood furniture. Standard threads on barrel (M14x1.0 left-hand) and a slant brake. Parkerized finish. Accepts the older milled style bayonets, not the newer AKM style. Built from Polish, Hungarian, or Bulgarian parts kits. Comes with one 30 round magazine.

EXC.	V.G.	GOOD
700	650	600

VECTOR AKUW

■ AKSW

This Vector AK47, 7.62x39, has a side-folding stock. Comes with black poly handguards or medium blonde wood handguards. Standard threads on barrel and a slant brake. Parkerized finish. Accepts the older milled style bayonets, not the newer AKM style. Built from Polish, Hungarian, or Bulgarian parts kits. The side-folder stock can interchange with a fixed stock if desired. Comes with one 30 round magazine.

EXC.	V.G.	GOOD
550	500	450

■ AKFP

This Vector AK47, 7.62x39, has a fixed black poly stock and black poly furniture. Standard threads on barrel and a slant break. Parkerized finish. Accepts the older milled style bayonets, not the newer AKM style. Built from Polish, Hungarian, or Bulgarian parts kits. The stock can interchange with a side-folding stock if desired. Comes with one 30 round magazine.

EXC.	V.G.	GOOD
550	500	450

■ AKFW

As above but with a blonde wood stock and handguard.

EXC.	V.G.	GOOD
550	500	450

■ AMD

The AMD, 7.62x39mm rifle. Made with the required U.S. parts including the extended flash hider that is welded on to achieve the 16-inch barrel length. Black poly furniture and parkerized finish. One 30 round mag included.

EXC.	V.G.	GOOD
650	600	500

■ RPD SEMI-AUTO

Now available from Vector, a drum/belt fed semi-auto RPD. Comes with a 100 round drum mag (with belts) and bipod. Made from Bulgarian parts kits on an American receiver. Fires 7.62x39 ammunition. ATF approved.

EXC	V.G.	GOOD
1950	1800	1650

VECTOR RPD SEMI-AUTO

VEPR

See: Robinson Armament.

VOLUNTEER ENTERPRISES
Knoxville, Tennessee

See: Commando Arms.

WALTHER
Ulm, Germany

Currently imported by Smith and Wesson.

■ MODEL G22

A 22LR semi-automatic rifle. Bullpup design has the action located in the buttstock. Adjustable sights and scope mount rails. 20-inch barrel. 10 round magazines.

NIB	EXC.	V.G.	GOOD
509	400	350	275

WALTHER G-22 RIFLE .22LR

WEAVER ARMS CORP.
Escondido, California

■ NIGHTHAWK CARBINE

A 9mm semi-automatic rifle that fires from a closed bolt. It has a 16-inch barrel. Collapsible shoulder stock. Magazines holding 25, 32, 40 or 50 rounds were available. Approximately 1500 were produced 1987-90.

EXC.	V.G.	GOOD
1000	850	700

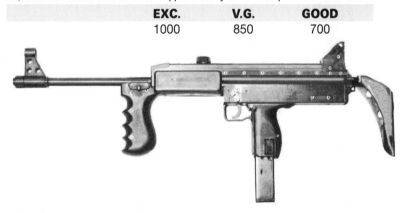

WEAVER NIGHTHAWK CARBINE

WILKINSON ARMS CO.
Covina, California/Parma, Idaho

Entrepreneur Ray Wilkinson manufactured a series of high capacity paramilitary designs. He started in Covina, Ca. and later mover to Parma, Idaho. His products were named after his daughters: Terry, Linda and Sherry. (The Sherry is a Baby Browning-sized .22 LR pistol.)

■ TERRY CARBINE

9mm semi-automatic rifle. It has a 16-1/4-inch barrel that ends with a cone shaped flash hider. Wood forearm. Synthetic or wood buttstock. 31 round magazine. This design first appeared in the 1960s and was manufactured by J&R Engineering of S. El. Monte, California, as the Model 68. Ray Wilkinson bought rights to the design and made some improvements.

EXC.	V.G.	GOOD
500	425	350

WILKINSON TERRY CARBINE

■ LINDA PISTOL

A 9mm semi-automatic pistol. A streamlined version of the Terry carbine action. 8-3/8-inch barrel. Wood forearm.

EXC.	V.G.	GOOD
550	475	400

WILKINSON LINDA PISTOL

■ LINDA CARBINE

A 9mm semi-automatic rifle. It has a 16-3/16-inch barrel with perforated alloy shroud. Detachable tubular buttstock.

EXC.	V.G.	GOOD
550	475	400

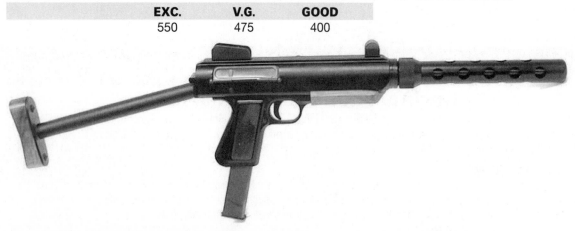

WILKINSON ARMS LINDA CARBINE 9MM

WILSON COMBAT

Berryville, Arkansas

Website: www.wilsoncombat.com

This manufacturer of precision 1911-A1 pistols also offers a line of AR-15 type rifles.

■ UT-15 TACTICAL CARBINE

Features include: forged upper (flat top) and lower receivers. Premium Wilson combat match-grade fluted barrel, 16-1/4-inch OAL with Wilson tactical muzzle brake. Free-float ventilated quad rail aluminum handguard. Ergo ergonomically correct pistol grip. Crisp 3-3.5-lb. trigger pull with JP trigger/hammer group. Premium mil-spec bolt and bolt carrier, NP-3 coated. Hard anodized finish on receivers and mil-spec black manganese phosphate (parkerized) on barrel and steel components. Six position mil-spec collapsible stock. Accepts all M-16/AR-15 style magazines. Includes one 20 round magazine.

MSRP	EXC.	V.G.	GOOD
1785	1500	1250	1000

■ M-4 T TACTICAL CARBINE

Features include forged upper (flat top) and lower receivers. 16-1/4-inch premium Wilson Combat match grade M-4 style barrel. Wilson tactical muzzle brake. Ergo ergonomically correct pistol grip. Crisp 3-3.5-lb. trigger pull with JP trigger group. Premium mil-spec bolt and bolt carrier. Hard anodize finish on receivers. Mil-spec black manganese phosphate (parkerized) on barrel and steel components or Armor-Tuff finish. Six position mil-spec collapsible stock. Accepts all M-16/AR-15 style magazines. Includes one 20 round magazine.

MSRP	EXC.	V.G.	GOOD
1785	1500	1250	1000

■ SS-15 SUPER SNIPER TACTICAL RIFLE

Features include forged upper (flat top) and lower receivers. Premium Wilson Combat match grade 20-inch super sniper barrel. Free floated aluminum handguard. Ergo ergonomically correct pistol grip. Crisp 3-3.5-lb. trigger-pull with JP trigger/hammer group, premium mil-spec bolt and bolt carrier. Hard anodized finish on receivers. Mil-spec black manganese phosphate (parkerized) or Armor-Tuff finish on steel components. Accepts all M-16/AR-15 style magazines; includes one 20 round magazine.

MSRP	EXC.	V.G.	GOOD
1799	1500	1250	1000

WISE LITE ARMS

Ft. Worth, Texas

Website: www.wlarms.com

This company builds a series of semi-automatic only versions of famous machineguns and sub-machineguns. All designs are BATFE approved. Their models feature a newly made receiver as well as original parts that have been rebuilt to function as a semi-automatic only. Most models are built in limited quantities due to shortages of imported parts. Prices fluctuate based on parts availability. Contact the manufacturer for current inventory. Other models can be custom built if the customer supplies a parts kit. Contact the manufacturer for a list of additional models. WLA states on their website as of July 5, 2010 they are "re-evaluating their business model and company direction." They have suspended new production and custom builds until further notice.

■ BROWNING MODEL 1919 .30-06

A semi-automatic version of the famous WWII era belt fed machine gun. Sideplates are riveted, as on the original guns. Matte blue or parkerized finish. Weight 35 lbs.

EXC.	V.G.	GOOD
1400	1200	1000

■ RUSSIAN DEGTYAREV DP28 LIGHT MACHINE GUN

These rifles look and feel just the like the original but will function only in a semi-automatic operation. The parts are of Polish origin. Each gun is fit with a patented semi-auto receiver and built to exacting standards with over 50 hours of hand fitting required for each gun. Each rifle comes fully assembled with four 47 round pan magazines, cover, sling, and wooden shipping crate. These guns are now shipping but in very low quantity. Only a limited number of rifles will be built.

EXC.	V.G.	GOOD
2600	2300	2000

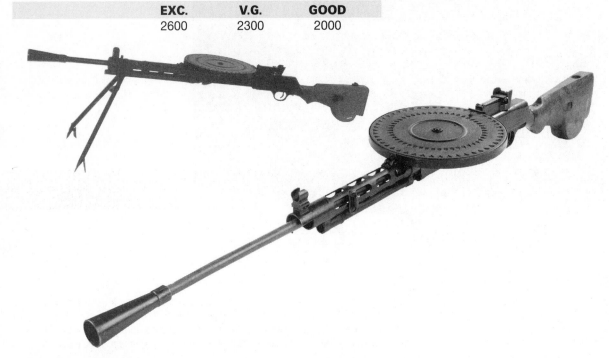

WISE LITE ARMS DP-28 SEMI AUTOMATIC RIFLE 7.62X54RMM

■ RUSSIAN PPSH-41 SEMI-AUTOMATIC RIFLE

Semiautomatic version of one of the most recognizable guns of WWII. The "papa-shaw" or burp gun was one of the best submachine guns ever produced, and saw extensive action from Stalingrad to the Chosin Reservoir. This rugged gun is chambered in 7.62x25mm and accepts 36 round stick or 50 round drum magazines. The barrel/shroud has been extended to 16-inch length to comply with BATFE regulations. Includes one 36 round round stick mag. Re-enactor's version also available with removable blank firing adapter. Weight is 12 pounds.

EXC.	V.G.	GOOD
800	700	600

WISE LITE ARMS PPSH-41 RIFLE 7.62X25MM

■ RUSSIAN PPS-43 SEMI-AUTOMATIC PISTOL

The WWII replacement to the PPSH-41, the model PPS-43 is made from stamped steel. Caliber is 7.62x25mm. In order to maintain the original appearance of this model, the over top folding stock is welded in the closed position. Accepts the 36 round stick magazines. Does not use the drum magazines. Re-enactor's version also available with removable blank firing adapter.

NIB	EXC.	V.G.	GOOD
775	700	600	500

WISE LITE ARMS PPS-43 PISTOL 7.62X25MM

■ FINNISH KP-44 SEMI-AUTOMATIC PISTOL

The Finnish KP-44 is chambered in 9mm Luger. It was copied from the Russian PPS-43. Stamped steel construction. In order to maintain the original appearance of this model, the over top folding stock is welded in the closed position. The barrel is 10 inches long, with an overall length of 24 inches. Accepts 36 round stick or 50 round drum magazines.

NIB	EXC.	V.G.	GOOD
775	700	600	500

YANKEE HILL MACHINE
Florence, Massachusetts
Website: www.yhm.net

Manufacturer of AR type Rifles.

Note: Most YHM-15 models are also offered in 6.8mm SPC. Add $75.00

■ YHM-15 BLACK DIAMOND SPECTER XL

Cal. 5.56mm. YHM 16-inch diamond fluted barrel, YHM Specter Xtra Length quad rail handguard, YHM flip front and rear sights, CAR stock. Weight: 7.1 lbs.

MSRP	EXC.	V.G.	GOOD
1429	1250	1100	950

YANKEE HILL MACHINE BLACK DIAMOND SPECTER XL RIFLE

■ YHM-15 BLACK DIAMOND SPECTER CARBINE

As above with mid-length Specter quad rail handguard.

MSRP	EXC.	V.G.	GOOD
1407	1250	1100	950

■ YHM-15 BLACK DIAMOND CARBINE

As above with carbine length quad rail handguard.

MSRP	EXC.	V.G.	GOOD
1369	1225	1100	950

**YHM BLACK DIAMOND CARBINE
5.56MM OR 6.8 SPC**

■ YHM-15 SMOOTH CARBINE

Cal. 5.56mm. YHM 16-inch diamond fluted barrel, YHM carbine length smooth handguard, YHM flip front and rear sights, CAR stock. Weight: 6.8 lbs.

MSRP	EXC.	V.G.	GOOD
1364	1225	1100	950

■ YHM-15 CUSTOMIZABLE CARBINE

Cal. 5.56mm. YHM 16inch diamond fluted barrel, YHM carbine length customizable handguard, YHM flip front and rear sights, CAR stock. Weight: 6.3 lbs.

MSRP	EXC.	V.G.	GOOD
1366	1250	1100	950

■ YHM-15 ENTRY LEVEL CARBINE

Cal. 5.56mm. YHM 16-inch diamond fluted barrel, Flat top receiver with no sights. YHM single rail gas block, CAR stock. Weight: 6.4 lbs.

MSRP	EXC.	V.G.	GOOD
1186	1050	900	800

YHM ENTRY LEVEL CARBINE

■ YHM-15 BLACK DIAMOND RIFLE

Cal. 5.56mm. YHM 20-inch diamond fluted barrel, YHM rifle length quad rail handguard, no sights, YHM single rail gas block, A2 stock. Weight: 8 lbs.

MSRP	EXC.	V.G.	GOOD
1357	1250	1100	950

■ YHM-15 CUSTOMIZABLE RIFLE

Cal. 5.56mm. YHM 20-inch diamond fluted barrel, YHM rifle length customizable handguard, no sights, YHM single rail gas block, A2 stock. Weight: 8 lbs.

MSRP	EXC.	V.G.	GOOD
1350	1250	1100	950

YHM CUSTOMIZABLE RIFLE

■ YHM-15 ENTRY LEVEL RIFLE

Cal. 5.56mm. YHM 20-inch diamond fluted barrel, YHM rifle length tubular handguard, no sights, YHM single rail gas block, A2 stock. Weight: 8 lbs.

MSRP	EXC.	V.G.	GOOD
1226	1150	1000	900

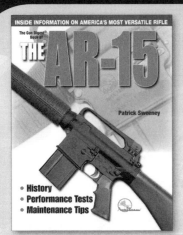
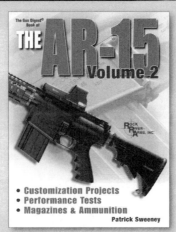
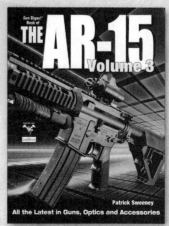
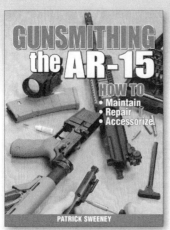
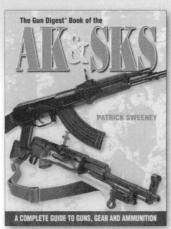

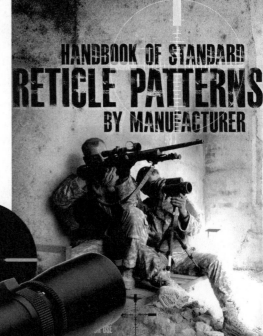